# SOURCES AND METHODS IN GEOGRAPHY

**Rivers**

## SOURCES AND METHODS IN GEOGRAPHY

**Series editors**

**M.A. Morgan** PhD
*Department of Geography, University of Bristol*

**D.J. Briggs** PhD
*Department of Geography, University of Sheffield*

## TITLES ALREADY PUBLISHED

# SOURCES AND METHODS IN GEOGRAPHY

# **Rivers**

**Geoffrey E. Petts** PhD
*University of Technology, Loughborough*

**BUTTERWORTHS**
London — Boston
Durban — Singapore — Sydney — Toronto — Wellington

First published 1983

©Butterworth & Co (Publishers) Ltd 1983

**British Library Cataloguing in Publication Data**

Petts, Geoffrey E.
    Rivers. — (Sources and methods in geography)
    1. Rivers
    I. Title      II. Series
    551.48'3    GB1203.2

ISBN 0-408-11070-8

Typeset by Illustrated Arts Ltd, Sutton, Surrey
Printed by Whitstable Litho Ltd, Whitstable, Kent

# FOREWORD

During recent years, geography has been undergoing considerable change. There have been many facets to this change, but one underlying theme is the adoption of a more rigorous approach to geographical enquiry, wherever this is appropriate. It has been reflected in numerous ways: in the greater emphasis which is placed upon quantitative and statistical methods of data collection and handling; in the attention given to the study of process as opposed to the description of form in human as well as in physical geography; and in the use of an inductive rather than deductive philosophy of learning.

What this means in practical terms is that the student and teacher of geography need to be acquainted with a wide range of methods. The student, both at school and in higher education, is increasingly becoming involved in projects or classwork which include some form of individual and original research. To be equipped for this type of study he/she needs to be aware of the sources from which he/she can obtain data, the techniques he/she can use to collect this information and the approaches he/she can take to analyse it. The teacher similarly requires a pool of empirical material on which he/she can draw as a source of class exercises. Both must be able to tackle geographical problems in a logical and scientific fashion, to construct appropriate explanatory hypotheses, and test these hypotheses in an objective and rational manner.

The aims of this series of books are therefore to introduce a range of sources which provide information for project and classwork, and to outline some of the methods by which this material can be analysed. The main concern is with relatively simple approaches rather than more sophisticated methods.

The reader will be expected to have a basic grounding in geography, and in some of the books a working knowledge of mathematical methods is useful. The level of detail and exposition, however, is intended to make it possible for the student, with little further reading, to gain a basic understanding of the selected themes. Consequently the series will be of particular interest and use to students and teachers involved in courses in which practical and project work figure as major components. At the same time students in higher education will find the books an invaluable guide to geographical methods.

M.A. Morgan  D.J. Briggs

*For N.K.S.*

## ACKNOWLEDGEMENTS

I wish to extend my sincere thanks to Jenny Jarvis for patiently typing the manuscript and to Anne Tarver, Helen Briars and Elspeth Cranston for allowing me to exploit their cartographic and photographic skills. Thanks too, to David Briggs and Michael Morgan for their constructive comments on a draft of the text.

I am also grateful to the following for their kind permission to reproduce copyright material:

*The Geographical Journal* for *Figure 6.14.*
*Environmental Conservation*, the *Foundation for Environmental Conservation*, and *Elsevier Sequoia, S.A.* for *Figure 6.12* and *6.13.*
*Zeitschrift für Geomorphologie* for *Figure 5.12.*
*John Wiley and Sons* for *Figures 6.3 and 6.5.*
*Journal of Sedimentary Petrology* for *Figure 4.14.*
*American Journal of Science* for *Figure 6.7.*
*Aerofilms Limited* for *Plate 5.3.*

# CONTENTS

# CHAPTER 1 THE NEED FOR FLUVIAL STUDIES

## 1.1 INTRODUCTION

Rivers are a fundamental feature of landscape. Each year rivers and streams carry enormous volumes of water and sediment, and for man their significance is considerable. Networks of river channels drain nearly seventy percent of the earth's land surface and their characteristics differ not only spatially but also over time at a single location. Indeed, rivers must be viewed as dynamic features because the flows, sediment loads and even the channel forms are changing constantly. Rivers have always provided a focus of attention for geographical studies, but the increasing **recognition of man as a significant geomorphological agent has given the subject a more applied bias and a new relevance**. In the past geomorphological studies concentrated upon the single examination of either landform, or process, or deposits and chronology. Today, the *measurement* and *modelling* of all three of these components provide an integrated approach for the interpretation of *spatial pattern* and *temporal change*. The purpose of this book is to clarify the nature of some important relationships between river processes, landforms and deposits, and to describe some simple approaches and techniques available for their study. Rivers are central to many environmental problems which require for their study the involvement of a range of specialists such as hydrologists, engineers and ecologists as well as geomorphologists. An awareness of the interdisciplinary nature of many contemporary problems and of the mutual concerns of these related disciplines will provide an improved appreciation of the need for the study of rivers.

### 1.1.1 The character of river systems

A river receives water and sediment from a *drainage basin*. Each basin is composed of slopes and bounded by a divide which separates it from adjacent basins. Water and sediment moving down the slopes are collected and concentrated in shallow hollows eventually to form streams and to provide the characteristic river flows and sediment loads. Such movements of water and sediment provide examples of geomorphic process: *fluvial processes* refer specifically to the movement of sediment and water in channels. In the course of transportation the processes of erosion and deposition fashion the *form* or *geometry* of the channel to produce a wide variety of fluvial landforms.

Rivers are characterised by one-way flows of water and sediment generated by gravity, and controlled by slope. Each drainage basin and the channel network enclosed within its boundary-divides is in reality composed of a hierarchy of channels and basins. Small drainage basins at the extremities of the system join to form a single but composite larger basin. Downstream more single and composite basins link together to form the typical drainage system. Thus, from headwater to mouth, many of the physical characteristics of

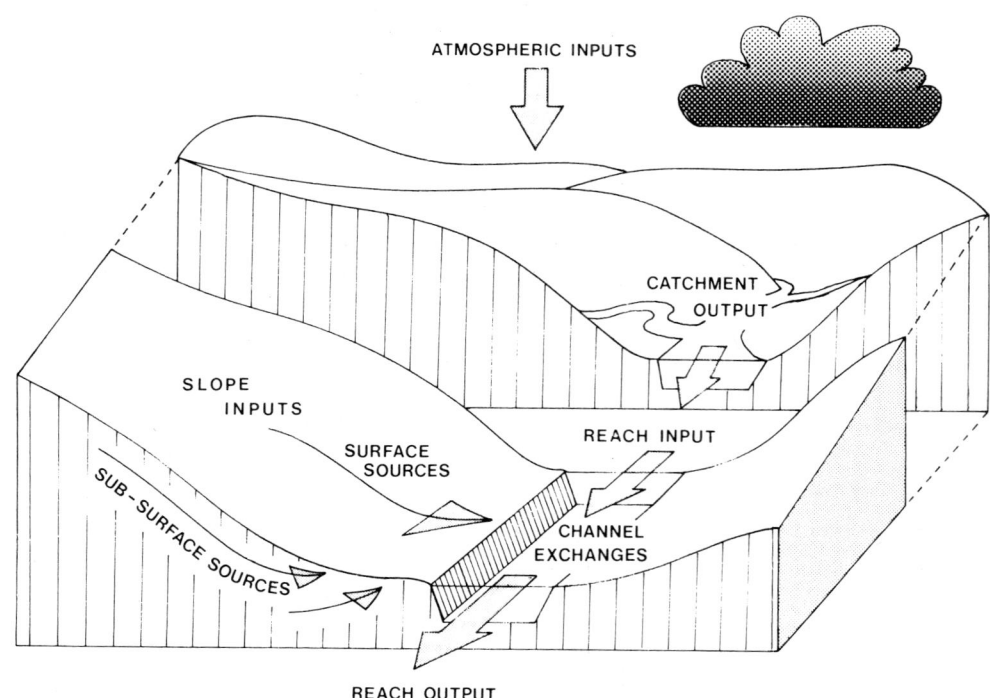

**Figure 1.1 Sources of water and sediment for a channel reach**

a river change progressively: the area of the drainage basin increases, the channel network is lengthened, the volumes of water and sediment transported increase, and the channel dimensions are enlarged.

Most channels are perennial, that is, they carry water all the year round, but many small headwater streams carry water for only part of the year (intermittent streams) and ephemeral rivers, such as found in semi-arid areas, carry water only after storm rainfalls. Nevertheless, each point along a river course will receive inputs of water and sediment from three sources (*Figure 1.1*). Firstly, from the atmosphere — water (rain, sleet and snow), dissolved chemicals and gases; secondly, from the neighbouring slopes where the water flowing over the surface and through the soil picks up solutes (dissolved substances), mineral particles and rock fragments together with dead organic matter from plants and animals; thirdly, from the slopes which form the drainage area upstream.

Rivers may be envisaged as vehicles for the transport of water and sediment from a source area to a place of collection or deposition (ultimately the oceans or an inland basin). Exchanges may be made within the channel — sediment may be deposited or eroded; water can be lost be transmission, that is by seepage into the bed and banks, as well as being input from neighbouring hillslopes; and water quality can be altered by contact with the boundary sediments and by the flora and fauna of the channel. Thus, the volume of water and sediment flowing past any point on a river during a known period of time, the *discharge* and *sediment load* respectively, will be controlled by climate, geology, drainage basin relief, soil character, vegetation and man; that is, by the character of the whole basin system.

## 1.2 NEEDS FOR FLUVIAL STUDIES

Rivers are controlled in order to reduce flooding and erosion damage; river water is abstracted for domestic, industrial or agricultural supplies and effluent is returned from sewerage works and power stations; but minimum flows — in terms of quantity and quality — must be maintained to cater for public health, fisheries and wildlife, navigation or recreational requirements. Thus the needs for information about rivers are many and varied.

## 1.2.1 Hydrological needs

Hydrology is concerned with the movement of water and its distribution in space and time. These are studied within the context of the **hydrological cycle** which describes the circulation of water from rain onto the land-surface via water flow over the surface and through the ground to streams, along channels to lakes and oceans, and its eventual evaporation back to the atmosphere. Throughout the history of civilisation the activities of man have been dependent to a large extent upon water supplies for domestic use, for agriculture and irrigation, for industry and power, and for transport. Early civilisations relied on floods for successful agriculture; water supply and land drainage schemes had been developed by 3200 BC; and dams were used commonly by Roman times to provide a reliable source of water and to prevent floods. Yet floodplain communities have frequently met with tragedy, for example in 1855 a flood on the Hwang Ho in China killed some 250 000 people. Moreover, problems of water-supply and flood-control are still increasing as man's need for water and floodplain land continue to grow.

Water as a natural resource is in great demand. In the UK, the average demand for water exceeds 300 litres per day per person, and this demand is increasing. However, the primary concern is with how the demand relates to supply. The natural supply is the amount of water available for use by man: that is the difference between the volume received from precipitation and the amount returned to the atmosphere by evaporation. For the UK the average annual available supply is about 515 million cubic metres per day ($m^3$ $d^{-1}$) as compared with a demand of 16 million $m^3$ $d^{-1}$ in 1976. Under extreme drought conditions, however, the demand may exceed the supply in many areas. Such a situation occurred in England and Wales in 1976; emergency pipelines were installed, bans were imposed on hosepipes, and water supplies were severely limited. On average there was a 10% shortfall in water supplies.

The major source areas for available supply are in the west and north of the country whereas the main demand areas, the major centres of population, are in central, southern and eastern England so that there exist major water management problems. These involve the consideration of ways to conserve water, and to transfer water from the areas of supply to those of high demand, whilst at the same time maintaining adequate river flows in order to assure sufficient dilution of effluents and to safeguard amenity and recreational interests and fisheries. It is necessary, therefore, to determine the annual water availability and its seasonal characteristics, and to assess the effects of changes within the drainage basin, resulting from human activity (such as land-use), which may alter these characteristics.

Floods may be defined as discharges which exceed the capacity of river channels and then proceed to flow over the adjacent valley floor (the floodplain). At the global scale, floods are responsible for about 30% of all natural disasters and 40% of the resulting fatalities. These high flows are commonly caused by prolonged or intense rainfall, sometimes augmented by snowmelt. In 1952, for example, the small town of Lynmouth in North Devon was devastated by an extreme flood (**see** Bleasdale and Douglas, 1972; Kidson, 1953). During the night of 15-16 August rain totalling up to 30 mm in some places fell onto a drainage basin that was already unusually wet after 90 mm had fallen during the preceding fourteen days. The rate of flow produced in this small basin, with an area of only 10.15 km$^2$, may have reached 650 cubic metres per second — almost as great as the highest recorded discharge for the River Severn at Bewdley, a drainage area of 4330 km$^2$.

Flood disasters, however, are man-made. Man has put himself at risk by continuing to use floodplains, and with increasing intensity, for settlement, agriculture and industry. In the USA, the yearly losses from flooding have more than doubled since 1936 when the Flood Control Act was passed despite increased expenditure on flood control schemes. Successful flood control and floodplain management require information for the adequate prediction and forecasting of flood characteristics. Needs exist to understand why flooding occurs and the factors which control flood *magnitude*, to determine how often floods occur at any location (the flood *frequency*), and to assess the impact of man upon these characteristics.

**1.2.2 Engineering needs**

The location of structures such as dams, bridges, culverts, navigation locks or buildings in, across or alongside a river requires an understanding of how and why the channel changes its form and of the rates at which these changes occur. Channel erosion may cause the structures to be undermined resulting, if allowed to go unchecked, in their collapse. Channel deposition can block drains and culverts, fill reservoirs, inhibit the operation of navigation locks and even increase flood problems. The ability of a river to erode and transport sediment, that is to do 'work', is dependent upon the available energy. Water flowing in a channel is subject to the force of gravity which induces downslope movement and the potential energy available is simply a function of the mass of water and the channel slope.

The conversion from potential to kinetic energy involves movement and it is this movement which gives water the 'power' to transport sediment and to produce landforms. Water flowing in channels expends most of the potential energy overcoming the frictional resistance of the channel bed and banks which tends to retard the flow, and only about 5% of the potential energy of a river is available for sediment transport. Nevertheless, three properties of water flow are important for the transport of sediment: velocity (the speed of flow), flow depth, and the discharge.

The river floodplain, the relatively flat area of land adjoining a river channel, is constructed as a result of the slow lateral migration of the channel, and is overflowed at times of high discharge. However, the persistent lateral migration of many river channels and the associated progressive erosion of the river bank, are potential hazards. Shifting channels may affect structures built on the floodplain, and because rivers are commonly used as boundaries debates over land ownership may arise. In Britain, more than £1 000 000 is spent annually in trying to overcome problems associated with shifting channels. One graphic illustration of river migration has been given by Mark Twain in *Life on the Mississippi* (1904, p. 3—4):

'More than once it has shortened itself thirty miles at a single jump! these cutoffs have had curious effects: they have thrown several river towns out into the rural districts and built up sand bars and forests in front of them. The town of Delta used to be three miles below Vicksburg . . . Delta is now two miles above Vicksburg.

'A cutoff plays havoc with boundary lines and jurisdictions: for instance, a man living in the State of Mississippi today, a cutoff occurs tonight, and tomorrow the man finds himself and his land over on the other side of the river, within the boundaries and subject to the laws of the State of Louisiana! Such a thing, happening in tbe upper river in the old times, could have transferred a slave from Missouri to Illinois and make a free man of him.'

One important observation made by Twain is that some channel changes can occur suddenly, particularly as a result of an extreme magnitude, rare flood. For example, Costa (1974) reported the erosional effects of a single tropical storm upon the Western Run, Maryland, USA. Hurricane Agnes struck the eastern coast in June 1972. Prior to the storm channel width was 16.8 m and the depth was 2.3 m. After the flood these had increased to 37.2 m and 7.6 m respectively and the storm caused damage exceeding $100 million.

Undesirably high rates of sediment supply to river channels may be derived from hillslope erosion within the drainage basin. The potential for rain to cause erosion is a function of its intensity and duration, and of the size and velocity of the raindrops, but the actual erosion is constrained by the slope characteristics, including vegetation cover and soil type, which resist the forces of raindrop impact and water flow. Within humid environments slope erosion rates are low under natural conditions but slope disturbance by man can have dramatic effects. Mining activity (e.g. for coal or china-clay) and agricultural and forestry practices provide large quantities of suspended solids for river systems, but building construction can have the greatest effects. Constructional activity involving soil disturbance, site preparation for houses, and the installation of sewer systems and road and pavement drainage, which affected only 25 percent of a small drainage basin in Devon, caused a ten-fold increase of the stream's sediment load (Walling, 1971).

Accelerated river channel deposition is an inevitable consequence of accelerated erosion and particular problems have arisen with regard to the life-expectancy of man-made lakes. Reservoirs for water-supply and flood-control are common features of river systems today and they provide large settling basins for the accumulation of the sediments transported by the inflowing rivers. Such sedimentation has commonly reduced the water storage capacity of reservoirs by less than 1% per year. However, several cases of accelerated sedimentation, associated with land-use change in the headwater basin, have produced excessive rates of storage loss which reduced the useful life of the reservoirs to less than twenty years.

The ability of a river, at any location along its course, to transport sediment is described by two important characteristics: the **competence** refers to the largest size of particle that can be moved by a discharge, and the *capacity* describes the maximum volume of sediment of a given size that can be transported. Any change of these two characteristics, or of the frequency with which discharges of particular competence and capacity occur, can produce accelerated rates of erosion or deposition. Even if the competence and capacity remain unaltered, a change in the rate of sediment supply to a river channel can induce a change of channel form. A need exists to understand not only the factors which influence sediment transport through a channel section but also the characteristics of the sediment source areas and particularly of the ways in which these characteristics are influenced by man.

### 1.2.3 Ecological needs

Ecology is concerned with the relationships between living organisms and their physical and chemical environment. The term *ecosystem* refers to the organisms and the environmental conditions in which they exist. A river and its drainage basin may be viewed as an ecosystem, that is as an integration of non-living (*abiotic*) and living (*biotic*) factors. Indeed, many organisms have adapted to a specific combination of physical and chemical conditions. An awareness of the running-water (*lotic*) ecosystem is necessary because it affects public health and the potential for amenity and recreation. Furthermore, examination of the lotic flora and fauna can provide an indication of the 'health' of a river and they can be used to identify rivers or sections of rivers which have been adversely affected by human activity. Indeed, the bottom-living (*benthic*) macro-invertebrates (*Figure 1.2*) provide a biotic index for assessing the character of a river. Hellawell (1978) provides information on the biological surveillance of rivers.

The lotic ecosystem receives energy from three sources, namely, solar radiation, allochthonous organic matter (organic material derived from 'outside' the channel, i.e. from vegetation on slopes within the drainage basin), and dissolved chemicals. Radiant energy is photosynthesised by plants and transformed into plant tissues which are utilised by higher organisms. The efficient running of an ecosystem depends upon the transfer of energy between organisms through the food web and involves the cycling of basic materials such as carbon, nitrogen and phosphorus. However, the primary energy source for all but the largest rivers is provided by allochthonous organic matter in dissolved form or as coarse particles, such as twigs, leaves, blossom, fruit and pollen. During trans-

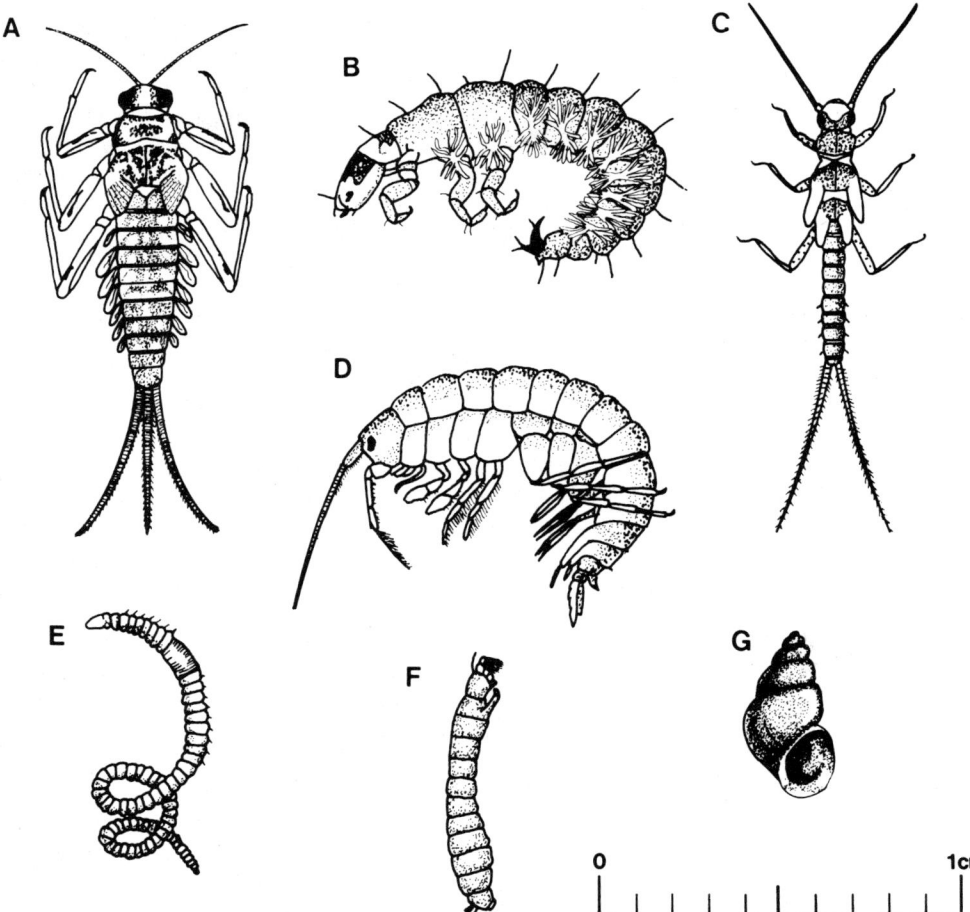

Figure 1.2 Common biotic indicators. Mayfly nymphs (A), caddis fly larvae (B), stone fly nymphs (C) and freshwater shrimps (D) dominate fast flowing, gravel-bed streams but are less common in polluted rivers where tubifex worms (E) are common. Blackfly larvae (F) commonly are associated with fast, shallow and clean-water sites while many molluscs (G) prefer slow currents and silty bed-sediments. Also, a healthy stream usually will have a high diversity of organisms in contrast to a polluted river which may be characteristised by a few tolerant species

port downstream the particulate organic matter is reduced in size by battering and abrasion, and as a result of alteration by the aquatic organisms.

Water flowing through a drainage basin transports organic debris and inorganic sediments, but it also acquires a *quality* as a result of the interaction of chemical, biological and physical processes. Water quality may be considered as comprising three factors: chemical composition, dissolved gas content and temperature. The chemistry of running water is largely determined by the composition of the rocks although a contribution will also be made by the atmosphere. Plants require three important elements for growth: potassium, nitrate and phosphate. Animals also have specific chemical requirements (for example calcium is required by molluscs for shell growth). Furthermore, most organisms have narrow *tolerance levels* for particular substances. Abnormally high levels of heavy metals, such as iron, lead and copper, can be highly toxic and can cause major changes of the biota within aquatic ecosystems.

Dissolved gases are vital to all organisms. The three most important gases — oxygen, nitrogen and carbon dioxide — are usually approximately in equilibrium with the atmosphere. Oxygen is also important for the aerobic chemical and microbial breakdown of organic molecules into simpler, stable end-products such as carbon dioxide, nitrogen, phosphate and water. Water temperature has an important direct control upon the fauna of lotic systems because many organisms can tolerate only a specific range of temperatures at least during part of their life cycles. Temperature also exerts an indirect control through its effect upon the concentration of dissolved oxygen: the solubility of oxygen in water decreases with a rise in temperature.

The sources of water, the pathways of water flow and the rates of water movement through a drainage basin to a large extent control the amount of organic matter, the concentration of dissolved chemicals and gases and the temperature conditions within a river channel. Thus, the hydrological characteristics of a drainage basin provide the overriding control of lotic habitats.

The movement of sediments and the size and shape of the river channel — itself designed by the movement of water and sediment in relation to the material which forms the bed and banks — are also important. The life cycles of many lotic species are often related to the seasonal variations of discharge, to the changes of flow velocity and to fluctuations of flow depth. Many species of plants and animals have adapted at least part of their life cycle to the movements of sediment within the channel. The form of the channel itself is another important factor, especially in relation to the spatial requirements of some species. The optimum discharge for salmonid spawning depends upon the form and particle-size composition of the channel bed (the **substrate**), while the efficiency with which different substrates trap organic debris affects the distribution of insect species. Information is needed, however, on how the various physical, chemical and biological characteristics of rivers interact both under natural conditions and in response to human activity.

### 1.2.4 Water quality needs

The interactions between man and water have always concerned geographers and have recently attracted even greater general interest with the growth of a wider public awareness of the problems of environmental pollution and control. Water pollution within lotic ecosystems is not new and is often undesirable.

Major pollution problems have arisen as a result of social and industrial developments since the industrial revolution. Enormous amounts of nutrients, particularly nitrate and phosphate, are derived from sewage effluents; trace metals are commonly discharged in industrial waste and drainage from mine spoil or from waste disposal pits can introduce toxic substances to the stream directly or via groundwater supplies. Even the use of salt for de-icing the roads has increased the chloride content of river discharges in some areas. The release of water used for cooling purposes in power stations, which is commonly 6–9 °C warmer than the natural river under conditions of low flow, often results in thermal pollution. Domestic and industrial effluent are identifiable **point sources** which are relatively easy to monitor and to control. **Diffuse sources** are more problematic. In industrial areas, for example, atmospheric pollution may result in a change of rainwater chemistry. Examples of emissions of sulphur dioxide, producing high acidity precipitation and a subsequent decrease in the pH of river waters, are particularly well documented.

Land-use changes and agricultural practices may, however, have produced the most widespread problems. The process of water enrichment with plant nutrients is known as **eutrophication**. Agricultural practices lead to the enrichment of water both as a result of vegetation removal, soil disturbance and changes of the pattern of water movement, and directly through the application of fertilisers. In many forests large quantities of nutrients are cycled through the vegetation, and in the humid tropical rainforests, particularly, the trees are a major nutrient store. Permanent removal of forests may result in increased nutrient inputs to rivers. The increased area and depth of modern ploughing accelerates the liberation of nitrogen and may change the pattern of water movement in the soil (and hence the degree of leaching of nutrients), thus adding to the eutrophication of rivers.

In England and Wales in 1972 over 3000 km of river were diagnosed as seriously polluted. Needs exist to quantify the contributions of nutrients from the various sources, to understand the processes governing their release from, and movement through, the soil, and to assess the impact of these contributions upon the lotic ecosystem. One major area of interest has been the assessment of the effects that agricultural practices have upon **nutrient budgets**. The annual nutrient budget refers to the difference between inputs from precipitation and fertiliser application within a drainage basin and the streamflow outputs. Examination of the nutrient budget enables the assessment of the effects of land-use changes in general terms although not giving information on the internal nutrient cycle between the soils and the vegetation.

Foster (1979), for example, has compared the streamflow outputs from different sources within a small 1.6 km$^2$ catchment in Devon. In the drainage basin, 14% is mixed deciduous woodland and the remainder is devoted to major crops of wheat and winter barley grown in rotation with root crops of swedes and potatoes. Streamflow derived from three different sources was sampled in order to investigate variations of solute concentration: a woodland stream, a subsurface tile drain and a surface drainage ditch — the latter two receiving water and sediment from cultivated areas. Measurements of the concentration of chloride, magnesium, sodium, potassium and nitrate-nitrogen in the discharges revealed significant differences between the source areas. For example, within the woodland stream the mean nitrate-nitrogen concentration was 2.7 mg$\ell^{-1}$, compared with 5.3 mg$\ell^{-1}$ and 11.1 mg$\ell^{-1}$ for the tile drain and drainage ditch respectively. Generally the higher concentration of solutes was associated with surface ditches draining cultivated areas. Although these high levels were thought likely to reflect the significance of surface fertiliser application, an explanation of the observed differences requires further knowledge of soil processes and of the ways in which agricultural practices such, as ploughing effect, the release of nutrients to the stream system.

## 1.3 THE BASIS OF FLUVIAL GEOMORPHOLOGY

Fluvial geomorphology is concerned with the processes of water and sediment movement in channels and with the channel forms produced by these processes. However, the discharges, water quality and sediment loads at a point on a river reflect the characteristics of climate, geology and land-use within the drainage basin. Thus, the ways in which water and sediment are supplied from their source areas is also of concern. The geographical approach has been founded upon a history of field research but attention to measurement and to quantitative data analysis is a product mainly of the past thirty years.

Many of the fundamental principles of water flow and sediment transport were established, and techniques for field measurement developed during the eighteenth and nineteenth centuries. These advances had been made, however, by geologists and engineers and were largely ignored by geographers until the 1950s. The first half of this century was dominated by the purely descriptive geomorphology of William Morris Davis. Davis expressed his ideas of landform evolution in the theory of the 'Cycle of Erosion'. This envisaged that landforms would change progressively through a continuous cycle of events, each cycle being initiated by a brief phase of uplift followed by the establishment and downcutting of rivers on the new exposed surface, and terminated by the reduction of the surface relief to a low, relatively flat 'peneplain'. Within each cycle, the rivers would pass through three stages from 'youth' (characterised by deep slopes, narrow valleys and relatively straight channels), through 'maturity', to 'old age' with very low slopes and highly meandering, slow flowing rivers.

A major criticism of the Davisian approach is that it concentrated upon landform description almost to the total exclusion of process and deposits. Yet, paradoxically, contemporary process-orientated and quantitatively-based studies developed out of the reactions to the Davisian ideas.

In particular, the work of R.E. Horton (1945) and A.N. Strahler (1952) demonstrated the advantages of a quantitative approach to the classification, description and analysis of landforms. Importantly their work established a direction to the study of process-form relationships and a linkage with the quantitative research of geologists and engineers. Major advances have occurred as a result of the work by L.B. Leopold and T. Maddock which used river data collected by engineers over the preceding seventy years to provide geomorphological evidence for an *equilibrium* condition controlled by discharge and sediment load and manifested by channels of different form.

One component of channel form which relates most apparently to the processes is channel width in cross-section, that is the width of a transverse profile or cut across the channel from bank to bank and perpendicular to the flow. At a single location, channel width may change during a year or between years but these variations will occur as fluctuations about an average value. Any change of the discharges and sediment loads produces an *adjustment* of channel width to a new equilibrium dimension. The existence of a balance between channel form and the prevailing processes, in which the channel dimensions in plan and cross-section are not constant, has been termed *quasi-equilibrium*.

One consequence of this improved view of a river was the rapid diversification of research to encompass short-term process rates, medium-term process-form relationships and long-term landform evolution and process change. In order to provide a common conceptual theme and a framework for the integration of these diversified research trends R.J. Chorley (1962) introduced the *systems approach* into geomorphology. The approach considers a river and its drainage basin as a set of forms which have particular attributes together with a set of relationships or linkages between the forms and between their attributes. A drainage basin can be viewed as an 'open system' because it continuously receives energy and mass (the input), determined primarily by the climate, and energy and mass (the output) is lost from a basin largely as the water discharges and sediment load of the river. A 'balance' may be attained within an open system whereby the import and export of energy and material are equated by means of an adjustment of the forms. The systems approach provides a way of describing complex real-world situations in simple terms and of identifying the full range of variables which affect the river system.

Importantly, a river is considered to be but one component in the drainage basin system of which man is the most influential part.

Fluvial studies have increasingly developed a more applied bias than required by landscape interpretation alone. This trend towards applied studies has been inspired by an improved awareness not only of the river as a resource (for water supply, navigation, amenity and recreation, and fisheries) and as a hazard (because of the problems caused by floods) but also of the sensitivity of rivers to human activities within the drainage basin. The downstream movement of water and sediment through the nested hierarchy of drainage basins, from the smallest headwater stream to the continental river system, facilitates the transmission of human impacts over potentially considerable distances, particularly in the downstream direction. Even the coastline may be affected. Dams built across rivers trap the sediment transported and on the River Rioni, USSR, for example, dams have reduced the sediment supplied by rivers to the Black Sea coastline and caused rapid beach erosion (Makkaveyev, 1970).

## 1.3.1 Objectives

The purpose of analysis in fluvial geomorphology has been envisaged by Gregory (1976) as the investigation of an equation which expresses landform ($F$) as a function of the processes ($P$) operating on earth materials ($M$) — the rocks, soils and sediments — during a period of time ($T$):

$$F = f(P.M.)dT$$

The equation provides a conceptual basis for the study of river channels by demonstrating the linkage between the four different objectives of river studies within fluvial geomorphology.

**1.   To measure (and then to understand) the different components of the equation.**
This requires independent studies of the processes, forms and materials to describe in detail the character of these components, their distribution in space and the way they vary over time.

**2.   To balance the equation.** That is to express the relationships between the three components for a particular geographical area and at a specific point in time. Field observations have shown that a given process operating on a particular type of material will produce a characteristic landform but such equilibrium relationships need more precise definition.

**3.   To differentiate the equation.** That is to identify the interaction between the elements of the equation over time. Continuous monitoring of each of the components would provide information on their interaction over short time scales but longer term interactions require the examination of historical data sources and sequences of deposits, or theoretical approaches for their study. Nevertheless, the available evidence suggests that process change will produce characteristic changes of landform.

**4.   To apply the equation.** That is to use the results from the preceding three levels of study in order to examine contemporary problems and particularly those associated with human impacts.

The study of rivers as fluvial geomorphology by geographers encompasses not only the objectives identified within the above equation but also the needs of hydrology, engineering and ecology. Considerable overlap exists with other disciplines and geographers must be aware of the needs of these disciplines. Just as we can learn from developments within these neighbouring subject areas, so geographers can often provide them with much useful information. One of the most challenging tasks for geomorphologists is to understand the mechanisms which effect channel change and to evaluate the factors which control and constrain these mechanisms.

The geographical perspective is necessarily broad but this breadth of interest is advantageous for two reasons:

1.   It provides for an improved awareness of the inter-relationships between the different components of the river system, and

2.   It provides for an improved appreciation of the sensitivity with which the different components react to human activity, and of the full range of river changes that may result from any given impact.

It is towards the development of predictive models for the anticipation of man-induced changes of rivers, and therefore for improved environmental management, that many contemporary studies of rivers are aimed. However, no matter whether we look at the large intercontinental river system or at a small local stream, our guesses, let alone our predictions, about the future must rely on the study of the present and the interpretation of the past.

# CHAPTER 2 DATA: MEASUREMENT AND ANALYSIS

Scientific explanation is based upon the testing of ideas through the measurement and analysis of carefully defined attributes. The ideas are speculations about the real world and involve the formation of an intuitive 'picture' of the nature of the reality under investigation. Such 'pictures' are used to formulate a model or representation of reality from which **hypotheses** may be developed by logical reasoning to account for certain facts. An hypothesis is a provisional statement which attempts to explain a problem and provides the basis for subsequent investigation, by which the hypothesis may be proved or disproved. Hypotheses cannot be proved absolutely, but by careful data collection, measurement and analysis it is possible to establish a certain degree of confidence in the theory proposed.

The study of rivers involves data collection by field observation and measurement, sometimes involving instrumentation, and by map interpretation, and by examination of aerial photographs, plans and historical documents. Laboratory models can provide useful control experiments, but by necessity they are unrealistically simplified so that confirmation of the findings realised must be achieved also by field observation and measurement. Furthermore, before such experiments can be designed a firm understanding must be gained of the character of the real world phenomena under investigation.

## 2.1 MEASUREMENT

To make the best use of the limited time and resources available for most studies, attention must be given to defining the properties to be observed and to selecting appropriate techniques and methods for measurement or classification. Observations are made for a purpose, and this determines the procedure for making the observation and the reliability of the observation as a description of the property concerned. However, certain operational definitions are first required. Rules must be specified in order to ensure that comparable data are collected: the property to be observed and the method of observation must be clearly defined. For example, in a study of the size characteristics of river bed sediments, to what does the word 'size' refer — mass, volume, length? How is it to be measured? Similarly in a study of channel slope, how is 'slope' to be defined? Over what distance is it to be measured? What equipment, if any, is needed?

In order to ensure a high level of **precision**, (i.e. repeatability of a measurement), the methods employed must be clearly specified. The methods should possess a degree of **objectivity** to allow for the unbiased measurement of a property and to enable anyone to obtain comparable data using the same method for measuring the same property. Also, the closeness of a measurement to the true value, that is the **accuracy** of the data, will depend upon the level of sophistication of the techniques used.

Some error will occur in numerical values obtained by repeated measurement of the same property, but these unpredictable **random errors** will be relatively small and will tend to be compensating so that the average value of the numbers will closely approach the true value. However, more serious errors can result from carelessness on the part of the observer in failing to comply with the rules of the measurement procedure. These errors will have a high magnitude but will be irregular in occurrence.

**Systematic** errors can result from the use of miscalibrated instruments or misinterpretation of the rules of the measurement procedure. The conclusions made at the end of a study will only be as good as the original measurements so that great care must be taken in the design and specification of a data collection procedure.

Measurement involves assigning a value to a property. Most data used for the study of rivers are observational (as opposed to experimental) and may involve either qualitative description or numerical measurement. Qualitative observations may be used, for example, to describe the character of the channel bed sediments as 'gravel', or 'sand'. No measurements are involved but the data may be converted to some sort of **nominal scale** whereby numbers or names are used to classify the information. The numbers or names can be chosen arbitrarily in that any number or name can be used to designate any individual class. Some data are suited to ranking on an **ordinal scale**. Numbers are assigned to classes in a sequence starting with one so that each successive number represents more (or less) of a given quality than the previous class. Ranking is merely sequential and the real magnitudes are not known in absolute terms. The interval between each rank is again arbitrary. Sediment size classes for example,

| (COARSE) | boulders | gravel | sand | silt | clay | (FINE) could be |
|---|---|---|---|---|---|---|
| | 5 | 4 | 3 | 2 | 1 | (increasing size) or |
| | 1 | 2 | 3 | 4 | 5 | (decreasing size) or |
| | 10 000 | 1 000 | 100 | 10 | 1 | etc. |

Qualitative observations are particularly useful before undertaking any measurement because they enable the description of an area and generate an awareness of the range of information available and of any associations which may exist say between land-uses, landforms, sediments and processes. Indeed, detailed sketch maps can provide useful information about the arrangement of landform elements, the character of deposits, the location of sites experiencing active erosion and so on.

Numerical measurement, as opposed to the numerical coding of qualitative observations, refers to the use of the more powerful *interval-* and *ratio-scales*. The former scale involves the assignment of values to classes which have an equal interval although no regard to zero. Temperature, for example, is measured using a scale based on equal increments of mercury expansion in a thermometer as temperature rises, but the zero point is arbitrary. The ratio-scale is the highest level of measurement, and is used when a zero point can be identified. Mass, length and velocity for example are all measured on this scale. In every case, zero indicates an absence of that property. All studies should use the ratio scale wherever possible but two measurement processes may often be used: primary measurements made using the ratio-scale are commonly classified, and usefully so, on a nominal scale.

Measurements can be used in two ways. Firstly, to provide improved descriptions of particular situations, and secondly, to infer that relationships exist between the different properties. Although direct interpretations can be made from the data such interpretations can be supported and improved by calculating statistics. Statistical techniques can be used to summarise the properties of a large data sample in a few numbers and enable valid inferences to be drawn from samples of data to the whole data set. However, in order to realise valid conclusions from any study one further question must be answered — where are the observations and measurements to be made?

## 2.2 SAMPLING

Rarely can we examine the whole of a river system in detail. It is therefore necessary to study a relatively small *sample of sites*, and the need arises to ensure that these are *representative* of the river system as a whole. For example, in a study of the particle-size characteristics of river-bed deposits the total number of particles is called the *population* but it is neither practicable nor necessary to measure all the particles (i.e. the complete population). For most purposes a perfectly adequate description of the size characteristics of the deposit can be obtained by measuring a *sample* of the population. The size of the sample is dependent upon the objectives of the study and the analytical procedures to be adopted but the basic concept in sampling is that of a *random sample*, which consists of a small number of observations chosen to be generally representative of a larger number that constitutes the *population* under consideration. A random sample is one in which every member of the population has an equal likelihood of being selected. Statistical theory is based almost entirely upon the assumption of random sampling. Therefore, in order to make valid use of statistics it is essential that random data samples are obtained.

A slight modification of random sampling, which preserves its theoretical advantages, is particularly useful for the study of rivers. Through a sound understanding of the fluvial system and using field observations or map data, a geomorphologist may be able to divide a population into subgroups, each of which is more homogeneous internally than the population as a whole. These subdivisions are known in statistics as *sampling strata*. A random sample should then be taken within each subgroup and the set of observations made is known as a *stratified random sample*, the sample being stratified within the whole population but random within each subgroup. However, taking a random sample is not as easy as it sounds; thought and planning are in fact required to select a truly random sample. Firstly, the population to be studied must be exactly defined and any sampling strata identified. Secondly, care should be taken to ensure that every member of the population is equally likely to be chosen to form part of the sample.

Random sampling in the context of a river system refers to data distributed in space. Such areal sampling problems are commonly solved by using a 'grid' which may be created in the field, but for study site location, for example, the National Grid on the

Ordnance Survey maps may be employed. In either case, the grid intersections are numbered, normally from left to right and from bottom to top so that numbers in both directions are at zero in the bottom-left corner which is designated 00. A sample of grid intersections is then made by reference to a *table of random numbers* (see Murdoch, and Barnes, 1974). For a grid size of less than 100 X 100 the two digits in the table would give the 'easting' (i.e. the number of grid lines to the right of the starting point 00), and the second pair of digits would give the 'northing'. The intersection of the two grid lines locates the sample point. If any of the co-ordinates provided by the random numbers lie outside the grid they should be rejected and new co-ordinates obtained until the required sample size has been reached. Some occasions arise, particularly for sampling linear features such as the river channel, when a *systematic* sampling technique may be desirable: sampling sites are selected systematically, at some regular and standard interval. This technique is valid and can be treated as a random sample provided that the data to be sampled do not have a periodic repetition at the same interval.

## 2.3 MAPS AS DATA SOURCES

Although fieldwork is arguably the most important part of river studies, maps often provide the first source of information upon which fieldwork is subsequently based, as well as providing an important data source in their own right. Topographic maps portray two fundamental characteristics of surface features: size (area or length) and spatial location (distance between points and the arrangement of these points). They have been widely employed for studies of rivers and not only provide a description of basin form, drainage pattern and channel slope (recorded by the contour spacing) but also act as historical data sources which may be compared with more recent field observations, maps or aerial photographs in order to identify changes within the system.

Although maps contain large amounts of valuable information, they are nevertheless subject to several sources of measurement error and data misrepresentation. Only a fraction of the information in the real world is recorded by maps, which must be viewed only as representations or models of that real world, and some of the information may have been recorded inaccurately. This is particularly true of old maps.

The transfer of information from field observation to a map involves the loss of data, a probable reduction in precision, and introduces the possibility of a misleading interpretation. The degree of accuracy with which a measured length can be shown on a map of given scale is termed the *plottable error*. On a map scale of 1:2,500 one millimetre represents 2.5 m on the ground; 25 m on a 1:25 000 map; and 250 m at a 1:250 000 scale. Considerable care must therefore be taken during map construction and during data abstraction. The *reduction in scale* from the real world 1:1 'ideal' ratio by necessity leads to a reduction in available information. The loss of information is known as *cartographic generalisation*, and this involves two considerations: selection and simplification. With decreasing scale linear detail must be drawn progressively more simply, so that it is often the case that a significant difference occurs between the length of a sinuous river measured on a map at one scale compared with the same river measured at a different scale.

On any map each symbol must occupy a finite area if it is to be legible. If a given map is reduced in scale in order to derive another, smaller scale map, the line widths, dimensions of point symbols and type size can only be slightly reduced and often remain more or less constant. It follows that each element of detail will occupy a proportionately greater area on the derived map than it did on the source material. Thus, in order to maintain the legibility of the derived map its content must be generalised. The measured length of a river system, for example, will become progressively shorter as the map scale is reduced because the features have not only to be simplified but also selectively omitted to leave space for 'more important' information. Small tributaries in particular may be selected for omission in order to maintain legibility or again to accommodate other detail. Both selection and simplification are based upon such qualitative factors as experience and geographical knowledge on the part of the map designer and by the purpose of the map production. So long as the limitations of maps as data sources are appreciated, however, they may be regarded as useful tools for the study of river systems.

In Britain between three and five complete revisions of the river systems have been made for large scale Ordnance Survey maps (1:10 560 series) but the 1:25 000 second series is used most commonly for studies of rivers at the present time. Irrespective of the series and map edition used as a basis for measurement, the edition and date of survey should be determined, and where possible standardised, because survey dates between individual sheets may vary considerably.

---

## 2.4 CHARACTERISTICS OF STATISTICAL DATA

When measurements of any given property are processed, the values will be found to vary even though the measurements represent the same property. For example, the size of the channel bed materials is found to vary markedly along a river, and between one river and another: the property which is observed to differ (i.e. the sediment size, in this example) is termed a *variable*. However, at any particular location the channel bed will contain sediment particles of different sizes. Such a *distribution* of values is characteristic of any data sample, whether it be measurements of sediment size, streamflow, drainage network or channel width.

If the data are grouped into classes, usually of equal size, the distribution may be depicted graphically as a histogram or frequency distribution curve (*Figure 2.1*). The latter is simply a smooth curve interpolated from the histogram, and describes the number, weight or proportion (%) — that is the *frequency* of the observations — that fall in each class. The data do not need to be collected in the classes used but may be subsequently grouped into them; for example, for each class the absolute frequency (the actual number or weight) or relative frequency (the percentage or proportion of all the observations that fall into a particular class) may be recorded. The histogram or frequency diagram describes the distribution of a large number of observations and is particularly useful when a huge table of values appears incomprehensible.

Frequency curves provide a useful way of describing a data set but for many purposes it is necessary to summarise the distribution in a quantitative manner. Four parameters are commonly used: mode, median, mean and standard deviation. The *mode* (or *modal class*) is the value of the measurement ( or class) which has the greatest frequency. The *median* value divides the area under the curve into two equal parts, (i.e. of all the measurements 50% are smaller and 50% are larger than the median). The **mean** ($\bar{x}$) is defined as the sum of the observations or measurements of a variable ($x$) divided by the total number of observations or measurements made ($n$), and is expressed

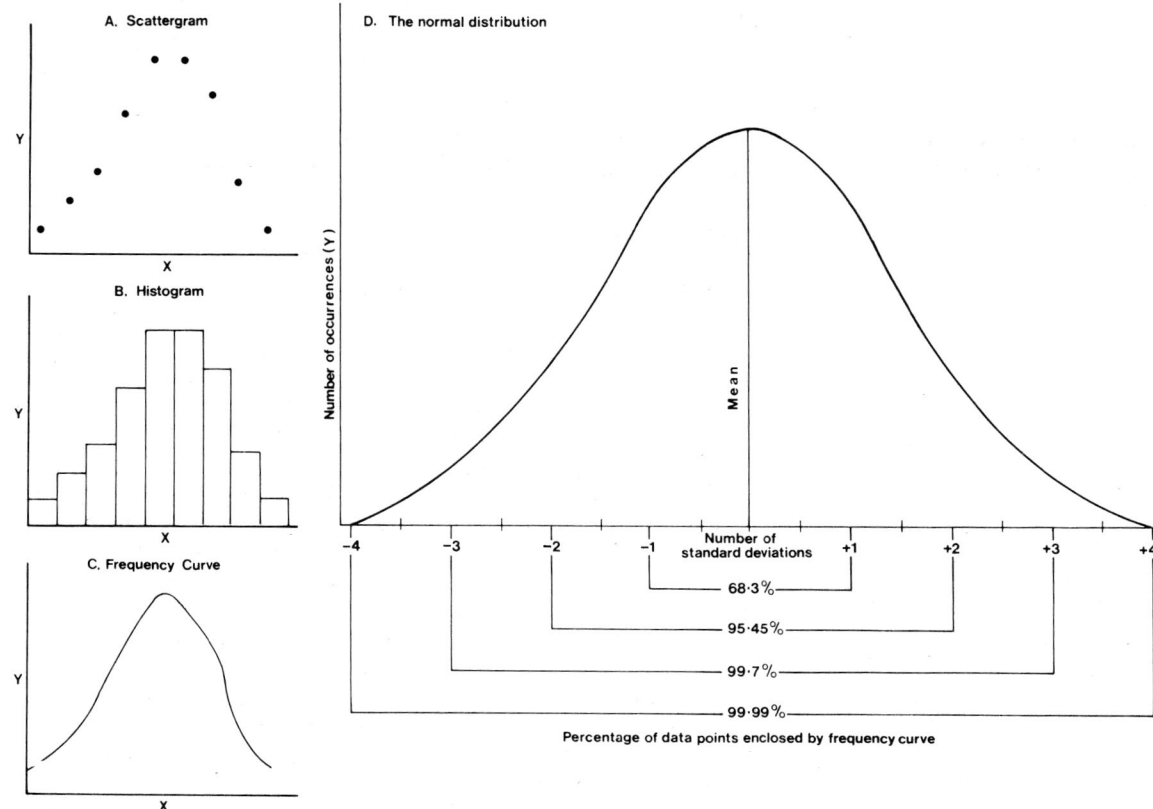

Figure 2.1 Presentation of data as frequency graphs

$$\bar{x} = \frac{\Sigma x}{n}$$

where $\Sigma x$ tells us to add together all the values of $x$.

The mean is the most commonly used estimate of the average value of a distribution. However for any data set, the actual values will differ from one another, and also from the mean so that some measure of the degree of scatter about the mean is also required if the character of the distribution is to be adequately summarised. The scatter or deviation of values about the mean is described by the standard deviation ($\sigma$) where

$$\sigma = \sqrt{\frac{\Sigma(x - \bar{x})^2}{n}}$$

A simple example is given in *Table 2.1*, where $d = x - \bar{x}$.

**TABLE 2.1 THE CALCULATION OF MEAN AND STANDARD DEVIATION FOR ANNUAL RAINFALL DATA FOR THE RIVER TER, ESSEX. (1970 – 1978)**

| Streamflow value $x$ (mm) | Deviation about mean $d$ | Deviation squared $d^2$ |
|---|---|---|
| 598 | 42 | 1764 |
| 523 | 33 | 1089 |
| 487 | 69 | 4761 |
| 491 | 65 | 4225 |
| 703 | 147 | 21609 |
| 566 | 10 | 100 |
| 477 | 79 | 6241 |
| 574 | 18 | 324 |
| 582 | 26 | 676 |
| $\Sigma x$ = 5001 | | $\Sigma d^2$ = 40789 |

$\Sigma x/n$ = Mean ($\bar{x}$) = 556. Standard deviation ($\sigma$) = $\sqrt{\dfrac{\Sigma d^2}{n}}$ = $\sqrt{\dfrac{40789}{9}}$ = 67

The shape of the frequency distribution curve obtained from any sample population usually approximates to one of only a few defined forms. For most statistical methods it is usually assumed that the frequency data is symmetrically distributed about the mean: and this is known as the *normal distribution*. Given a normal curve the distribution of data about the mean is predictable irrespective of the actual values of the mean and standard deviation (*Figure 2.1D*). Thus, for a normally distributed data set, about two-thirds (precisely, 68.3%) of the measurements will be within one standard deviation of the mean, and about 95 percent will lie between $+2\sigma$ and $-2\sigma$; in other words for a sample of 100 measurements of a given variable only five values will be more than two standard deviations greater or smaller than the mean.

On the assumption that a data set conforms to a normal distribution it has been shown above that the percentage of measurements which occur within certain limits can be determined by reference to the mean and standard deviation. The chance or *probability* of particular values occurring in a sample can then be predicted. Also, it is possible to assess the probability that a given value is likely to be equalled, exceeded or not reached, and the probability that certain events are likely to occur at given intervals. For example, there is a 50% probability of values being greater than the mean, i.e. there would be an equal chance of a value being above or below the average.

The probability ($p$) of an event occurring is expressed as a value of between one and zero. If $p$ = 1 that value will always be obtained; 100% of the measurements lie within the outer limits of the distribution so that the probability of a measurement within these limits is 1.0. If $p$ = 0 then the value will never occur. A probability of 0.8 means that a value, or event chosen at random from a population, is likely to occur on average eighty times in each sample of 100 values or events whilst $p$ = 0.2 suggests that a value or event is relatively unlikely (twenty occurrences in every hundred on average). New observations may occur outside the limits of a frequency distribution but the chance of such a measurement occurring obviously depends upon the sample size: for distributions based upon a large sample the chance is infinitesimally small. A probability scale is commonly seen to range from 0.00001 to 0.99999 (*see Figure 3.14* for an example).

The concept of probability is fundamental to statistical analysis and data need to be described by a normal distribution in order to enable rigorous statistical testing. Parametric statistics are the most powerful and these use interval and ratio-scale measurements of variables which are known to be normally distributed. However, data for many variables in the earth science, in general, and for those describing the characteristics of rivers in particular, do not satisfy this requirement. The distribution is often *skewed*, that is, it is asymmetrical with the median having a different value from that of the mean.

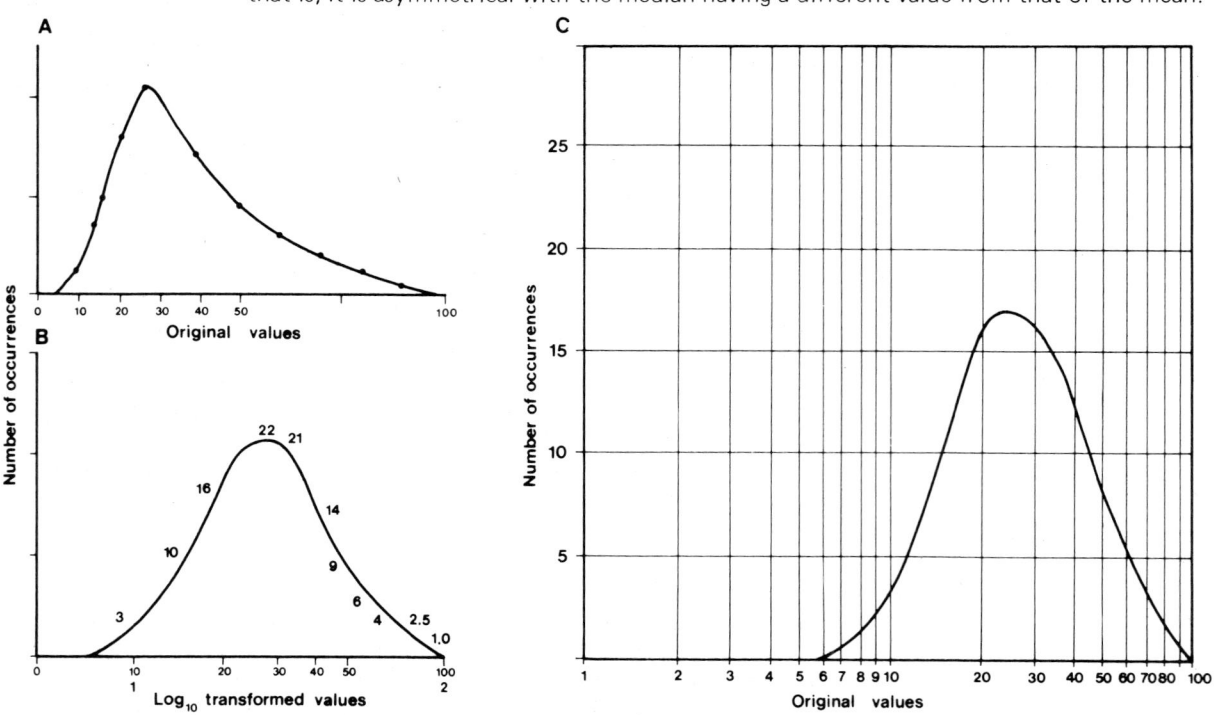

Figure 2.2 The transformation of a positively skewed distribution (A) using logarithms to the base 10 (B) and by plotting directly onto log-normal graph paper in order to normalise the distribution (C)

In these cases either less powerful non-parametric statistics, which use nominal and ordinal measurements, must be employed or the data must be manipulated in a way so as to normalise the distribution. Such manipulation can be effected by the process of *transformation*.

For many variables the data display a marked positive skewness with a peak clearly to the left of the mean — with a maximum frequency at the lower end of the scale (*Figure 2.2*). These data in fact show log-normality and an approximately normal distribution will result by transforming the data into logarithms ($\log_{10}$). Although the logarithm of any number can be obtained from standard mathematical tables (e.g. *Four Figure Mathematical Tables*, Macmillan), specially drawn logarithmic graph paper may be used and the arithmetic values plotted directly (*Figure 2.2C*). The logarithmic axis is divided into 'cycles' each numbered from 1 to 9. Any number of cycles may be used and within each successive cycle the values increase to the power of 10. For example, on four-cycle graph paper the first cycle scale might read 0.1, 0.2, 0.3 . . . 0.9; the second cycle would then be 1, 2, . . . 9; the third 10, 20, . . .90; and the fourth 100, 200, . . . 900.

As will be seen later, the value of logarithmic plots is that positively skewed distributions are shown as more-or-less straight lines on bivariate scattergrams. Plotting the normal data on arithmetic graph paper would reveal a curved relationship. It is *the ability to derive linear bivariate relationships that has considerable importance for the study of rivers*.

___

## 2.5 DATA ANALYSIS

### 2.5.1 Detecting relationships

Many geomorphological studies attempt to establish relationships and associations between the measurements of form and/or process. In reality the concept of 'cause and effect' is very hard to substantiate because of the multivariate character of natural systems. Nevertheless, useful information can be gained from the examination of bivariate relationships. Simple graphs (or scatter diagrams) can on their own illuminate inter-relationships between variables. In *Figure 2.3* the variable *X*, known as the *independent variable*, is suggested to have *caused* the form of *Y*, the dependent variable. The strength

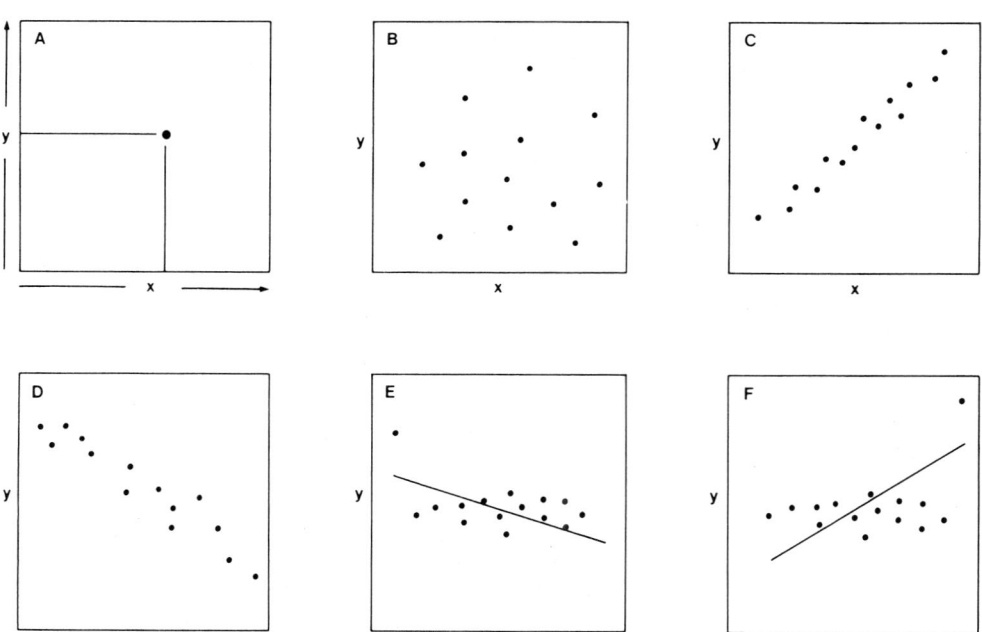

Figure 2.3 Common bi-variate relationships. A simple relationship is shown in A; a sample of points may show a wide scatter and a weak correlation (B), or a strong positive (C) or negative (D) correlation. However, the direction of correlation may be biased by a single extreme value (E and F)

of the relationship between any pair of parameters, that is, the degree of connectivity, is commonly revealed by *correlation analysis*. The wide scatter of points suggests that no apparent relationship exists between the two variables in *Figure 2.3B*, but in C or D a relationship is observable. In C, for example, an increase in the value of *X* produces an increase in the value of *Y* and this is known as a positive correlation; in D, *Y* is reduced as *X* increases, giving a negative correlation.

In order to determine the strength of a relationship between two variables (*x* and *y*) the correlation coefficient ('*r*') may be calculated. For many geomorphological problems the Pearson product-movement coefficient is employed and this may be expressed in a form which allows easy computation:

$$r = \frac{A}{\sqrt{B \times C}}$$

where $A = \Sigma xy - (\Sigma x \times \frac{(\Sigma y)}{(n)})$

$B = \Sigma x^2 - (\Sigma x \times \frac{(\Sigma x)}{(n)})$

$C = \Sigma y^2 - (\Sigma y \times \frac{(\Sigma y)}{(n)})$

Determination of the correlation coefficient therefore requires the calculation of only five different sums: the sum of the $x$ values ($\Sigma x$), the sum of the $y$ values ($\Sigma y$), the sum of the $x$-squared values ($\Sigma x^2$), the sum of the y-squared values ($\Sigma y^2$) and the sum of the $x$ times $y$ values ($\Sigma xy$), and the mean values of $x$ and $y$. The derived value of '$r$' can vary between +1 and −1. Values of zero mean that there is no relationship between $X$ and $Y$, but as the values approach +1 or −1 the strength of the correlation increases: $r = -1$ expresses a perfect negative correlation and $r = +1$ expresses a perfect positive correlation.

For example, it may be suspected intuitively that a relationship exists between channel width (form) and a discharge (process). Field measurement may support this idea, but the relationship can be statistically tested by calculating the correlation coefficient (*Table 2.2*). The value of '$r$' squared ($r^2$) should also be determined because it provides an indication of the proportion of the total variance of the dependent variable ($Y$) that is explained by the independent variable ($X$). In the example in *Table 2.2*, $r^2 = 0.9773$ so that the *degree of explanation* of the total variance of $Y$ by $X$ is 97.7 percent. However,

**TABLE 2.2 COMPUTATION OF THE DEGREE OF CORRELATION BETWEEN DISCHARGE (X) AND CHANNEL WIDTH (Y) FOR THE RIVER ERME, DARTMOOR, UK**

| X | $\log_{10} X$ | $(\log_{10} X)^2$ | Y | $\log_{10} Y$ | $(\log_{10} Y)^2$ | $\log_{10} X \times \log_{10} Y$ |
|---|---|---|---|---|---|---|
| 1.8 | 0.2553 | 0.0652 | 2.8 | 0.4472 | 0.1999 | 0.1142 |
| 2.7 | 0.4314 | 0.1861 | 4.2 | 0.6232 | 0.3884 | 0.2688 |
| 2.9 | 0.4624 | 0.2138 | 4.8 | 0.6812 | 0.4641 | 0.3150 |
| 3.9 | 0.5911 | 0.3494 | 5.2 | 0.7160 | 0.5127 | 0.4232 |
| 5.4 | 0.7324 | 0.5364 | 8.6 | 0.9345 | 0.8733 | 0.6844 |
| 5.7 | 0.7559 | 0.5714 | 8.1 | 0.9085 | 0.8253 | 0.6867 |
| 6.9 | 0.8388 | 0.7036 | 11.0 | 1.0414 | 1.0845 | 0.8735 |
| 7.4 | 0.8692 | 0.7556 | 12.4 | 1.0934 | 1.1955 | 0.9504 |
| Sum | 4.9365 | 3.3815 | | 6.4454 | 5.5437 | 4.3162 |
| Mean ($n$ = 8) | 0.6171 | | | 0.8057 | | |

$$A = 4.3162 - (4.9365 \times 0.8057) = 0.3389$$
$$B = 3.3815 - (4.9365 \times 0.6171) = 0.3352$$
$$C = 5.5437 - (6.4454 \times 0.8057) = 0.3506$$

$$r = \frac{0.3389}{\sqrt{0.3352 \times 0.3506}} = 0.9886$$

*Note*: A sample of only eight values is used here for demonstration purposes. A sample of **at least** fifteen values should normally be used.

it is important actually to plot scatter diagrams of the samples **X** and **Y** to ensure correct interpretation of the correlation coefficient. For example, a single extreme value can markedly bias the correlation coefficient (*Figures 2.3E and F*).

**2.5.2 Testing for significance**

Assuming that two variables are normally distributed it is possible to determine if the value of '*r*' represents a statistically significant relationship. It may be that the relationship has occurred by chance. Such chance relationships may result especially from some partiality in data collection; different relationships would then be obtained by the examination of a new or enlarged sample of the same population. In tests of significance a *null hypothesis* is set up. This states the hypothesis to be tested in a negative way and is designated Ho. For the relationship between channel width and discharge the null hypothesis would be expressed thus:

Ho: there is *no* significant relationship between discharge and channel width.

The alternative hypothesis (H1) would then be:

H1: there *is* a significant relationship between discharge and channel width.

The null hypothesis is then tested: if it is rejected it can be assumed that the relationship shown by the correlation coefficient is not a result of chance and H1 is accepted.

The significance of a particular relationship is determined by comparison of a test statistic with standard tables (e.g. Murdoch and Barnes, 1974). These tables give critical levels for the test statistic at different significance levels and for different sample sizes. The tables give the critical values of the test statistic required for the null hypothesis to be rejected at a specified significance level.

The critical significance level is selected prior to the test and determines the *confidence* with which the null hypothesis can be rejected. For example, a critical significance level of 0.05 is commonly used and this means that the null hypothesis will be correctly rejected on 95 occasions out of 100, and wrongly rejected on only five occasions. A higher level of confidence can be attained by using critical significance levels of 0.01 or 0.001 which means that the rejection of the null hypothesis is likely to be wrong once in one hundred and once in one thousand occasions respectively.

The significance test varies according to the nature of the original hypothesis and depends upon whether the null hypothesis is directional of non-directional. Tests for significance in a predicted direction are termed 'one-tailed' and those which test for differences in either direction are termed 'two-tailed'. The significance may be determined by comparison of the value of '$r$' with the critical value at a chosen significance level and for a given number of degrees of freedom ($n - 2$; where $n$ = sample size). Here the sample correlation coefficient '$r$' is positive so that the alternative hypothesis H1 states that the population correlation coefficient ($p$) is greater than zero. For a negative '$r$' the hypothesis would be H1 ($p < 0$). In either case we are testing a relationship versus the null hypothesis Ho ($p = 0$) in a predetermined direction and a one-tailed test is used. Only if the computed value of '$r$' at that significance level exceeds the critical value should the null hypothesis be rejected. In the example, with 13 degrees of freedom, the correlation coefficient ($r = 0.98$) is greater than the critical value of 0.48 at the 0.05 significance level and the null hypothesis can be rejected.

Alternatively, and particularly for large sample sizes, the Student's t-distribution may be employed. The t-test is expressed as

$$t = r \sqrt{\frac{(n-2)}{(1-r^2)}}, \text{ with } n - 2 \text{ degrees of freedom}$$

For this example

$$t = 0.98 \sqrt{\frac{15-2}{1-0.96}} = 17.67, \text{ with 13 degrees of freedom.}$$

Using a one-tailed Student's t-distribution at the 0.05 significance level, again as published in the standard tables, the null hypothesis can be rejected if '$t$' is greater than 1.77. Thus, such a strong correlation coefficient could be produced by chance on far fewer than five in a hundred times, and H1 is accepted: channel width is related to discharge.

**2.5.3 Testing for differences between samples**

Frequently, data are recorded as classes, or a simple observation of the presence or absence of a feature may have been made. For example, an hypothesis may be stated: the solute load of streams is related to land-use type (*see* **Section 4.1.3** for discussion). To compare independent samples which include *nominal data* a contingency table is set up to describe the data distribution (*Table 2.3*). *Table 2.4* gives the frequency of occurrence of the three dissolved load classes measured as specific electrical conductance for two different land-uses on Devonian rocks in south-west England. The null hypothesis (Ho) that there is no significant difference between the dissolved loads of the streams

**TABLE 2.3 A CONTINGENCY TABLE**

|  | A | B | Total |
|---|---|---|---|
| Group 1 | a | b | a + b |
| Group 2 | c | d | c + d |
| Total | a + c | b + d | a + b + c + d |

**TABLE 2.4 OBSERVED AND EXPECTED VALUES OF STREAM DISSOLVED LOADS FOR DIFFERENT LAND-USES. (EXPECTED FREQUENCIES ARE GIVEN IN BRACKETS)**

| Reference Class | Dissolved load | Specific electrical conductance ($\mu$mhos cm$^{-1}$ 25 $^\circ$C) | 1 Woodland | 2 Moorland | Totals |
|---|---|---|---|---|---|
| A | Low | 30 — 70 | 3 (10.4) | 20 (12.58) | 23 |
| B | Intermediate | 70 — 110 | 9 ( 7.70) | 8 ( 9.3) | 17 |
| C | High | 110 — 150 | 12 ( 5.89) | 1 ( 7.11) | 13 |
|  | Totals |  | 24 | 29 | 53 |

After Walling and Webb, 1975

(i.e. that the observed differences could have arisen simply by chance) is tested using *chi square*. This involves calculating the expected frequencies.

Since out of a total of fifty-three sites, twenty-three were within Class A, 23 ÷ 53 of the samples *should* be in this class if they were randomly distributed. The probability of a woodland stream having a dissolved load of Class A is then:

| proportion of total sample in Class A | X | proportion of total sample woodland | X | size of total sample |
|---|---|---|---|---|

(23 ÷ 53) X (24 ÷ 53) X 53 = 10.4

This is the expected frequency. To test Ho:

$$\text{Chi square } (\chi^2) = \sum_{i=1}^{r} \sum_{j=1}^{k} \frac{(O_{ij} - E_{ij})^2}{E_{ij}}$$

where $O_{ij}$ = observed values

$E_{ij}$ = expected values

$r$ = rows, and $k$ = columns

$$\sum_{i=1}^{r} \sum_{j=1}^{k} = \text{sum values over all rows and all columns:}$$

*References to Table 2.4* = A1, A2, B1, etc.

$$\underbrace{\frac{(3-10.4)^2}{\left(10.4\right)}}_{\text{A1}} + \underbrace{\frac{(20-12.58)^2}{\left(12.58\right)}}_{\text{A2}} + \underbrace{\frac{(9-7.70)^2}{\left(7.70\right)}}_{\text{B1}} + \underbrace{\frac{(8-9.3)^2}{\left(9.3\right)}}_{\text{B2}} = \underbrace{\frac{(12-5.89)^2}{\left(5.89\right)}}_{\text{C1}}$$

$$+ \underbrace{\frac{(1-7.11)^2}{\left(7.11\right)}}_{\text{C2}} = 21.632 \text{ with } (r-1) \times (k-1) \text{ degrees of freedom}$$

$$(3-1) \times (2-1)$$

**2** d.f.

Using tables of chi-square values we find that our value of 21.632 for 2 degrees of freedom is greater than the critical value for a probability of 0.01 ($\chi^2_{(0.01,2)} = 9.21$).

This means that such a distribution of frequencies would arise by chance less than 1 in 100 times. The null hypothesis is therefore rejected and it can be concluded that land-use has a significant influence upon the dissolved load of the streams.

## 2.5.4 Empirical models

Empirical models are based upon an essentially inductive approach whereby a general law can be assumed because particular cases that seem to be examples of the law are observed to exist. The models use statistically significant relationships between variables measured in the field or from map sources and describe the change of a dependent variable for any particular variation of the independent (control) variable. The relationships are defined using techniques of *regression* analysis. Many variations of the classical regression technique are available for deriving the line-of-best-fit through any scatter of data points. Most commonly a least-squares fit is applied: the best-fit line is drawn such that the sum of the squares of the $Y$ variation for any value of $X$ (the vertical deviations about the line) is a minimum. For simple arithmetic data, the regression line may be expressed as:

$$Y = a + bX$$

then, using logarithmic data:

$$\log_{10} Y = a + b.\log_{10} x$$

where $a$ = the sample estimate of the intercept describing the value of $Y$ for $X$ equal to unity;

$b$ = the sample estimate of the slope of the line which describes the rate of change of $Y$ on $X$, expressed as a power function;

$Y$ = the estimated average $Y$ for the given value of $X$

Using the same notation as employed for determining the correlation coefficient (Section 2.3.5) the regression line may be simply calculated:

the slope , $b = A \div B$

the intercept, $q = y - (b \times \bar{x})$

Therefore for the relationship between discharge and channel width along the River Erme on Dartmoor:

A = 0.3389 B = 0.3352 C = 0.3506
$b$ = 0.3389 ÷ 0.3352 = 1.011
$a$ = 0.8057 − (1.011 X 0.6171) = 0.1818

It is now possible to draw a regression line on the scattergram (*Figure 2.4*) and to determine the 'best estimate' of channel width (*W*) for any given discharge (*Q*):

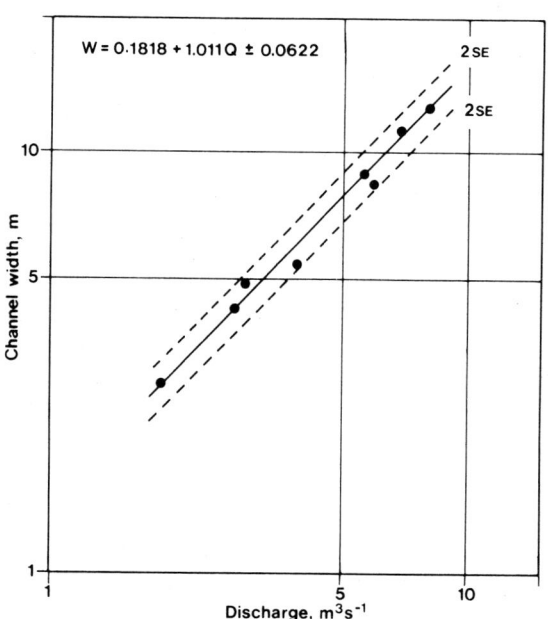

Figure 2.4 Double-log scattergram and regression for the relationship between discharge and channel width, River Erme (*see Tables 2.2 and 2.5*)

so that for $Q = 1$ m$^3$ s$^{-1}$;

$\log_{10} W = 0.3037 + (0.8207 \times 0) = 0.3037$;

$W = 2.01$ m

for $Q = 10$ m$^3$ s$^{-1}$;

$\log_{10} W = 0.3037 + (0.8207 \times 1) = 1.1244$;

$W = 13.32$ m.

Such simple empirical models (say between discharge and channel width, runoff and sediment yield or drainage area and drainage network length) provide no information about why the relationship exists or what controls the relationship. Nevertheless, the slope of the regression curve, the '*b*' exponent, is a most useful descriptor for comparison between rivers and for the examination of changes in a river's character downstream or over time. The greater the change of the dependent variable ($Y$) for any given change of the independent variable ($X$), the greater will be the deviation of the '*b*' exponent from zero.

It must be stressed that the regression lines are only *the best estimates* of the relationship between two variables. In the example of the River Erme, therefore, the relationship between discharge and channel width is imperfect (all the data do not fit exactly onto a straight line) and with an imperfect relationship we cannot define a single absolutely correct answer. Therefore it is useful to assess the range within which actual estimates are likely to fall. This is achieved by calculating the *standard error* ($E$) of the estimate of the dependent variable ($Y$):

$$E = \sigma y \sqrt{1 - r^2}$$

where $\sigma y$ = standard deviation of $Y$; and $r$ = correlation coefficient. For the River Erme data where $\sigma y = 0.2066$ and $r = 0.9886$:

$$E = 0.2066 \times \sqrt{(1 - 0.9886^2)} = 0.0311$$

The standard error relates to the regression estimate in the same way that the standard deviation relates to the mean, that is, there is a 68 per cent probability that the actual values will differ from the regression line value by **not more than** one standard error; and there is a 95 per cent probability that the actual values will lie within two standard errors of the estimate. Using the standard errors it is possible to construct **confidence limits** of the regression. Thus, for the River Erme (**Table 2.2**) the regression equation may be written thus:

$$\log_{10} Y = a + b \log_{10} X \pm 2E$$
$$\log_{10} W = 0.1818 + (1.011 \times \log_{10} Q) \pm 0.0622$$

The confidence limits are added to the graph (**Figure 2.4**); for a discharge of 10 m$^3$ s$^{-1}$ 95% of channel width measurements will be between 17.99 m and 13.51 m, and 68% between 16.75 m and 14.51 m.

# CHAPTER 3 STREAMFLOW

Streamflow comprises the movement of water over the surface of the earth within a well-defined course and under the influence of gravity. Water flowing in channels, which may range in size from the small rivulet to the large river, is supplied by water moving in a diffuse manner through the soils and rocks or over the hillslopes within the source area, (i.e. within the drainage basin). In Britain, long-term streamflow data are available from the regional water authorities for most major rivers and many small streams. The **Surface Water Year Book**, for 1966–70 published by HMSO, London, contains data for 782 measurement stations and **The Water Data Unit**, at Reading, Berkshire, has the responsibility for collecting, processing and storing river-flow records on a national basis. Rainfall data also are given for most gauged catchments. On a global scale, streamflow data is summarised in **Discharge of selected Rivers of the World**, UNESCO/HID, Paris, 3 volumes, 1969.

Streamflow is conventionally described as a **discharge** — the volume of water passing through a channel cross-section per unit time (cubic metres per second ($m^3 s^{-1}$) or litres per second ($\ell s^{-1}$), or as the **runoff** from a drainage basin. Some examples of river discharges are given in **Table 3.1**. The annual volume of runoff transmitted by a river is closely related to the area of the drainage basin, which determines the total amount of rainfall caught. Therefore, for comparison between rivers, it is usual to divide the measure of discharge by the drainage area. This is expressed as cubic metres per second per square kilometre ($m^3 s^{-1} km^{-2}$) if the mean annual discharge is used, or as a depth of water over the basin (mm) if the total annual discharge is employed. The latter represents the amount of rainfall that became streamflow. However, the percentage of rainfall that reaches the channel may vary from more than ninety to less than ten percent. This variability relates to the character of the hydrological cycle.

## 3.1 THE GLOBAL HYDROLOGICAL CYCLE

Streamflow is but one component of the hydrological cycle which describes the movement of water between the oceans, atmosphere, and the land. The hydrological cycle may be

## TABLE 3.1 SOME EXAMPLES OF STREAMFLOW CHARACTERISTICS

| River and location | Drainage area (km$^2$) | Mean flow (m$^3$ s$^{-1}$) | (m$^3$ s$^{-1}$ km$^{-2}$) | Highest flow (m$^3$ s$^{-1}$) | (m$^3$ s$^{-1}$ km$^{-2}$) |
|---|---|---|---|---|---|
| Congo, Central African Republic | 3 475 000 | 40 400 | 0.012 | 59 200 | 0.017 |
| Mississippi, USA | 2 964 300 | 16 200 | 0.005 | 39 200 | 0.013 |
| Ob, USSR | 2 430 000 | 14 000 | 0.006 | 43 800 | 0.018 |
| Mackenzie, Canada | 1 570 000 | 8 000 | 0.005 | 26 100 | 0.017 |
| Volga, USSR | 1 350 000 | 7 250 | 0.005 | 27 500 | 0.020 |
| Mekong, Thailand | 391 000 | 9 000 | 0.023 | 31 400 | 0.080 |
| Niger, Mali | 340 000 | 925 | 0.003 | 1 750 | 0.005 |
| Yukon, Canada | 275 000 | 2 100 | 0.008 | 6 970 | 0.025 |
| Uruguay, Uruguay | 238 900 | 5 050 | 0.021 | 27 000 | 0.113 |
| **Britain** | | | | | |
| Thames | 9 870 | 67 | 0.007 | 1 064 | 0.108 |
| Trent | 7 490 | 83 | 0.011 | 790 | 0.105 |
| Tay | 4 590 | 156 | 0.034 | 1 387 | 0.302 |
| Severn | 4 330 | 62 | 0.014 | 654 | 0.151 |
| Wye | 4 040 | 70 | 0.017 | 906 | 0.224 |
| Great Ouse | 3 030 | 14 | 0.005 | 310 | 0.102 |
| Avon | 1 600 | 20 | 0.013 | 365 | 0.228 |
| Swale | 1 350 | 19 | 0.014 | 255 | 0.189 |
| Test | 1 040 | 13 | 0.013 | 38 | 0.037 |
| Cam | 811 | 3.5 | 0.004 | 73 | 0.090 |
| Exe | 601 | 16 | 0.027 | 495 | 0.824 |
| Tweed system | 4 390 | 83 | 0.019 | 1 186 | 0.270 |
| | 2 080 | 47 | 0.023 | 792 | 0.380 |
| | 1 500 | 38 | 0.025 | 605 | 0.403 |
| | 694 | 16 | 0.023 | 480 | 0.692 |
| | 373 | 9.3 | 0.025 | 266 | 0.713 |
| | 23.7 | 0.75 | 0.032 | 29 | 1.224 |

viewed at the global scale as a closed system within which the same mass of water is conserved. Within the cycle, water moves between the principal **storages** — the atmosphere, ocean, ice and groundwater — mostly by three processes of mass transfer: evaporation, precipitation and streamflow.

The oceans cover some 70% of the earth's surface and store over 97% of the total available water supply. Evaporation provides the moisture supply for the atmosphere and it is the character of this storage which determines the precipitation input to a drainage basin and controls streamflow. Although the atmosphere stores only a small fraction of 1% of the available water at any one time, this small amount serves as a continuing source of precipitation because of the continuous replenishment through evaporation. Only about 23% of the precipitation (rain, hail, sleet, snow) falls onto the land surface and not all of this becomes streamflow (**Figure 3.1**). Some may be returned

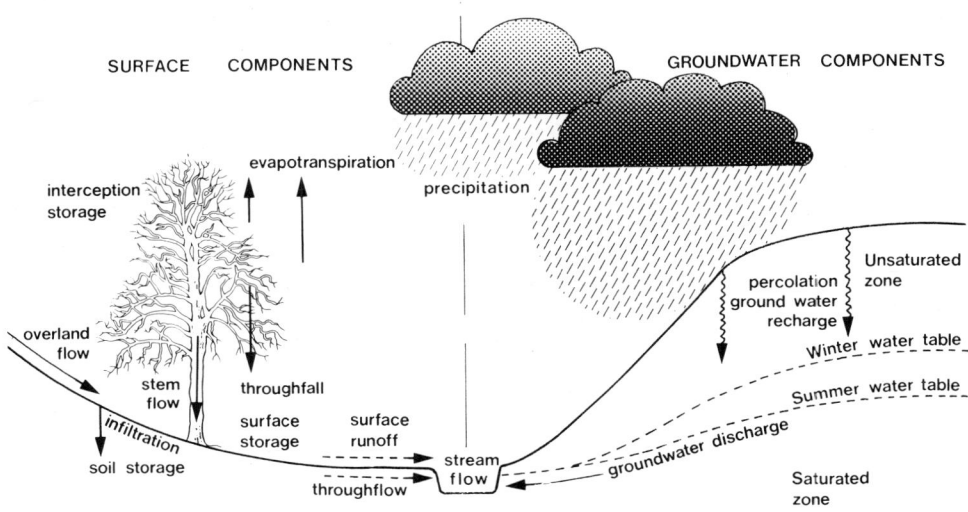

**Figure 3.1 Components of drainage basin hydrology**

to the atmosphere by evaporation either immediately or after interception or surface storage, and some may percolate to the groundwater zone to replenish subsurface storages.

The amount of rain falling at a particular location is almost entirely independent of the amount of evaporation taking place there. Comparison of annual precipitation data with the evaporation values within latitudinal zones shows that in the subtropics evaporation tends to dominate whilst in low- and mid-latitudes precipitation is the major factor. Large scale air-movements are required to explain such variations.

These movements may be viewed as producing convergence (net moisture input) and divergence (net moisture output). Convergence dominates in the inter-tropical and mid-latitude areas so that in general terms a zonal distribution of precipitation over the earth may be observed. Variations within this essentially latitudinal distribution are due to two primary factors — dominant wind direction and orographic influences. Mountain ranges will tend to accentuate local precipitation amounts, because air rising over a mountain range is cooled; condensation and then precipitation may be induced. Coastal areas receiving dominantly onshore winds may receive high levels of precipitation, being 'nearest' the primary source of precipitation water. Inland, this effect will decrease rapidly and areas of extremely low rainfall commonly are found in the continental interiors.

Similarly, coastal areas receiving offshore winds may receive only low precipitation amounts. On reaching the ground surface precipitation will be distributed in two ways — by evaporation back to the atmosphere or by streamflow to the oceans. The rate of transfer, however, will be influenced by storage within the soils and rocks which compose the drainage basins, and may be delayed for periods of days, months or even years where the precipitation falls as snow. Further variations will result where the annual melting of glacier ice forms a major component of annual runoff. Indeed, glaciers and ice-sheets may store water for tens, hundreds or even thousands of years.

Evaporation occurs when some of the molecules which comprise a given mass of water accelerate their movements to such a rate that they are able to escape into the overlying air. The kinetic energy of movement is derived from solar radiation. Because radiation is the dominant control, the process of evaporation has a general spatial pattern related to latitude which, for the oceans, varies from less than 600 mm per year in high latitudes to over 1500 mm per year within the tropics. Whereas in the case of open water bodies, moisture is always available, evaporation from the land-surface is **supply limited**; that is, it is governed by the availability of water near the surface. In dry soils, for example, evaporation will be zero. Thus, during dry periods the evaporation from a bare soil will be considerably less than that from an open water surface, although as the frequency of surface wetting by rain increases the rate of evaporation will approach that from open water.

Over most of the land-surface a more or less complete vegetation cover exists and water is lost from the plant surfaces, a process known as transpiration. For practical purposes it is impossible to separate transpiration from evaporation and they are generally considered together as **evapotranspiration**. The highest annual losses of water from the land by evapotranspiration occur primarily in the equatorial zone in response to high solar radiation inputs and the growth of a dense surface vegetation cover. The rate of water loss from the land, however — the **actual** evapotranspiration — is commonly limited by deficiencies of water supply so that it will be less than the **potential** evaporation from an open water surface. The losses rarely exceed 1000 mm and the losses from the land surfaces are commonly less than 50% of those from the oceans in the same latitudes.

The available supply of water for streamflow may now be defined as the annual precipitation minus the actual evapotranspiration, known as the **residual rainfall**. In tropical areas, despite high evapotranspiration rates, precipitation is dominant to give high values of annual runoff in excess of 1000 mm. High values are also produced in cool maritime areas where rates of evapotranspiration are low. Even within a relatively small area such as the UK, extreme variations of runoff may be found. The spatial patterns of annual precipitation and evapotranspiration interact to produce a wide range of residual rainfalls from over 2500 mm at locations in the west to less than 125 mm in some southeastern areas.

Consideration of annual data can conceal, however, the true nature of the precipitation-evapotranspiration relationship and lead to an underestimate of the annual runoff. For example, in a river basin with an annual precipitation of 1000 mm and an annual potential evapotranspiration of 800 mm it would be assumed that the annual runoff would amount to only 200 mm. However, if 750 mm of rain fell during winter when the evapotranspiration losses were only 150 mm then 600 mm of runoff would be produced; the 250 mm of summer rain would be lost by evapotranspiration but the total annual runoff would be three times higher than initially expected and the supply-limited actual evaporation would reach only 400 mm.

Rivers commonly display a seasonal pattern of streamflow which reflects the interaction of precipitation and evaporation during the year. Such patterns, known as 'runoff regimes' (*Figure 3.2*) provide a means of classifying rivers and they may be revealed simply by drawing a graph of discharge against time using monthly- or daily-mean flow data. Tropical rivers receive high rainfall inputs during the summer but experience a marked dry season during winter. Evapotranspiration is high all year so that the streamflow tends

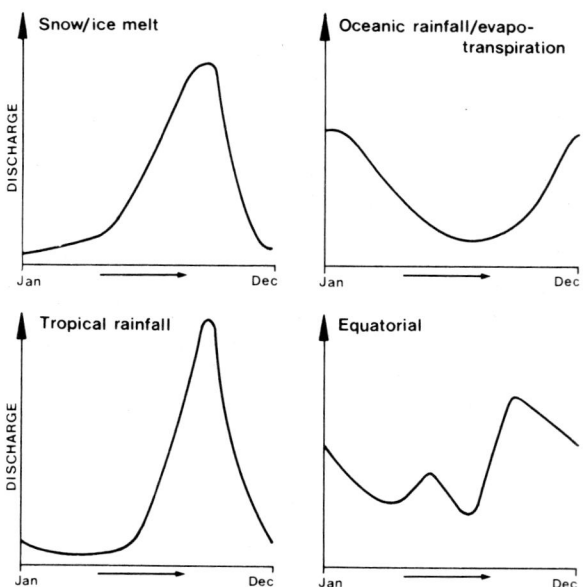

**Figure 3.2 Characteristic runoff regimes**

to reflect the variable rainfall conditions which are often associated with the monsoons. In temperate, oceanic areas precipitation occurs all year with a maximum in winter or autumn, but the runoff regime is more the reflection of the marked peak of evapotranspiration during the summer months. A more complex regime describes equatorial rivers because the rainfall which occurs throughout the year has two clear peaks at the equinoxes. A fourth general type of runoff regime may be recognised for rivers dominated by snow and ice-melt which produce a major peak of streamflow during the late spring or early summer.

In reality, many rivers display a more complex flow regime related to the interaction of several factors; for example, a late spring snow-melt followed in the autumn by convectional storms. Furthermore, large rivers may receive runoff from several climatic zones so that the regime of the main stream will show a complex variation reflecting the superposition of the runoff regimes of each of the major tributaries. British rivers are small by international standards and have relatively simple regimes characterised by a summer peak of evapotranspiration. However, even within Britain the timing of the runoff maxima varies from December in the 'hard-rock' west, to February in the 'soft-rock' east; a reflection of the greater water holding capacity of the porous rocks.

## 3.2 THE BASIN HYDROLOGICAL CYCLE

Within particular climatic zones the annual runoff and the general character of the runoff regime will be generally similar for different catchments. In detail, however, considerable differences will be observed which particularly relate to differences in geology and landuse. These factors may be examined using the water balance approach by reference to average annual data or by reference to short term variations. The **water balance** refers to the balance between water inputs to a river basin as precipitation ($p$) and water outflow by evapotranspiration ($ET$), streamflow ($Q$) and change in groundwater storage ($\Delta S$):

$$P = ET + Q \pm \Delta S$$

It is conventional to use the **water year** (October 1 to September 30). To avoid problems of changing groundwater storage, the water year commences with the winter wet season and outflow from the groundwater reserves will occur during the second half of the year — the summer dry season. In this way the change of subsurface storage ($\Delta S$) may be considered as negligible.

Rainfall onto the catchment surface is characteristically irregular in space, time and amount, but the pattern of streamflow is comparatively regular. This contrast between the behaviour of streamflow and rainfall from which it is derived results from the existence of storages within the catchment which serve to regulate the release of water to the streams. Some of these storages act to slow down the movement of water to streams by only minutes, others by hours and yet others by days, weeks or even months. To explain differences in the pattern of discharge between streams requires, therefore, an understanding of the character of these storages and of how each storage effects water movement. In general terms streamflow is derived from two sources distinguished by the rate of water transfer to the channel — baseflow and storm runoff.

### 3.2.1 Baseflow generation

For all streams, groundwater releases provide the base-flows upon which storm runoff is superimposed. In fact the saturated sub-surface zone constitutes 21% of the world's fresh water and 97% of all unfrozen fresh water. Groundwater is derived primarily from precipitation but percolation from lakes and rivers may be important in some areas. For example, in some deserts streamflow from adjacent uplands may provide the major source of groundwater recharge. Nevertheless, in most areas the slow release of water from the groundwater storage serves to maintain streamflow during dry periods.

Rock type is the fundamental factor controlling the volume of water that can be stored and the rate of ground water movement. Water is stored in the voids within the rocks: the spaces or pores between the individual grains, such as found in sandstones for example, the joints and fissures within massive rocks such as granite or limestone, and the bedding planes between rock layers. The water table is the limit below which all the voids contain water, that is the limit of rock saturation.

The total volume of a rock body which is represented by voids is known as the *porosity*. Porosity is related to the shape, arrangement and degree of sorting of the particles, and to post-depositional modifications arising from solution, weathering, cementation, compaction, fracturing and faulting. Each groundwater store, or *aquifer*, can be characterised by the volume of water which it will retain against the force of gravity if it is allowed to drain after being saturated. The percentage of the total volume of the saturated material which drains under gravity is known as the *specific yield*: the specific yield then describes the amount of water available for streamflow.

During the winter or wet season the rate of aquifer recharge exceeds the rate of water release to streamflow, the volume of stored water increases and the water table rises. As the water table rises, its slope is steepened so that the rate of groundwater discharge is increased. During dry periods the water table is lowered and water drains rapidly from the larger voids (for shallow aquifers water may also be lost through evapotranspiration).

However, because *capillary forces* within the voids resist water release and the effect of these forces increases as the void size decreases, the rate of release is progressively reduced. Capillary forces refer to the support of a vertical column of water by surface tension such as can be observed in narrow glass tubes. Therefore, for example, a highly porous clay having very fine pores, in which strong forces can hold the water, will have a low specific yield although a high porosity; in a well jointed rock, sands or gravels the voids are so large as to provide little capillary resistance and the water is freely released. The term *permeability* is used to describe the characteristics of a rock which influence the flow of water through it. Permeability depends mainly on the size of the voids in contrast to the porosity which describes the total volume of voids. Permeabilities range from $10^6$ md$^{-1}$ for unconsolidated gravels to less than one millimetre per day for clays and igneous rocks, although locally these may be increased if fissures, joints or faults are present. Groundwater discharge occurs where the water table intersects the ground surface either in a diffuse manner or at well-defined locations as seepage and springs respectively.

A graph of runoff plotted against time is termed a *hydrograph* and although within the same climatic zone the annual flow regime may appear to be markedly similar, consideration of the mean daily discharges reveals different degrees of *flow variability* related to the different geologic character of the drainage basins. For example, the River Derwent in the Derbyshire Peak District drains a relatively impermeable shale-sandstone catchment and clearly has a different streamflow character from that of the

**TABLE 3.2 STREAMFLOW CHARACTERISTICS OF IMPERMEABLE AND PERMEABLE BASINS**

| River | Geology | Drainage area (km$^2$) | Average annual rainfall (mm) | Average annual runoff (mm) | Minimum recorded flow (m$^3$ s$^{-1}$) | Maximum recorded flow (m$^3$ s$^{-1}$) |
|---|---|---|---|---|---|---|
| Derwent | sandstone-shale (impermeable) | 127 | 1220 | 940 | 0.47 (0.0037 m$^3$ s$^{-1}$ km$^{-2}$) | 150.60* (1.19 m$^3$ s$^{-1}$ km$^{-2}$) |
| Wye | limestone (permeable) | 154 | 1150 | 810 | 1.05 (0.0068 m$^3$ s$^{-1}$ km$^{-2}$) | 37.80* (0.25 m$^3$ s$^{-1}$ km$^{-2}$) |

*Recorded from the same rainstorm on 09.12.65.

neighbouring River Wye which drains highly permeable Carboniferous Limestone (*Table 3.2*).

Although having similar drainage areas, annual rainfalls and annual runoff values the degree of flow variability is markedly different. The greater significance of the groundwater storage, and correspondingly less significant surface runoff, has regulated the rate of streamflow and reduced the short term fluctuations of the River Wye so that the maximum flow on record is only about 25% of that produced by the impermeable Derwent catchment, but the minimum flow is greater. In both cases however the fluctuations produced by surface runoff are superimposed on an overall seasonal variation which is closely related to changes of groundwater discharge (*Figure 3.3*). Streams, such as the Wye, draining very permeable catchments will respond only very slowly to rainfall; most of the water will percolate through the soil to the underlying groundwater zone; flow will be relatively slow in comparison to that over the ground surface; and a low variability hydrograph will be produced. Impermeable basins on the other hand such as that of the River Derwent will generate streamflows that are highly sensitive to rainfall inputs.

**3.2.2 Storm runoff production**

During rainfall water may flow rapidly to the stream over the ground surface or through

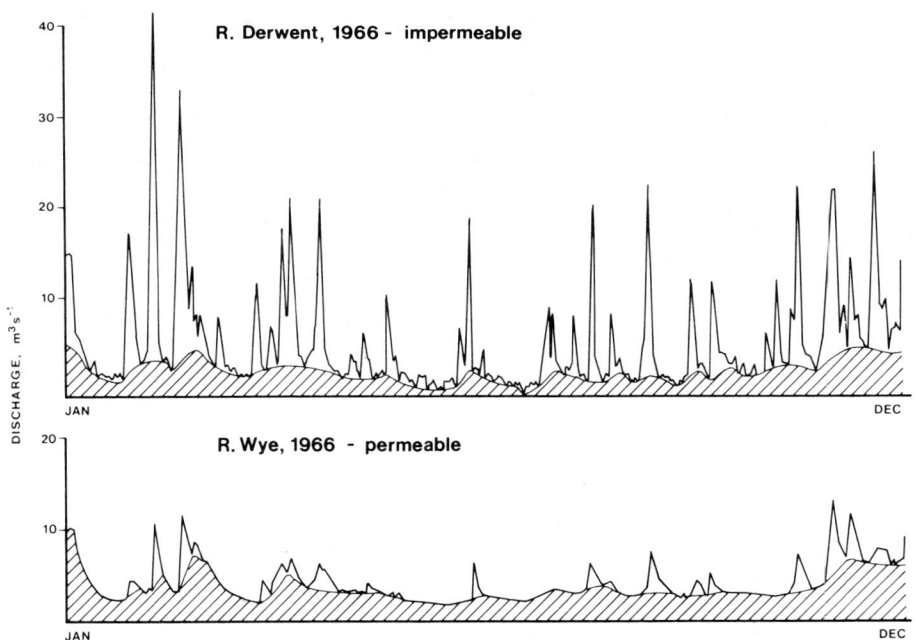

**Figure 3.3 Flow variability within permeable and impermeable catchments — flood peaks are superimposed on a relatively constant base-flow (shaded)**

the soil. To a large extent the pathway taken is determined by the character of the soil itself. A soil's character is related to the interaction of rock-type (or more strictly parent material), climate and biotic and topographical factors. These control three independent processes of water movement: entry through the soil surface (infiltration), storage within the soil, and transmission through the soil (*see* Finlayson and Statham, 1980).

Storm runoff is produced primarily by relatively rapid flow over the ground surface or through the soil and four pathways have been identified (*Figure 3.4*) — Hortonian overland flow, subsurface stormflow, return flow and direct precipitation onto saturated areas. Horton envisaged that surface runoff would occur when rainfall intensity exceeded the infiltration capacity of the soil. Water would accumulate on the surface of the soil and fill small depressions but eventually this detention storage would be exhausted; water would begin to flow downslope as an irregular sheet, or as a series of tiny rivulets. Infiltration capacities range from less then 5 mm hr$^{-1}$ for clay loams to 50 mm hr$^{-1}$ for loamy sand and experience has shown that where there is an appreciable vegetation cover, and especially where there is a humus or litter layer, Hortonian overland flow will occur only rarely during the most extreme storms (Kirkby and Chorley, 1976). Nevertheless, this mechanism of runoff production may occur on areas of bare soil where

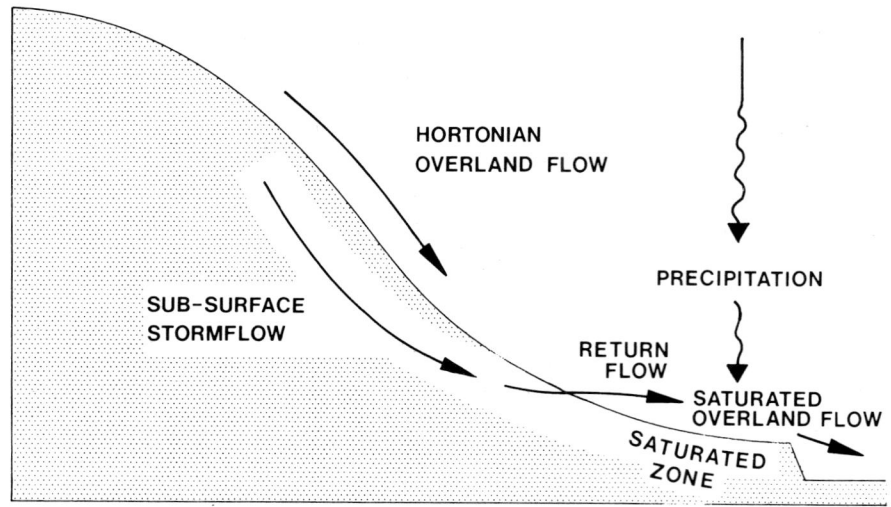

**Figure 3.4 Storm runoff production on hillslopes**

compaction and the infilling of pores by fine particles can significantly reduce the infiltration capacity of the surface. Hortonian overland flow has been identified in semi-arid areas and on areas of barren soil such as cultivated fields, spoil heaps and compacted tracks, and peak rates of flow up to 200 mm $hr^{-1}$ may be generated.

Within most humid environments, characterised by a diverse vegetation cover, rainfall intensities rarely exceed the infiltration capacity of the soil so that Hortonian overland flow will not occur. Prior to rainfall the water table will slope towards the channel at a shallow angle and a continuous small baseflow will be provided to the stream. Downslope the water table will be at a progressively shallower depth and the moisture content of the soil will be higher. These two factors combine to ensure that the percolation of water during the early part of a rainstorm will cause a rise in the water table near the base of the slope. Higher up the slope the greater depth of the water table and the drier soil will mean that some water will be held in the soil and that the passage of water downwards to the groundwater zone will take a relatively long time. At the base of the hillslope the water table will steepen in response to the supply of water and the rate of groundwater discharge will increase producing subsurface stormflow.

If the surface layers become saturated subsurface water can escape from the soil and flow to the channel on the surface. This 'return flow' can supply water to the channel at faster rates than achieved by subsurface flow, and it will be supplemented by direct precipitation onto the saturated surface. As the storm progresses the saturated area expands upslope so that more of the catchment contributes to **saturated overland flow**. The saturated area also expands and contracts seasonally so that the initial condition of the catchment at the start of a rainstorm, and the amount and timing of the runoff produced by a rainstorm of given intensity and duration, will vary between seasons. This model of storm runoff generation was developed as the **variable source area concept** (Hewlett and Hibbert, 1967). The saturated zone which produces rapid runoff occupies only a small proportion of the catchment area so that even small changes in the size of the saturated area may produce significant differences in the volume and rate of runoff when rain occurs.

The relative importance of the three main mechanisms of storm runoff production may be summarised thus:

|                          | *Dominant location* |
|--------------------------|---------------------|
| **Subsurface stormflow** | humid climate; dense vegetation; steep straight slopes; deep permeable soils; narrow valley bottoms |
| **Saturated overland flow** | humid climate; dense vegetation; gentle concave footslopes; thin soils of variable permeability; wide valley bottoms |
| **Hortonian overland flow** | arid to sub-humid climate; thin vegetation; or impermeable soils |

### 3.2.3 The role of vegetation

It has already been noted that the vegetation cover can significantly influence the infiltration capacity of the soil surface but in many areas rainfalls may be intercepted and stored by the vegetation cover before reaching that surface. The significance of interception storage depends not only upon the character of the vegetation, particularly the form, density and surface texture of the leaves, twigs and other surfaces, but also the precipitation characteristics.

The duration and intensity of the rainfall may have a particular effect. Rain moves through the canopy by two pathways, throughfall and stemflow. Rain falling onto the plant surfaces is caught and stored but may be displaced by further rain to the next, lower layer of vegetation. Throughfall represents water that has passed to the ground either by passing through spaces between the leaves or by dripping from the surfaces. Stemflow refers to the movement of water from storage by movement down the stems and trunk to the ground. During and after rainfall the water held by interception storage will be returned to the atmosphere by evaporation. Furthermore, if evapotranspiration is supply-limited, trees with deep root systems will tap a relatively larger supply and yield higher actual evapotranspiration losses during summer than say from a grassland catchment.

Comparison of data from two neighbouring catchments on the slopes of Plynlimon, mid-Wales, demonstrates the significance of vegetation differences for both annual

**TABLE 3.3 STREAMFLOW WITHIN WOODLAND AND MOORLAND CATCHMENTS**

| River | Vegetation type | Drainage area (km$^2$) | Average annual rainfall (mm) | Average evapo-transpiration (mm) | Average annual runoff (mm) | Maximum recorded flow (m$^3$ s$^{-1}$) |
|-------|-----------------|------------------------|------------------------------|----------------------------------|----------------------------|----------------------------------------|
| Wye | moorland | 10.55 | 2606 | 442 | 2164 | 65.4 (6.2 m$^3$ s$^{-1}$ km$^{-2}$) |
| Severn | 67% forested | 8.70 | 2380 | 799 | 1581 | 41.0 (4.7 m$^3$ s$^{-1}$ km$^{-2}$) |

Data provided by The Institute of Hydrology.

runoff and flow variability (*Table 3.3*). In 1973 the Institute of Hydrology established the moorland basin of the Upper Wye and the headwater of the adjacent River Severn, which was 67% forested, as experimental basins. The basins were intensively instrumented to monitor all the major components of the hydrological cycle. Within the forested catchment, mean evapotranspiration losses were found to be twice as great; the mean streamflow was correspondingly smaller; and the flow variability was noticeably less. Thus, the storage provided by the forest canopy plays an important role in regulating streamflow.

Differences may, however, be expected between coniferous and deciduous woodland, not least because the seasonal characteristics of the deciduous tree canopy will influence the pattern of streamflow through the year. Within the Hubbard Brook experimental basin, New Hampshire, USA, Likens and Bormann (1972) found that during the warm summer months high evapotranspiration rates associated with maximum forest growth produced low stream discharges but in the autumn the deciduous trees shed their leaves, the transpiring surfaces were lost and the streamflow increased.

## 3.3 MEASUREMENT OF STREAMFLOW CONTROLS

Streamflow at any point within a drainage network reflects the interaction of two primary groups of control variables describing the form of the drainage basin and the climatic characteristics. At a smaller scale, hillslope form and composition in terms of soil type and surface cover also exert an important control; for techniques of measuring infiltration and throughflow rates reference should be made to Finlayson and Statham (1980).

### 3.3.1 Drainage basin form

The drainage basin is the fundamental unit of all river studies. Basin form can be described by three parameters: size, shape and relief. Size is normally defined as **basin area** and this acts as a scale factor for all the other basin characteristics because it influences the volume of runoff available to a river system. Measurements are normally derived from topographic maps or from aerial photographs but may be supplemented by field observations.

First the drainage basin must be delimited. This requires the careful definition of the watershed which surrounds all the drainage lines in a basin and describes the divide between adjacent basins (*Figure 3.5*). The area of the basin can then be measured by overlaying graph paper and counting the squares contained within the watershed, by planimeter or by using a digitiser linked, for example, to a micro-computer. Caution must be exercised when defining watersheds of basins underlain by very permeable rocks because the topographic divide may not coincide with the groundwater divide. On the Carboniferous limestone in Derbyshire, for example, several square kilometres of the River Wye basin drain into the basin of the River Noe to the north.

**Basin shape** and **relief** have an important influence upon streamflows by affecting the timing of water delivery at the basin outflow point. The measurement of shape has proved problematic because of the difficulty of distinguishing between two basins of similar shape but having the outlet in different positions: the implications of this for streamflow are demonstrated in *Figure 3.5B*. Assuming uniform rainfall over the drainage basin, the close proximity of the major proportion of the area to the basin outflow in B2, shown by the higher rate of drainage area increase for progressively longer basins, will produce a quicker delivery of runoff. Basin length may be defined in two ways; as

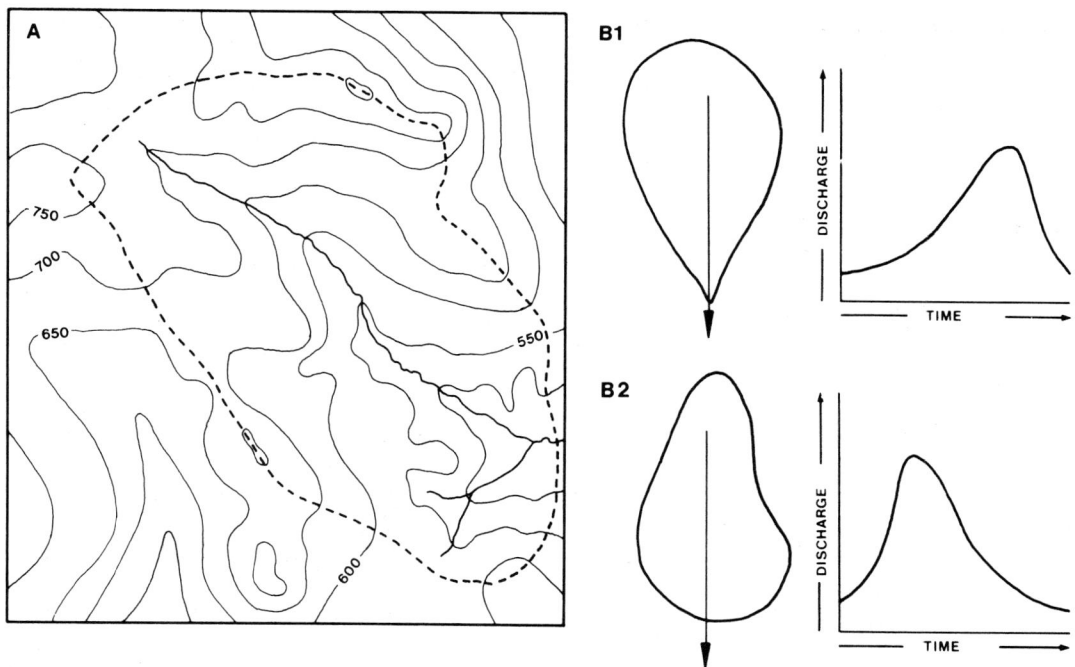

**Figure 3.5 Catchment shape, delimited from contours (A), and its influence on the flood hydrograph at the outflow point assuming a uniform distribution of storm rainfall (B)**

the maximum straight line distance between the catchment outlet and a point on the divide or as the distance along the centre line of the valley and parallel to the main drainage line. Two common parameters defining basin shape use measures of basin length ($L$), perimeter length ($P$) and drainage area ($A$) to determine the degree of circularity and elongation:

$$\text{Circularity} = \frac{4\pi A}{P^2}; \quad \text{Elongation} = \frac{A}{L^2}$$

The measurement of basin relief is also more problematic than might perhaps be imagined because of the difficulty in describing a three dimensional basin in a very simple form. Nevertheless, several indices of relief may be easily determined. The maximum relief ($H$) is defined as the difference between the highest point on the watershed and the altitude of the basin outflow. A relief ratio ($RH$) has been more frequently used, where

$$RH = H \div L$$

but this measure of basin relief is only a very crude estimate of slope because the long profile of a river tends to be concave upwards. In order to take account of this characteristic, a preferred measure of slope has been defined as the difference in elevation ($h$) between two points located at 10 and 85% of the mainstream length ($S_{1085}$):

$$S_{1085} = \frac{h10 - h85}{L10 - L85}$$

## 3.3.2 Rainfall and evapotranspiration

Rainfall inputs and evapotranspiration losses in terms of their absolute annual values, seasonal patterns and short term variations exert the major control upon streamflow. Records of rainfall for most areas of Britain have been collected for nearly 100 years and a few sites have longer sequences. Field measurement of rainfall and evapotranspiration is relatively straightforward but the measurements will relate only to a very small area and this will, of necessity, be assumed to represent the inputs and losses over much larger areas.

Various types of instrument have been developed for recording rainfall but the simplest is the standard raingauge which collects the rain falling through an orifice of known area. However, the data must be treated with some caution. Normally the gauge stands 305 mm above ground level. The very presence of the gauge may affect the local air flow pattern in the vicinity of the orifice and the actual catch may be less than that which would have reached the ground if the gauge had not been there. Studies using raingauges having the orifice at ground-level suggest that the standard raingauge may underestimate rainfall by up to 20%, although an error of 5% is commonly accepted. Such errors may arise particularly at windy sites and for exposed windy locations the most successful solution has been to install the raingauge in a shallow pit so that its rim is level with the surrounding ground surface and the space between the rim and the edge of the pit is spanned by a metal or plastic grid to prevent splash into the gauge and to minimise the effect of the pit upon the airflow around the orifice.

The measurement of evapotranspiration losses is perhaps the most difficult component of the basin hydrological cycle to quantify. Estimates of evaporation from an open water surface can be obtained by using small tanks of water in which the lowering of the water surface or the amount of water required to maintain a constant level are recorded, taking into account any input from rainfall. Various types of evaporation tank or pan are in use. The standard British tank is 610 mm deep and is 1.83 m square installed with its rim protruding 76 mm above the surface, and filled so that the water level is approximately level with the ground.

The determination of evaporation from bare soil or of evapotranspiration from a vegetated surface require the construction of a lysimeter (**see** Trudgill, 1983). Most lysimeters consist of a container embedded in the ground so that the rim is level with the ground surface. The container is normally filled with the soil removed when excavating the pit in such a way as to replicate, as closely as possible, the undisturbed soil conditions. Disturbed soil will normally be less compact and will have a higher permeability so that the soil may have to be compacted. A drain in the bottom of the container conducts percolating water into a second smaller container at the base of the pit. The soil in the drum is watered daily using a measured volume of water to maintain the soil at *field capacity* and the percolate is measured so that

$$ET = W - D, \text{ where } W = \text{water added and } D = \text{drainage}$$

Small lysimeters can be lifted easily so that small changes of storage can be detected by weighing, and changes in weight equivalent to less than 0.5 mm can be recorded. The installation of two lysimeters, the second not being irrigated after the initial watering, would enable the study of the effects of limited water availability upon the actual evapo-transpiration rate.

For most small basins a single instrumentation site may be practicable but care must be taken to ensure that the location of the instruments is as representative of the average basin characteristics as possible. The values obtained from the single instrumentation site will then be used to describe the rainfall and evapotranspiration characteristics of the whole catchment. Within large basins variations of altitude, aspect, slope and surface cover may cause important differences of precipitation and evapotranspiration between locations so that multiple instrumentation sites should be used. A stratified sampling procedure should be employed: the basin is divided into areas of like character and gauges sited at points representative of these units. At the Plynlimon research basins of the Institute of Hydrology, a basic raingauge network was designed by dividing the catchments into a number of units based upon four classes of altitude, four of aspect, and three divisions of slope. A raingauge was installed at a randomly chosen site each unit constituting more than 2% of the total area of the catchment. This resulted in a total of about 50 gauges in the two catchments — a total area of less than 20 km$^2$.

## 3.4 WATER FLOW IN CHANNELS

The rate of water flow within a channel is influenced by the channel slope, the channel shape in cross-section and the roughness of the channel boundary. Channel shape can be described by the *hydraulic radius* of the water cross-section, and is defined as the area of water per unit of channel-water contact (area ÷ wetted perimeter). Channel roughness is related to the size and shape of the channel boundary materials, but also to any obstructions within, or protruding into, the flow such as aquatic plants, roots or fallen trees. Channel slope ($S$) hydraulic radius ($R$) and boundary roughness ($n$) are related to the mean velocity of flow ($\bar{v}$) measured in metres per second by the Manning equation:

$$\bar{v} = \frac{R^{0.67}\,S^{0.5}}{n}$$

Manning's roughness coefficient is notoriously difficult to determine but may be estimated visually and a guide is given in **Table 3.4**. The effects of boundary resistance upon the flow is clearly shown by the velocity distribution within the cross-section (**Figure 3.6**). Lines of equal velocity, known as **isovels**, are often closer together and the actual current velocity is lower nearer the bed and banks, while the highest velocity occurs in the centre of the channel below or extending below the surface. The pattern displayed by the isovels, however, also reflects the shape of the channel both in terms of width and depth, and symmetry.

Streamflow is rarely stable for long periods and the way in which the flow changes, and the characteristics of the flow at any single point in time, vary between cross-sections of different shape. That is, at a short time-scale the character of the flows will be controlled by the morphology of the channel itself. At any one point in time the streamflow within a cross-section, the discharge ($Q$) may be described as the combination of the water area ($A$) and the average speed of flow or velocity within that area ($v$), so that:

$$Q = A \times \bar{v}$$

If the water density remains the same along a river section and if no more water is received either from seepage or tributary inflows or is lost from the channel, then the discharge will remain the same at different cross-sections (1, 2, 3) so that

$$Q = A1.\bar{v}1 = A2.\bar{v}2 = A3.\bar{v}3, \text{etc}$$

The relative magnitude of the two components ($A$ and $\bar{v}$) may differ, but the product of ($A \times \bar{v}$) must remain constant. This is a form of the **continuity equation** which expresses the notion that water discharge is constant in successive reaches assuming neither import nor export of water. The equation also describes the relative behaviour of the two primary variables of area and velocity. In order to maintain continuity the mean velocity within a cross-section must change in an inverse manner to the cross-sectional area at that location. For example, for a discharge of 2 m³ s⁻¹ the flow within a cross-sectional area of 4 m² must have a velocity of 0.5 m s⁻¹, but if the water area within a cross-section is

**TABLE 3.4 A GUIDE TO CHANNEL ROUGHNESS ESTIMATION**

| Bed profile | Vegetation (tree roots, aquatic weeds, etc.) | Sand and gravel | Bed-material size Coarse gravels | Boulders |
|---|---|---|---|---|
| Uniform | None | 0.020 | 0.030 | 0.050 |
| Undulating* | None | 0.030 | 0.040 | 0.055 |
| Uniform | Some | 0.040 | 0.050 | 0.060 |
| Undulating* | Some | 0.050 | 0.060 | 0.070 |
| Highly irregular | None | 0.055 | 0.070 | 0.080 |
| Highly irregular | Extensive | 0.080 | 0.090 | 0.100 |

*Undulating = pools and riffles well developed (see Section 5.3.2. and **Figure 5.9**).

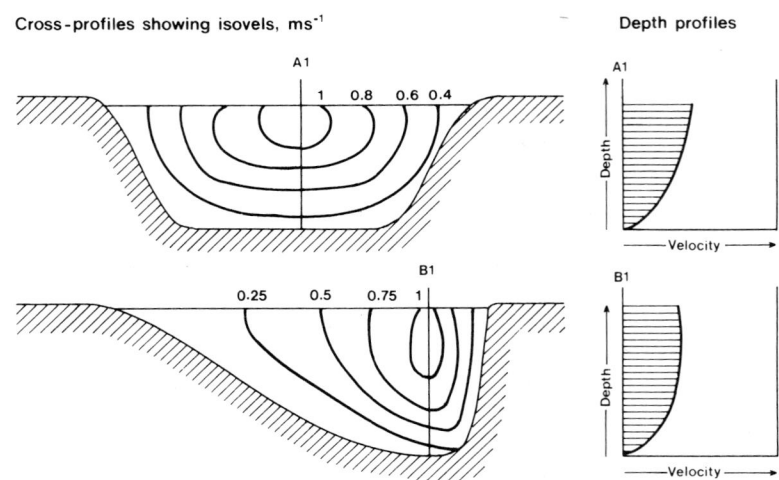

Cross-profiles showing isovels, ms$^{-1}$

Depth profiles

Figure 3.6 Velocity distributions within symmetrical and asymmetrical channel cross-sections

reduced to 1 m² a short distance downstream the velocity must have increased to 2 m s⁻¹. So, within a reach, any change of area is compensated for by an opposing change of mean velocity.

The water area within a cross-section is itself the product of the width and mean depth of flow so that the continuity equation may be re-written as:

$$Q = W \times \bar{d} \times \bar{v}$$

Again differences in any one parameter between cross-sections must be matched by opposing changes of one or both of the other two variables. Thus

e.g. $Q = 2 \text{ m}^3 \text{ s}^{-1} = W$ (8 m) $\times \bar{d}$ (0.5 m) $\times \bar{v}$ (0.5 m s⁻¹)

$= W$ (4 m) $\times \bar{d}$ (0.5 m) $\times \bar{v}$ (1 m s⁻¹)

$= W$ (4 m) $\times \bar{d}$ (1 m) $\times \bar{v}$ (0.5 m s⁻¹)

$= W$ (4 m) $\times \bar{d}$ (0.25 m) $\times \bar{v}$ (2 m s⁻¹)

The relative magnitude of the three components therefore describes the character of the channel cross-section. The way in which these components vary at a cross-section as discharge changes has been described as the **at-a-station hydraulic geometry** (Leopold and Maddock, 1953). Different channel shapes will produce different changes of the width, depth and velocity components in order to accommodate variations of discharge. For example, a narrow and deep channel with vertical banks will accommodate changes of discharge primarily by a change of water depth, a triangular channel will adjust all three components — **w. d.** and **$\bar{v}$**. whilst in wide shallow channels with gently sloping banks width will be the most important component. The at-a-station variations are described by the regression exponents (**Table 3.5**) and these may be represented graphically for comparison between sites (**Figure 3.7**). World-wide data are summarised by Park (1977).

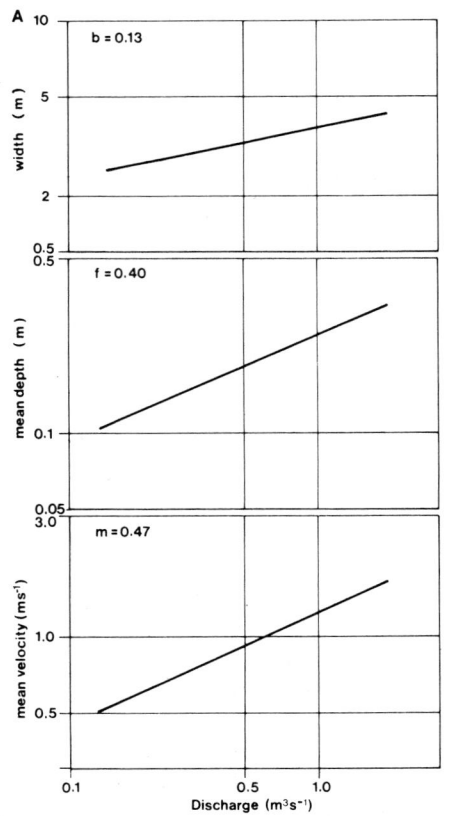

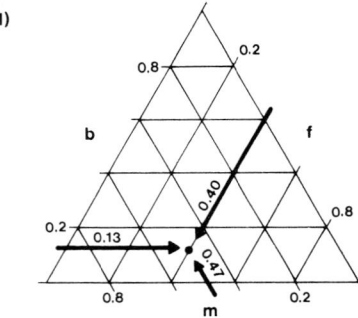

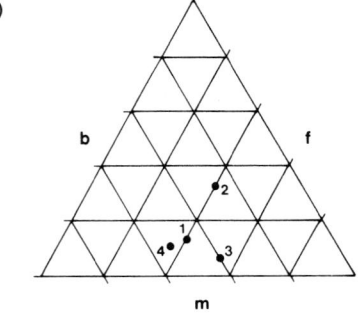

Figure 3.7 The representation of hydraulic-geometry data using double logarithmic plots (A) and triangular diagrams (B): the plotting method is shown in B(1) and the data for *Table 3.5* is shown in B(2)

**TABLE 3.5 AT-A-STATION HYDRAULIC GEOMETRY: REGRESSION EXPONENTS (WIDTH $\propto Q^b$; DEPTH $\propto Q^f$; VELOCITY $\propto Q^m$)**

| Key to Figure 3.10 | River, location and characteristics | $b$ | $f$ | $m$ |
|---|---|---|---|---|
| 1 | R. Langedalen, Norway (steep banks) | 0.13 | 0.40 | 0.47 |
| 2 | R. Langedalen, Norway (low-angle banks) | 0.32 | 0.40 | 0.28 |
| 3 | R. Hodder, UK (very steep banks) | 0.08 | 0.52 | 0.40 |
| 4 | Small, high gradient stream with boulder bed, Dartmoor, UK. | 0.12 | 0.37 | 0.51 |

Note that $b + f + m = 1.0$ in order to maintain continuity.

## 3.4.1 Flood discharges

Within short time scales streamflow is seen to respond to storm rainfalls and this response is described by the *flood hydrograph* (*Figure 3.8*). The hydrograph has two main characteristics: size and shape.

'Size' refers to the volume of water contained within the curve whilst the 'shape' describes the distribution of that volume over time. Under low-flow conditions the base-flow decreases slowly until rain falls when the rate of streamflow will increase rapidly. This is described by the steep rising limb of the hydrograph which represents rapid runoff from surface and shallow sub-surface sources. Initially, runoff is supplied by the basin area nearest to the measurement point and this is added to sequentially by runoff from more remote source areas. Discharge continues to rise until the peak is reached a short time after the peak of rainfall — the time difference between the peaks is known as the basin lag. The hydrograph peak represents the point in time when the rate of water draining the catchment reaches a maximum; thereafter flow is controlled largely by the

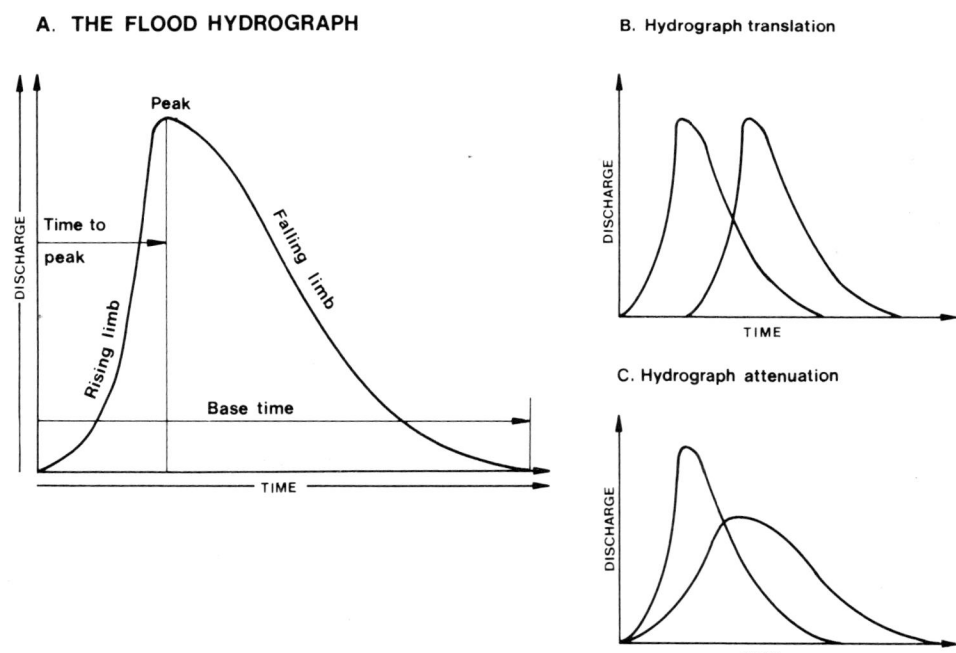

## A. THE FLOOD HYDROGRAPH

Peak

Time to peak

Rising limb

Falling limb

Base time

DISCHARGE

TIME

### B. Hydrograph translation

DISCHARGE

TIME

### C. Hydrograph attenuation

DISCHARGE

TIME

**Figure 3.8 The flood hydrograph (A) and its downstream translation (B) and attenuation (C)**

amount of water in storage and the rate of water release from these storages. Discharge decreases quickly at first as the rapid runoff sources become depleted and then less quickly as the deeper subsurface sources continue to drain. Thus, in the absence of further rain, discharge falls at progressively decreasing rates to become dominated again by groundwater releases. For small basins, runoff from the different parts of the basin will be superimposed so that the hydrograph has a short duration and high peak. But, at points receiving runoff from large drainage areas, the addition of runoff contributions from the different tributary streams will be staggered and this produces longer duration and less peaked hydrographs.

The character of the flow within a cross-section changes during the passage of a flood discharge and depends upon whether the discharge is increasing or decreasing. The movement of storm runoff along a river channel appears in the form of a wave which changes its shape as it moves downstream. The flood wave will be influenced by two opposing processes: *translation* and *attenuation* (*Figure 3.8B* and *C*). Translation refers to the movement of the flood wave downstream without any change of form and requires high velocities and steep, straight channels. Within very low slope channels, ponding may occur. When water flows into a channel reach it does not flow out or displace an equal volume of water immediately but a part of the flow will be stored within the reach, raising the water level and causing the outflow to increase. Because the inflow, in part, is stored to increase the water depth, the outflow rate cannot be as high as the rate of inflow. When the rate of inflow falls the stored water within the reach will continue to drain relatively slowly. Thus, the outflow hydrograph will be attenuated: the peak flow rate will be reduced and the time-to-peak and the duration of the flood flow will be increased.

Rivers generally are affected by both of these processes so that the passage of a flood wave will be associated with a condition intermediate between the two extreme states described above. As the flood wave is translated downstream a proportion of the water will be stored within the channel and the wave will be attenuated. Generally the larger the channel and lower the slope the greater will be the attenuation. The effect of attenuation will be increased particularly by floodplain storage when water flows over-bank. Indeed the floodplain is a very significant component of the river system for the storage of flood waters especially within lowland rivers.

The variation of discharge at-a-station in response to the passage of a flood wave is described in a simplified form in *Figure 3.9*. Assuming that the discharge has not caused any change of the channel form, for a given water depth, the flow width and area will be the same on both the rising and falling limb of the hydrograph. However on the rising limb the slope of the water surface is relatively steep and the inflow to the section will be greater than the outflow. The reversed slope on the falling limb indicates that the

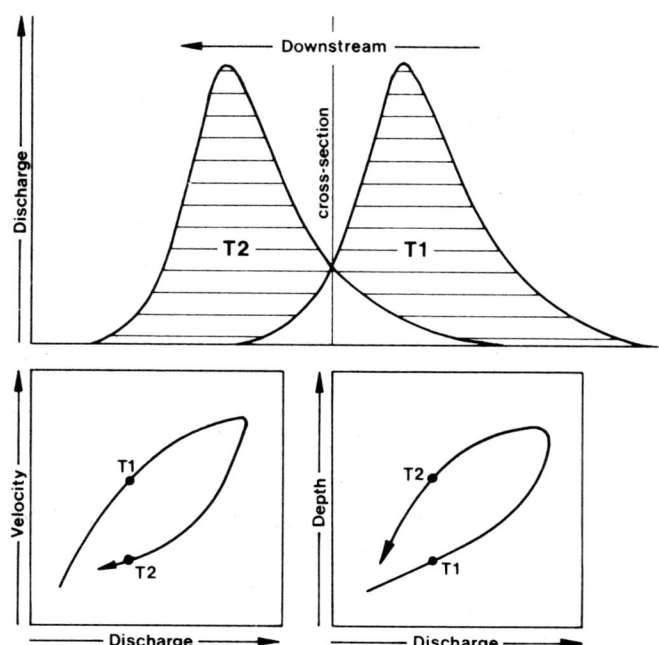

**Figure 3.9 Flow variation at-a-station during a flood. The flow characteristics during flood-wave passage past a single cross-section are exemplified for two points in time (T1 and T2)**

opposite will be true, that is, the rate of water inflow will be less than the water outflow. Also, because of the slope of the water surface, the velocity for a given water depth will be greater on the rising limb of the hydrograph than on the falling limb, and because the water area is constant then the discharge on the rising limb will be greater than on the falling limb for the same water depth. Similarly, for a given discharge, on the rising limb the width and depth will be lower and the velocity higher than on the falling limb. Such a relationship, known as a hysteretic curve, is found particularly in channels with low slopes. The difference between the rising and falling limbs decreases as the channel slope becomes steeper.

## 3.4.2 Measurement of streamflow

The measurement of streamflow is obviously the most important component of any study, not just because it comprises a major output from catchments but also because it is closely linked to the processes of sediment transport which are responsible for the formation of the different fluvial landforms. Moreover, studies of streamflow alone can illuminate the effects of varying catchment characteristics in comparative studies of two or more drainage basins, or in studies concerned with the downstream pattern of streamflow variation. The measurements themselves are relatively easy to make because water movement is confined within the narrow boundaries of the channel.

### 1. Velocity — area methods

The stream discharge at a single point in time is a function of two parameters: water area and the mean flow velocity within a cross-section. Measurement techniques involve the observation of changes in both water area and mean flow velocity or by controlling velocity artificially so that discharge may be computed from a simple observation of water area. In either case the measurement of water depth is the essential element of discharge measurement. The expression of water depth above a defined datum level, which may be the stream bed, the surface of a man-made structure such as a weir, or an arbitrary level, is referred to as the *stage*. Stage measurements are used in conjunction with a survey of the channel cross-section at the measurement location in order to determine the water area. The cross-section of the channel is simply measured by stretching a tape horizontally across the channel from bank to bank and then measuring the vertical distance from the tape to the channel bank and bed at regular intervals so as to describe the channel shape with reasonable accuracy (*see* section 5.2.2). Measurements of stage, using the streambed as the datum, can then be converted to values of water area by simply referring to the graphed cross-section (*Figure 3.10A*).

The simplest way of measuring stage is to use a calibrated stage pole or board having clearly painted divisions. Although turbulence may be a problem, these can normally be read quickly by eye to an accuracy of 5 mm or better. A board or pole can be easily

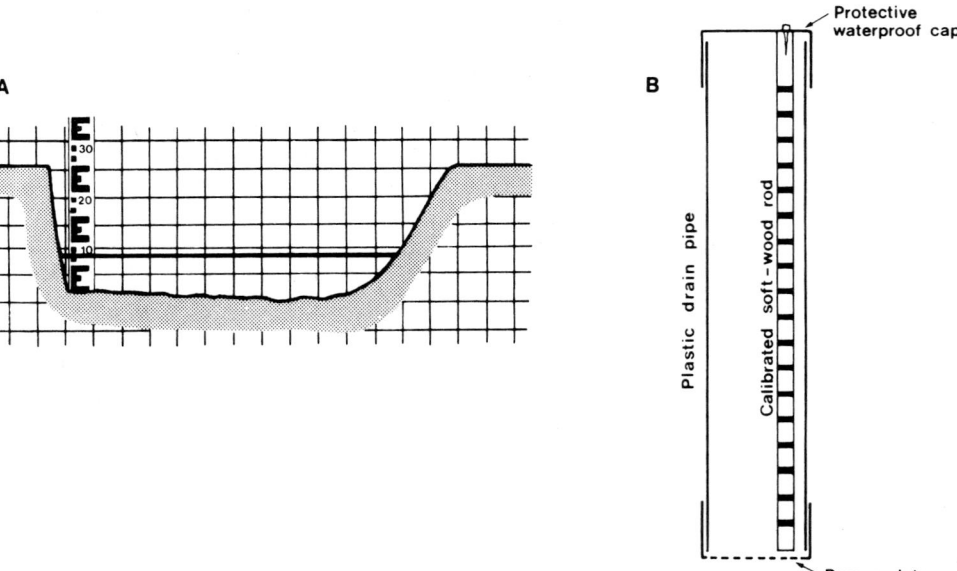

**Figure 3.10 Stage measurement using a calibrated staff (A) can be supplemented by the construction of a crest-stage recorder (B)**

fixed into the bed and bank if repeated observations are to be undertaken at a location. Flood peaks, however, commonly occur at 'inconvenient' times and permanent stage boards which are read at a constant interval (ie. weekly or daily or even hourly for short periods) can be usefully supplemented by a crest-stage gauge which records the stage of the highest flow during any period between observations. The crest stage recorder (*Figure 3.10B*) simply uses the 'tide-mark' principle. Various forms may be constructed but the most common consists of a length of piping or tubing containing an index rod and floatable material such as sawdust or powdered cork, and has its base covered with a fine wire mesh or other suitable material to keep the sawdust in but also to allow the simultaneous response of the water level inside the tube to changes of stage. As the stage rises the water level inside the tube will rise, carrying with it the sawdust which adheres to the index rod as the stage falls, leaving a record of the maximum stage reached during a storm event. After each observation the index rod is wiped clean and the floating material should be replaced at regular intervals to prevent waterlogging.

The conversion of stage data to discharge values requires measurement of velocity. Velocity can be determined using several methods depending upon the size and character of the channel and the accuracy required. Floats provide a very simple means of obtaining an estimate of flow velocity especially if materials which float just below the surface are used so as to reduce problems of wind interference. The time required for the float to travel a fixed distance (normally 10–50 m) is recorded and the average of several runs is employed to represent the surface velocity of the section; a conversion factor of 0.80 is commonly used to obtain a mean velocity estimate. Floats, however, provide no information on the point velocity distribution within a cross-section; for this a current meter is employed. Commonly this consists of a propeller which rotates at a speed proportional to the flow velocity. The revolutions are recorded and counted by means of an electric counter. The number of revolutions within a predetermined time interval, (commonly 60 seconds) is used to provide a representative value of the point velocity by reference to a calibration equation or graph. The meter may be mounted on a wading rod or for larger rivers suspended from a cableway.

The mean velocity for the cross-section is determined from a number of point measurements. The basic procedure is to select a series of verticals spaced at known intervals across the section, and to determine the depth and mean velocity of each vertical. As a general rule, the interval between each vertical should not exceed 5% of the total water width, although for channels of uniform shape a smaller number of verticals may suffice. At each vertical, water depth ($D$) is measured and the mean velocity ($v$) is calculated from velocity measurements made at specific depths. For verticals less than 600 cm deep the point velocity is measured at a depth of 0.6 x$D$. At verticals having greater water depths, point velocities should be measured at 0.2 x$D$ and 0.8 x$D$ and the mean velocity is then determined from these two measurements. These data can then be converted into a value of discharge using the simple mid-section method (*Figure 3.11*). Each vertical is viewed as being in the centre of a segment; the discharge of each segment is calculated, and the

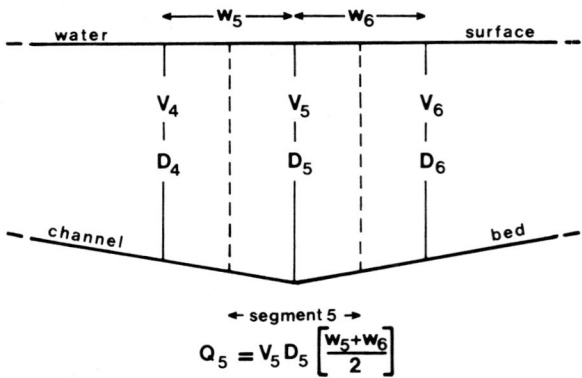

**Figure 3.11 The mid-section method for calculating discharge**

$$Q_5 = V_5 D_5 \left[\frac{w_5 + w_6}{2}\right]$$

total discharge is the sum of the segment discharges.

The velocity-area technique described above gives a value of streamflow at the time of observation. When done in detail and to a high level of accuracy, it is very time-consuming. Where repeated observations are required, therefore, discharge may be directly determined from stage data by reference to a rating curve which describes the relationship between discharge and stage. The rating curve is obtained by applying the velocity-area technique to a selected range of discharges so that a graph can be produced of stage and discharge (e.g. *Figure 3.12*). When plotted on log-log graph paper this relationship tends to approximate to a straight line. The accuracy of the rating curve depends upon the number of data points used for its construction and upon the stability of the channel cross-section. Periodic checks should be made by re-surveying the cross-section and using the velocity-area technique.

Controlled cross-sections are sometimes used to overcome the problems of bed scour at high flows. Natural controls, such as the outcrop of a hard rock band across the stream, may be utilised to provide a stable relationship between discharge and stage. Alternatively, the channel may be lined by paving slabs, giving a flat bed and sides sloping at 45° or 60°.

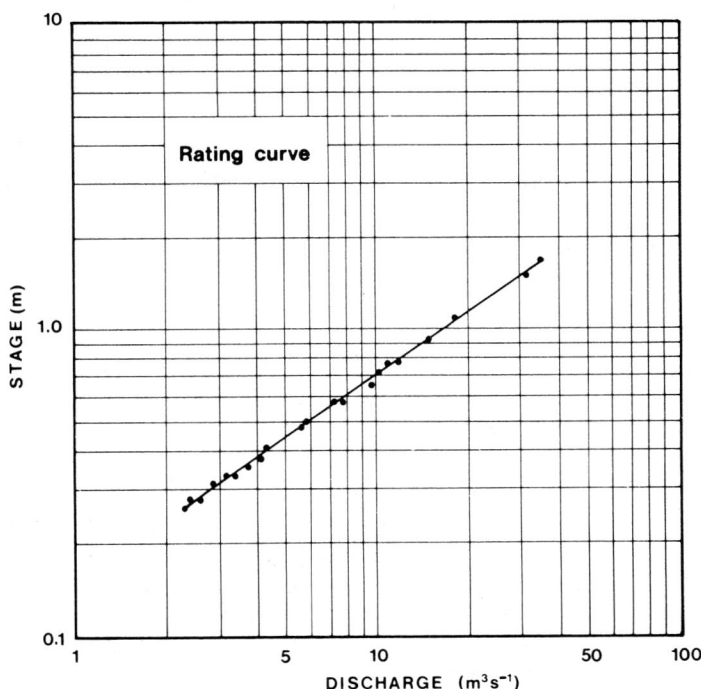

**Figure 3.12 A stage-discharge rating curve**

However, for very small channels the use of a float or current meter can be problematic. Discharge may be calculated instead from the degree of dilution of a tracer solution such as sodium chloride (NaCl), of known concentration injected into the stream at constant rate. A practical working guide for the application of dilution gauging to natural channels has been presented by Browne and Foster (1978).

For accurate repeated measurements of discharge, artificial structures should be used

**Plate 3.1 A trapezoidal flume at the Blackbrook gauging station, Leicestershire**

to control the rate of outflow from a reach (*Plate 3.1*). A wide variety of structures have been designed but all are based on the same principle: that is, the cross-sectional area and the flow velocity are known from a simple measure of water stage and are controlled by the dimensions of the structure through or over which the water flows (*Figure 3.13*).

Although most structures are expensive to install, in small catchments various types of sharp-crested weir can be constructed cheaply and effectively. The weir is constructed out of a thin metal plate. It acts as a dam placed across the stream and the flow passes through or over a notch or crest of known dimensions. The weir impounds the water upstream

**Common forms of gauging structure**

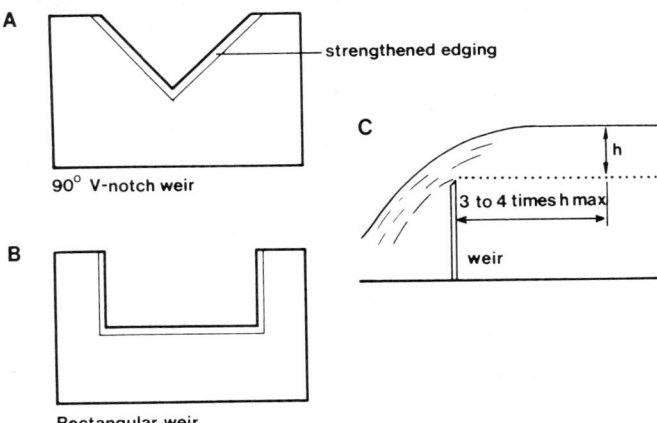

Figure 3.13 Flow control structures. A 90° V-notch weir (A) or a rectangular weir (B) can be used to control the head of water (h) so that discharge can be calculated from measurements of stage alone

such that a constant relationship exists between the head of water above the base of the notch or above the crest and the rate of outflow over the weir. In order to avoid the effects of drawdown, however, the measurement of the head should be undertaken at a distance of two or three times the maximum head behind the crest.

Triangular notch weirs are generally used for very small streams and streams characterised by small changes of stage, while rectangular forms are used where a larger discharge capacity is required. Gregory and Walling (1971) describe the construction of an inexpensive yet adequate V-notch weir made from aluminium sheet or marine ply, with the notch edged by a sharpened metal strip and installed across the channel using metal and wooden stakes. It is important that the upstream side of the weir is made watertight with polythene sheet, sandbags and clay to prevent seepage under or around the structure. Immediately downstream of the weir, the channel bed should be lined with large stones or concrete blocks to prevent erosion and the possible undermining of the structure.

**TABLE 3.6 APPLICATION OF SIMPLE FLOW CONTROL STRUCTURES TO SMALL STREAMS**

| Structure type | Top width (cm) | Maximum depth (cm) | Maximum discharge measureable ($m^3 s^{-1}$) | Workable minimum discharge ($m^3 s^{-1}$) |
|---|---|---|---|---|
| 90° V-notch | 40 | 20 | 0.025 | 0.0002 |
| | 60 | 30 | 0.068 | — |
| | 80 | 40 | 0.138 | — |
| | 100 | 50 | 0.240 | — |
| Rectangular | 50 | 20 | 0.083 | 0.005 |
| | 50 | 30 | 0.153 | — |
| | 100 | 30 | 0.305 | 0.010 |
| | 100 | 40 | 0.470 | — |
| | 150 | 30 | 0.458 | 0.015 |
| | 150 | 50 | 0.986 | — |
| | 200 | 50 | 1.315 | 0.020 |
| | 300 | 50 | 1.973 | 0.030 |

The rectangular weirs may have the banks of the channel as the vertical sides of the notch. Alternatively, the width of the crest may be less than the channel width in order to increase the head of water flowing through the weir and consequently to exaggerate changes in head with changes in discharge. For a given water area and velocity, the narrower the crest width the greater the depth, and the more sensitive will be changes of stage to changes of discharge.

Some guidelines are given in *Table 3.6*. Whichever method is used, the conversion of river stage data into values of discharge using the rating curve or rating equation can be tedious, but the increased use of micro-computers has greatly improved the efficiency of data processing.

### 3.4.3 Analysis of hydrological data

Analysis is required for the purpose of extracting and determining the major characteristics of streamflow at each measurement location. The techniques employed may be classified according to the objectives of the analysis — to identify any long-term trends;

or to examine the flow variability, the extreme flow data, or the form of individual flood hydrographs.

If a long record of rainfall or streamflow data is available a regression or, more simply a running-mean, technique may be applied to annual or monthly mean flow values (*Figure 3.14A*). Commonly, 5-year running means and 12-monthly means are employed to reduce the influence of short-term fluctuations, to smooth the data and to illuminate any trends. To generate a graph of 5-year running means the first five annual means are averaged and the value obtained is entered against the third year. Then starting with the second annual mean the next five years' values are averaged and the discharge obtained is plotted against the fourth year. This stepwise averaging is continued until all the data is used.

**A**

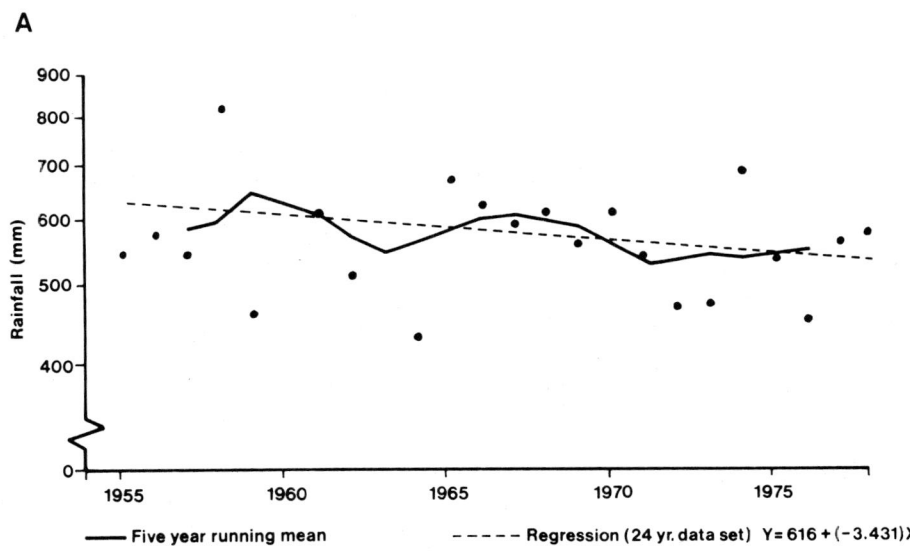

Figure 3.14A Analysis of
hydrological data: long-term trends
can be identified using regression
or moving average techniques

—— Five year running mean          - - - - Regression (24 yr. data set) $Y = 616 + (-3.431)X \pm 95$

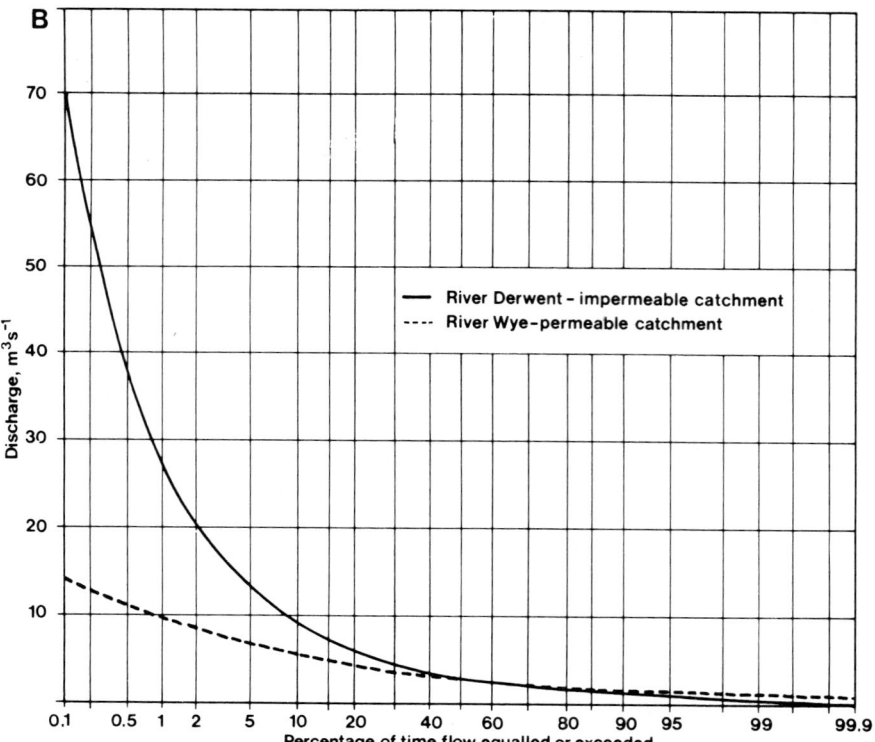

**Figure 3.14B Flow variability can be synthesized using a duration curve**

Records of sufficient length for the examination of temporal changes in streamflow pattern are often unavailable but data suited to the characterisation of streamflow within particular rivers are readily obtained. Streamflow may be characterised by the degree of flow variability and this can be determined in a standard way so as to facilitate comparison between rivers. The data are processed in the form of a cumulative frequency graph known as the *flow duration curve* (*Figure 3.14B*). Daily mean flow data for at least one year and ideally five years or longer are rearranged into their order of magnitude. The data are then converted so as to describe the number of times that each discharge was equalled or exceeded, expressed as a percentage:

i.e. $(x/n) \times 100$

where $n$ is number of days of record and $x$ is number of times (days) the specified flow was equalled or exceeded.

Alternatively, for long records, the flow values may be grouped into a number of predetermined classes before being converted into cumulative percentages. If a simple duration curve is plotted using normal $x$ and $y$ co-ordinates, the area beneath the curve will be directly proportional to the total discharge but the detail concerning the low flows is effectively obscured. In order to avoid this problem and to provide detail at the extreme ends of the duration curve, logarithmic values are used for the flow magnitudes on the $y$-axis and the flow durations on the $x$-axis are expressed as probability values. To facilitate visual comparison between the duration curves from two or more catchments, the discharge values should be expressed as a ratio to the mean flow $(q/\bar{q})$. The mean flow can be simply read off the duration curve — that flow which is equaled or exceeded 50% of the time — or abstracted form the ordered data.

The extremes of the flow duration data, that is the rare floods and droughts, may be analysed using *frequency* or *probability analysis*: an important tool not only for describing hydrological data but also for flood and drought prediction and the design of water supply and flood control schemes. The technique does not describe the actual incidence of an event in real time but relates the magnitude of an event to the frequency with which it is likely to occur. Statistically, the probability of the event happening is determined. Thus, it is possible for example to estimate the magnitude of a flood which is likely to be equalled or exceeded on average once during fifty years; or to predict the likely frequency of a flood which would inundate a particular area of floodplain such as a proposed development site.

The flood which is likely to be equalled or exceeded on average once every fifty years is also said to have a recurrence interval of fifty years and is termed a 50-year flood. The maximum discharge during each year of record is extracted (creating an *annual series* of data) and placed in rank order with the largest annual peak ranked number one. The recurrence interval or probability is then determined for each of the discharges as shown in *Table 3.7*. The recurrence or probability values may then be plotted against their respective discharge or flow values. In an applied sense concern is for very extreme events say with a recurrence interval of one hundred years but hydrological records are seldom of sufficient length so that the available data must be used to extrapolate the magnitude of such rare events. This may be achieved using the Theory of Extreme Values as applied by E.J. Gumbel. Simply the theory proposes that no matter how high the maximum recorded flood an even higher flood will occur sometime in the future. If the data in any record conforms to the theory when plotted as a graph on Gumbel plotting paper the data will conform to a straight line. However, a

**TABLE 3.7 CALCULATION OF THE RECURRENCE INTERVAL AND PROBABILITY OF EXTREME EVENTS. DATA FOR RIVER DERWENT, DERBYSHIRE, UK**

| Year | Maximum discharge $(m^3\ s^{-1})$ | Rank $(r)$ | Rank order of discharges $(m^3\ s^{-1})$ | Recurrence interval $(T) = (n + 1)/r$ | Probability $(P) = r/(n + 1)$ |
|------|------|------|------|------|------|
| 1 | 43.04 | 8 | 150.65 | 12 | 0.08 |
| 2 | 72.21 | 4 | 99.11 | 6 | 0.17 |
| 3 | 64.85 | 5 | 87.50 | 4 | 0.25 |
| 4 | 61.73 | 6 | 72.21 | 3 | 0.33 |
| 5 | 150.65 | 1 | 64.85 | 2.4 | 0.42 |
| 6 | 10.48 | 11 | 61.73 | 2 | 0.50 |
| 7 | 44.46 | 7 | 44.46 | 1.7 | 0.58 |
| 8 | 39.08 | 9 | 43.04 | 1.5 | 0.67 |
| 9 | 28.32 | 10 | 39.08 | 1.33 | 0.75 |
| 10 | 99.11 | 2 | 28.32 | 1.2 | 0.83 |
| 11 | 87.50 | 3 | 10.48 | 1.09 | 0.92 |

$n = 11$

good approximation to a straight line is often shown by data plotted on a normal probability scale and either logarithmic or linear discharge ordinates (*Figure 3.15*).

Two particular discharge frequencies have been repeatedly used in studies of river systems: namely, the *mean annual flood* which has a recurrence interval of 2.33 years and the *most probable annual flood* having a recurrence interval of 1.58 years, using

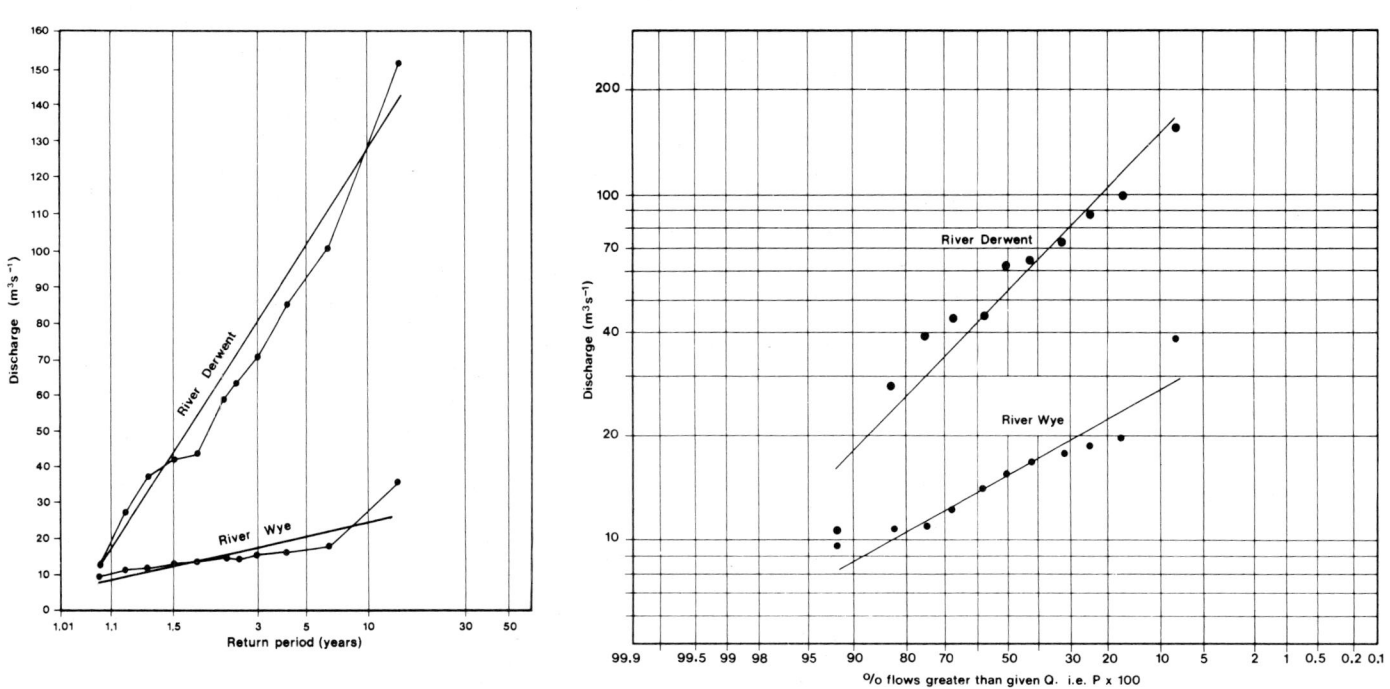

**Figure 3.15 Extreme flow data represented as a return period (or recurrence interval) (A) or as a probability (B)**

an annual series of data, and symbolised as $Q_{2.33}$ and $Q_{2.58}$ respectively. Such values may be realistically obtained from ten years of record; the record length should normally be at least twice as long as the recurrence interval of the largest flood for which data are required. However, it must be noted that a flood having a recurrence interval of one hundred years does not imply any regularity of recurrence in real time, it will not occur regularly every hundred years. Two hundred-year floods may occur in two consecutive years while there is nothing to prevent a five-hundred-year flood occurring in a hundred year time span. Indeed, a five-hundred-year flood is to be EXPECTED on average during one in every five one-hundred year time spans.

From short periods of streamflow observation, differences between catchments may be examined through the study of the flood hydrograph. The examination of the relationship between storm rainfall and the storm runoff produced requires that the storm runoff component is separated from the background base-flow discharge. The simplest procedure for hydrograph separation is based upon the assumption that the beginning of hydrograph rise is the result of the arrival of rapid runoff (or quickflow) in the stream channel (*Figure 3.16*). A separation line is then drawn from the point of hydrograph rise to a point on the recession limb. To fix the precise point requires the identification of an inflection point or of a subtle change of curvature of the hydrograph recession. It is, therefore, rather arbitrary although various mathematical and chemical procedures have been developed.

One procedure for small drainage basins (up to 50 km$^2$) involves drawing a theoretical separation line from the point of initial hydrograph rise: a line rising at 0.01 m$^3$ s$^{-1}$ per square kilometre of drainage basin per hour has been employed (Hewlett and Hibbert, 1967). Once separated, the volume of the quickflow component can be determined and related to the rainfall characteristics as a simple graph. It may be of interest to calculate the runoff percentage, defined as the proportion of storm rainfall occurring as storm runoff, so that the effect of rainfall intensity, antecedent rainfall and seasonal factors upon the volume of storm runoff may be examined. Because the shape of the storm hydrograph is influenced by the catchment characteristics, standardisation of the effects of different rainfall intensities and durations could isolate a characteristic hydrograph shape for each catchment.

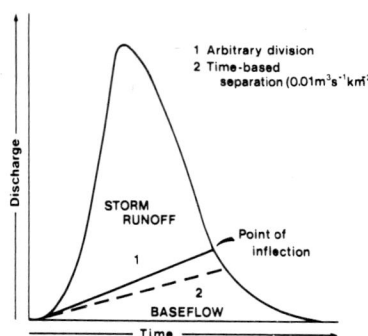

**Figure 3.16 Hydrograph separation**

The shape of the hydrograph, is related to several basic characteristics which are fixed from storm to storm — basin area, basin shape, relief, geology etc. Because of the constancy of these controls each basin may be expected to produce characteristic hydrographs for rainstroms of specific duration. The method of hydrograph analysis uses a concept first described by Sherman (1932); the concept of the **unit hydrograph**, which is based upon three principles:

1. rainfalls of the same duration produce runoff of the same duration irrespective of the rainfall intensity;
2. rainfalls of the same duration but of different intensities produce a hydrograph with ordinates (ie. discharge at various times) which are in the same proportion to each other as the rainfall intensities (ie. a rainfall of 2 cm will result in a hydrograph whose ordinates are twice those of the 1 cm unit hydrograph);
3. the hydrograph produced by a series of rainfalls will be a composite hydrograph formed by the super-position of rainfall related individual hydrographs (ie. the hydrograph due to three separate but clearly spaced storms will be the sum of the three separate hydrographs).

Note that the 'duration' refers to that of effective rainfall which generates the hydrograph and not to the duration of the hydrograph: a 2-hour unit hydrograph is produced by a 2-hour rainfall; the duration of the storm runoff may exceed twenty hours. However, the unit hydrograph is not very sensitive to variations in storm duration so that a range of storm durations may be used, say between one and three hours to obtain the 2-hour unit hydrograph. A simple procedure for constructing unit hydrographs has been presented by Dunne and Leopold (1978). A unit hydrograph can be produced from four or five single peaked streamflow hydrographs produced by short duration storms of intense moderately uniform rain (**Figure 3.17**).

### Procedure:
Plot the hydrographs on graph paper and draw a line to separate storm runoff from the base-flow component (**A**);
Determine the volume of storm runoff (**V**) in cubic metres by simply counting squares on the graph paper (**B**);

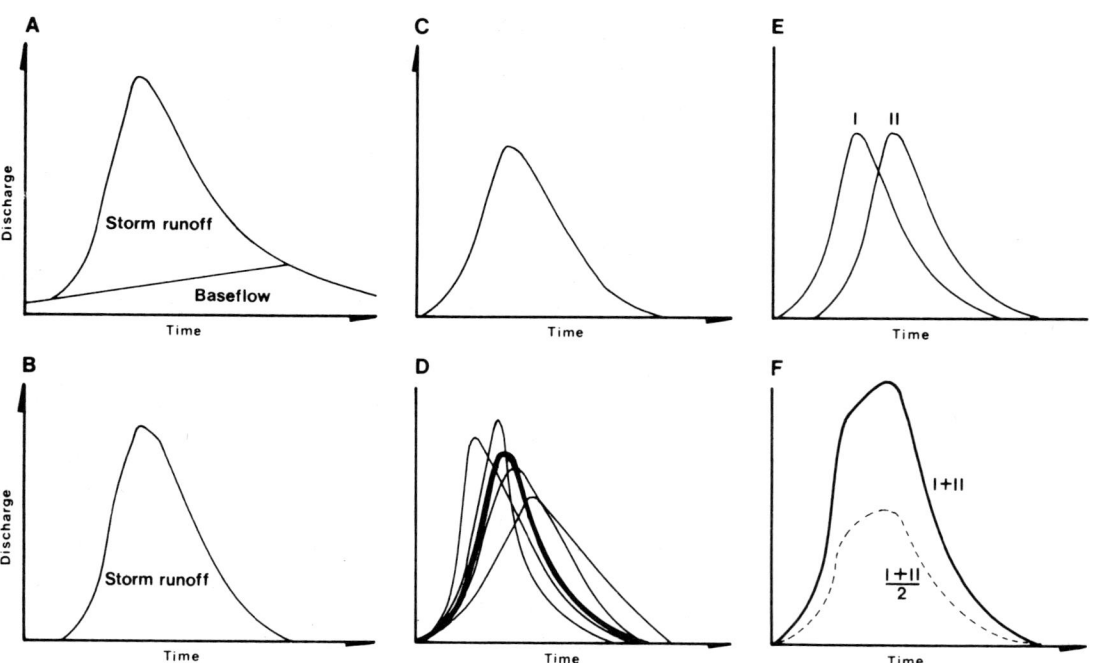

Figure 3.17 Unit hydrograph construction (*see* text for discussion of steps)

Reduce the ordinates of the storm runoff graph to their equivalent values for one centimetre of runoff (*C*);

$$q_i = Q_i \times \left( \frac{1}{((V \div A) \times 100)} \right)$$

where $q_i$ = unit discharge at each time interval ($i$) in m$^3$ s$^{-1}$;

$Q_i$ = storm runoff at each time interval ($i$) in m$^3$ s$^{-1}$;

$A$ = drainage area in m$^2$;

$V$ = storm runoff volume in m$^3$;

Plot and superimpose each of the reduced hydrographs so that each begins at the same time (D);

Determine the time to peak of each hydrograph, average the values obtained, plot this "average peak" and sketch the unit hydrograph to conform to the average shape of the reduced hydrographs passing through the 'average peak' and having a volume equal to 1 cm of runoff:

Having obtained a unit hydrograph for a particular stream and a particular duration of rain, the runoff from any other rainfall of the same duration may be predicted. Effective rain of 4 cm, for example, would produce a unit hydrograph whose ordinates are multiplied by four. This storm runoff would then be added to the estimated base-flow to produce the streamflow hydrograph. Longer duration unit graphs may also be generated. A 4-hour unit hydrograph may be extended to an 8-hour unit hydrograph by assuming two 4-hour rainstorms, the second immediately following the first. The two rainstorms will produce identical unit hydrographs but the second will lag behind the first by four hours (*Figure 3.17E*). The two unit hydrographs are then added together and the total hydrograph obtained represents runoff from 8 hours of rain. However, the volume of runoff represented by the hydrograph will be 2 cm so that the ordinates must be divided by two in order to derive the 8-hour unit hydrograph (*F*). The longer time-base and lower peak is to be expected because the same 'unit' volume of rain has fallen at a lower intensity for a longer time.

# CHAPTER 4  SEDIMENTS IN RIVER SYSTEMS

Each year rivers transport large quantities of sediment in particulate form, that is as individual grains and rock fragments, and in solution. The rate at which sediment is moved is called the sediment discharge, measured in weight per unit time ($t.yr^{-1}$). On the global scale the average sediment discharge per year — the average sediment yield — varies widely (Holeman, 1968): for example,

| | | | |
|---|---|---|---|
| R. Ching, China | $8040\ t\ km^{-2}\ yr^{-1}$ | R. Kosi, India | $3130\ \ t\ km^{-2}\ yr^{-1}$ |
| R. Colorado, USA | $424\ t\ km^{-2}\ yr^{-1}$ | R. Amazon, Brazil | $67\ \ t\ km^{-2}\ yr^{-1}$ |
| R. Danube, USSR | $27\ t\ km^{-2}\ yr^{-1}$ | R. Rhine, Holland | $3.5\ t\ km^{-2}\ yr^{-1}$ |

For Britain the average long-term sediment yield is $33\ t\ km^{-2}\ yr^{-1}$ although extreme values range from 0.8 to $488\ t\ km^{-2}\ yr^{-1}$. The relative proportion of the sediment discharge composed of particulate sediment and solutes also varies widely. Either component can form between 5% and 95% of the total load. In the UK, Walling (1971) observed that the average sediment discharge of streams in south-east Devon is composed of 40% particulate sediment (2.5% bedload and 37.5% suspended load) and 60% solutes. The sediments transported by rivers are derived from the rocks, soils, and superficial deposits within the drainage basin. Climate predominates as the control of sediment yield on the global scale because climate controls weathering and runoff rates, and the character of the vegetation cover. However, rivers with high sediment yields are associated also with areas of high relief and on a smaller scale with human activities, particularly vegetation-clearance and land cultivation.

Sediment is continually being eroded from drainage basins and transported to basins of deposition. The sequence of events involving uplift — erosion — transportation — deposition — conversion into rock (compaction, metamorphism or even melting) — uplift is known as the Geologic Cycle. Rocks are, for the most part, formed under conditions of high temperature, high pressure, and in the absence of large quantities of water and air. At the earth's surface the minerals change their character under the conditions of low temperature and low pressure and in the presence of air and water. These changes are produced by the processes of **weathering** which alter the rock-forming minerals until they come into equilibrium with the surface or near-surface environment. Weathering processes can be categorised as physical and chemical; the former produce the mechanical breakdown of rocks into smaller fragments, and the latter produce the chemical decomposition of the rock-forming minerals into different materials. Further discussion is given by Trudgill (1983). The products of these weathering processes supply the sediment load of rivers.

The removal of these weathered rock materials by rivers as the sediment discharge describes the rate of landsurface denudation. For the Earth as a whole, the average sediment discharge is about 125 $t$ km$^{-2}$ yr$^{-1}$ and this represents a lowering of the land surface by 30 mm in every thousand years. In addition to direct contributions from crystalline rocks, river sediments may contain large proportions of grains whose immediate source is older sediments. Material in solution may be transported rapidly to the ocean basins but the movement of particulate sediment is intermittent. Some particles may "rest" for thousands of years in temporary storages (floodplains, alluvial fans or lake deposits) during which time they may be altered further by mechanical breakdown and chemical decomposition.

## 4.1 THE SOLUTE LOAD

Rivers transport large amounts of material in solution. Indeed, for some rivers the dissolved or solute load can be several times greater than the solid load; for these catchments, chemical erosion will form the major component of landscape denudation. The water of streams and rivers may contain a wide range of chemical constituents which originate from several sources, particularly from the atmosphere and from the weathering of bedrock. Precipitation does not provide chemically pure water to the catchment surface but contains materials in solution. Dry fallout from the atmosphere also provides a measureable input to the land surface. This involves relatively large dust particles which fall due to gravity. It is, however, difficult to separate the solutes contributed by precipitation and dry fallout in any sample analysis and these sources are normally considered as **bulk precipitation** inputs. Significant concentrations of chloride, sodium, calcium and sulphur commonly are contributed to the dissolved load of streams by precipitation. Chloride and sodium are derived primarily from sea-water so that particularly high concentrations of the elements may be found in coastal locations. On the other hand, calcium and sulphur have a terrestrial origin and their significance increases for inland areas. Today, sulphur concentrations are especially influenced by atmospheric pollution.

At the global scale, the chemical composition of surface water has been related to climate (atmospheric precipitation, and evaporation) and to geology (Gibbs, 1970). Each of the three controls appears to dominate a well-defined geographical region and to produce characteristic solute loadings; low solute loads dominated by atmospheric precipitation; very high solute loads influenced by evaporation; and intermediate loads dominated by rock and soil sources (*Figure 4.1*). The tropical rivers of Africa and South

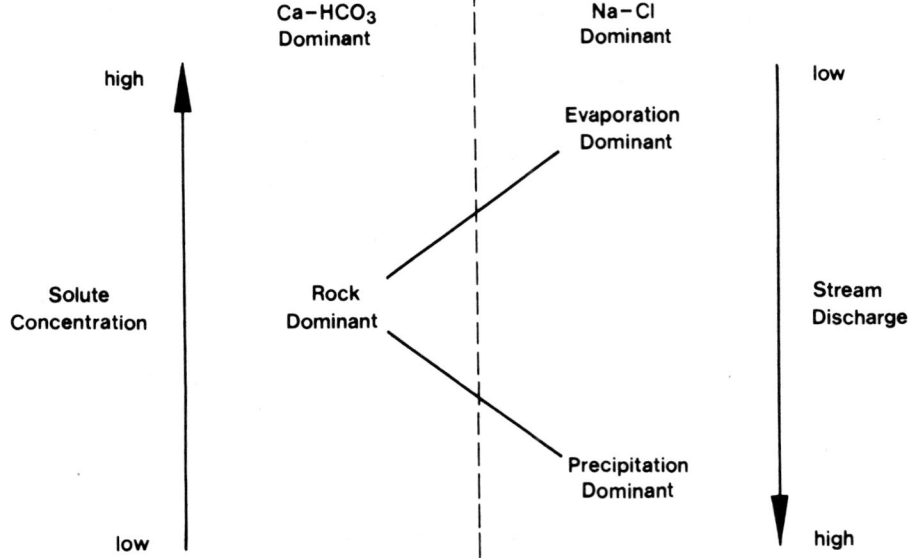

**Figure 4.1 Chemical composition of surface waters. (After Gibbs, 1970)**

America, in areas of low relief, receive water from thoroughly leached soils; the solute loads are low (up to 30 mg$\ell^{-1}$), and controlled by precipitation. The composition of many of the tropical tributaries of the Amazon River, for example, are similar to that of the sea, being dominated by sodium and chloride. In hot, arid regions, streamflow concentrations of dissolved solids may exceed 2000 mg$\ell^{-1}$. These high loads transported, for example, by the River Jordan, are influenced by the processes of evaporation which increase the salinity of the water. However, within this type of environment calcium carbonate is precipitated from solution so that the composition of the water is dominated by sodium and chloride. The third category — areas having intermediate solute loads — are characterised by calcium and bicarbonate dominated water which is closely related to the composition of the rocks of the drainage basin.

### 4.1.1 Solutes in streamflow: sample collection and analysis

The study of a river's dissolved load obviously requires the collection of water samples but this apparently simple operation introduces the major source of error. For studies of the spatial variation in streamwater solute loads within or between catchments, the selected sampling points should 'represent' areas of relatively uniform climate, rock-type, relief and land-use.

A general rule is to select small streams; the solute loadings of streams draining large catchment areas will reflect the mixing of water from various sources so that the effects of clearly defined source areas will become masked.

Secondly, the sample must be representative in the time-dimension. The solute load of stream discharges at any point is constant only during periods of stable base-flow and varies in response to seasonal storm-related changes in solute production and discharge. For spatial surveys care must be taken to ensure comparability in hydrological terms, and sampling should be undertaken under low-flow conditions. Computation of annual solute loads and the study of seasonal variations have been based upon daily or even weekly samples, whilst the examination of changes of solute loads during storm events requires a much more intensive sampling frequency, commonly of between ten minutes and one hour. Continuous monitoring of solute levels largely overcomes problems of deciding upon a sampling frequency but the equipment is costly and is often unavailable.

Thirdly, care must be taken to ensure that the sample is not contaminated. The need for clean sample containers is obviously fundamental because contamination may severely alter the character of the dissolved load, particularly if the water sampled has a low solute content. In general the larger the sample taken the lower will be the effects of contamination. A one-litre bottle has been commonly used. Borosilicate glass sample bottles have often been employed and milk bottles have proved suitable, but screw-top polyethylene containers which are both light and flexible are most popular. The sample should be analysed as soon as possible after collection because for some water types chemical changes may occur within the sample bottle due, for example, to chemical precipitation or to the activity of aquatic organisms.

Determination of the concentration of total dissolved solids (TDS) requires a sample size of between 0.5 and 1 litre. For some stages of flow the water samples collected will contain high concentrations of suspended solids and these should be removed by filtering the sample (*see* section 4.2.4). A filter pore size of 0.45 $\mu$m is commonly employed. After removal of the suspended matter the sample should be evaporated to dryness at between 100 °C and 105 °C, transferred to a desiccator and, after cooling, weighed. Frequently the weight of the dry residue is small so that extreme care must be taken during weighing.

1.  **Equipment:**
Oven capable of maintaining a temperature of between 100 and 105 °C.
Balance capable of weighing to at least 0.001 g.
Large evaporating dishes or other suitable container.
Desiccator.

2.  **Sample:**
500 to 1000 ml.

3.  **Procedure:**
Weigh the sample container at room temperature ($W$1 mg).
Add known volume of between 500 and 1000 m$\ell$. water sample ($V$ m ).
Evaporate sample to dryness in a drying oven at between 100 °C and 105 °C.
Transfer container to a desiccator and allow to cool.
Reweigh sample container ($W$2 mg) to at least three decimal places.

$$\text{Concentration of total dissolved solids (mg } \ell^{-1}) = W1 - W2 \times \frac{1000}{V}$$

Alternatively, the specific electrical conductance (SEC) may be measured. This parameter describes the ability of a solution to carry an electric current and, measured in micromhos/cm ($\mu$mhos cm$^{-1}$) or in microsiemens per millimetre ($\mu$s mm$^{-1}$) directly reflects the TDS content of the water being tested. SEC is dependant, however, upon temperature and values are usually reported at a standard temperature of 25 $^\circ$C. Measurement requires the use of a field or laboratory conductivity meter but provides a reliable, and relatively cheap method which avoids a large number of laborious TDS determinations. Based upon at least ten careful TDS determinations a relationship can be established with SEC of the form:

TDS = SEC X constant

The constant is the coefficient derived from a regression analysis which relates TDS and SEC. The correlation coefficient should also be determined in order to ensure that the relationship obtained is significant. A usable relationship is easier to establish if the range of conductivity and TDS values employed is large; at low ranges insignificant correlations commonly occur.

The annual solute load of a stream is effectively the product of the volume of streamflow and the average solute concentration:

1.  total discharge X mean concentration = load
    (m$^3$)             (mg $\ell^{-1}$ X 1000)      (mg yr$^{-1}$)

Alternatively:

2.  mean discharge X mean concentration X  31.54 = load
    $\ell$ s$^{-1}$              mg $\ell^{-1}$                       kg yr$^{-1}$

either equation requires only a few measurements of solute concentration made throughout the year.

Such estimates of annual solute load describe the rate of chemical denudation within a drainage basin. Chemical denudation rates are normally expressed either as a rate of ground-surface lowering in millimetres per thousand years (mm $1000 \, \text{yr}^{-1}$) or as a volumetric rate in cubic metres per square kilometre per year ($\text{m}^3 \, \text{km}^{-2} \, \text{yr}^{-1}$); the two expressions are directly equivalent. The conversion of annual load to denudation rate requires an estimate of particle density (mass $\div$ volume, i.e. $\text{kg m}^{-3}$). Although such

estimates of basin denudation based upon mean values must be treated with caution, they provide valuable information for comparative studies concerned with streams draining different rock-types and land-uses.

## 4.1.2 The catchment scale: lithological controls

The chemical composition of water derived from the soils and rocks within a catchment are characterised by variable concentrations of four cations — calcium ($Ca^{2+}$), sodium ($Na^+$), potassium ($K^+$) and magnesium ($Mg^+$) — and three anions — bicarbonate ($HCO_3^-$), sulphate ($SO_4^{2-}$) and chloride ($Cl^-$). It is clear that the different solubilities of the rock-forming minerals are an important control on the solute load and its chemical composition. Coarse crystalline silicate rocks are relatively insoluble and the streamflows will be characterised by only small solute loads: granite rocks, for example, commonly yields waters with less than 100 mg $\ell^{-1}$ of dissolved material. Limestone and other calcareous rocks can produce higher solute loads of between 100 and 1000 mg $\ell^{-1}$, but extreme values may be produced by shales and mudstones (often more than 2000 mg $\ell^{-1}$). These rocks often contain salt deposits and large amounts of organic matter, producing high levels of sulphate, sodium and potassium.

The length of time that water is retained in the soil or rock is a critical factor governing the solute load of streamflows. The *residence time* determines whether a weathering reaction (*see* Trudgill, 1983) is allowed to proceed to the point where the solution is in equilibrium: the slower the rate of water movement (ie. the longer the residence time) the greater the opportunity for the water to achieve equilibrium with the surrounding rock. The significance of 'residence time' has been demonstrated by Newson (1971) who measured dissolved sediment concentrations in limestone streams before, during and after underground flow under a variety of flow conditions. Limestone is mainly composed of calcium carbonate (calcite) which is highly soluble particularly in the presence of a weak carbonic acid, and weathers by solution:

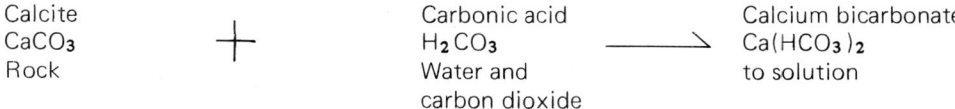

| Calcite | | Carbonic acid | | Calcium bicarbonate |
|---------|---|---------------|---|---------------------|
| $CaCO_3$ | $+$ | $H_2CO_3$ | $\longrightarrow$ | $Ca(HCO_3)_2$ |
| Rock | | Water and carbon dioxide | | to solution |

In massive limestones the calcite crystals are tightly packed giving only a low porosity and solutional processes are confined to the ground surface and to cracks and fissures. Sub-surface solution is often more intense just below the water table where chemical reactions and water flow are both maximised. Streams emanating from limestone sources receive water that has moved through the bedrock in two ways: firstly, water which collects on the surface during storms can be channelled rapidly through a network of conduits (including caves and smaller passages) and, secondly, diffuse flow which percolates slowly through the limestone. At the point of resurgence, the dissolved load concentrations will reflect the relative proportions of conduit flow, having a chemical composition similar to that of the rainwater but modified by passage through the superficial soil, and diffuse flow having higher concentrations of solutes. The highly permeable nature of the limestone, however, may allow the domination of percolation water for all but the highest floods so that solute concentrations in the resurgence water are high and fairly constant. Nevertheless, those resurgences receiving relatively large proportions of conduit flow will show very different changes of dissolved load (*Figure 4.2A*). As the proportion of conduit flow in the resurgent discharge increases so the dissolved load decreases.

The variability of total dissolved solids concentration is closely related to the water discharge. An inverse relationship is commonly found between solute concentrations and discharge (*Figure 4.2B*), produced by the dilution of solute-rich base-flow by storm run-off with shorter residence times and lower solute concentrations. A slight peak of solute concentration may be associated with the initial rise of the storm hydrograph. This is related to the displacement of 'old water' stored in the soil by 'new water' (i.e. the infiltration of precipitation). The dilution effect is affirmed by the consideration of

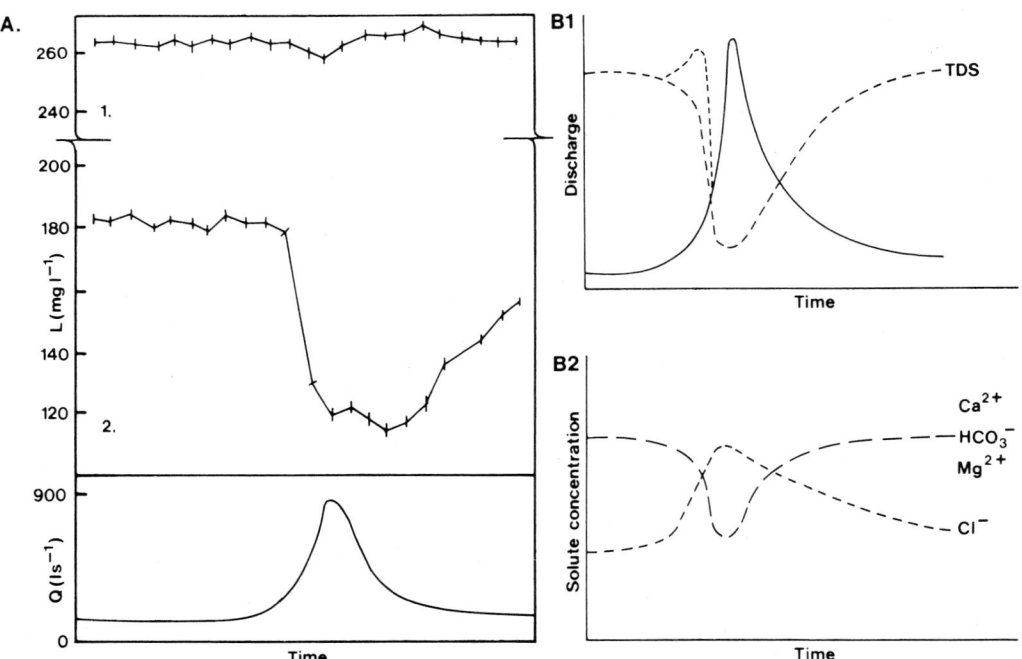

Figure 4.2 Variation of solute concentration (L) with discharge (Q). The effect of residence time (A) is shown by streamflow dominated by percolation water (1) and by conduit flow (2). During storm rainfall (B) rapid runoff will dilute the concentration of total dissolved solids (1) and most ions (2)

individual ions. Ions derived from long-residence base-flows moving through rocks (bicarbonate, magnesium and calcium, for example) are diluted, whilst water derived from storm runoff, having a short residence time, will reflect the quality of the rainfall and the ions (e.g. chloride) can have a direct relationship with discharge. Seasonal variations in solute concentrations are related similarly to the prevalence of high or low flow conditions at particular times of the year and TDS behaviour. High concentrations will occur during summer when water derived from sub-surface sources dominates and low concentrations will be found during winter — the season of greatest dilution. However, this seasonal pattern is very generalised and will be complicated by storm runoff events.

## 4.1.3 Assessing rock controls on solute loadings and catchment denudation (After Walling and Webb, 1975)

The 1462 km$^2$ drainage basin of the River Exe, Devon, extends over a variety of geological strata and provided the study unit for an evaluation of the extent, significance and controls of spatial variations in solute concentrations. The altitude of the drainage basin extends up to over 500 m on Exmoor and the pattern of relief is reflected by the variation of mean annual rainfall from over 1700 mm in the north to less than 850 mm in the south.

A sampling programme was designed to document the spatial variation in solute concentrations. Water samples were collected simply by dipping polythene containers into the stream at over five hundred sites throughout the stream network but concentrating on streams draining small catchments in order to illuminate local extremes. A number of samples were also taken along the major channels in order to evaluate the mixing of water from different sources and the progressive change in water quality along the course of the River Exe. The period of sample collection was chosen to coincide with a spell of dry weather during early July so as to ensure hydrological comparability between sites. Because of the large number of sites selected and the need to analyse the samples within thirty hours of collection to avoid sample deterioration, the analysis was restricted to the determination of specific electrical conductance values corrected to 25 °C.

The data demonstrated a marked variation in solute loadings as reflected by values of specific electrical conductance of less than 40 $\mu$mhos cm$^{-1}$ to maximum values of 1000 $\mu$mhos cm$^{-1}$. However, within this broad range a marked spatial pattern was apparent with low values of less then 150 $\mu$mhos cm$^{-1}$ particularly associated with the area of Exmoor and the Brendon Hills to the north, and the highest values exceeding 400 $\mu$mhos cm$^{-1}$ concentrated in the south-east of the basin. Moreover, analysis of the results by the Chi Square test indicated that this pattern significantly reflects the underlying geological units (*Table 4.1*). Particularly high values of specific electrical conductance (1070 $\mu$mhos cm$^{-1}$ or 700 mg $\ell^{-1}$) were found for streams draining marls containing abundant calcareous material or salt deposits. On the other hand minimum values of only 38 $\mu$mhos

**TABLE 4.1 SOLUTE LOADS FOR STREAMS DRAINING DIFFERENT ROCKS WITHIN THE EXE BASIN (AFTER WALLING AND WEBB, 1975)**

| Specific electrical conductance ($\mu$mhos cm$^{-1}$) | Total dissolved solids (mg$\ell^{-1}$) | Lithology |
|---|---|---|
| 400 | 260 | Permian and Triassic rocks: marls, sandstones, breccies, conglomerates. |
| 150 < 400 | 98 < 260 | Upper carboniferous, culm measures; shales and sandstones. |
| 150 | 98 | Devonian, Cretaceous and Eocene: clay with flints, gravel, greensand, sandstones, silt-stones and slates. |

cm$^{-1}$ (23 mg $\ell^{-1}$) reflect the occurrence of insoluble rock materials having a high, relatively inert, silicious content. Assuming a particle density of 2500 kg m$^3$ denudation rates were obtained, ranging from 2.0 to 100.0 mm 1000 yr$^{-1}$, highest values being found for basins underlain by Permian rocks and lowest values for Devonian rocks on Exmoor.

At a smaller scale, it was suspected that SEC variations between streams from a single lithological group might be related to different land-uses within each of the small drainage basins. In order to test this hypothesis statistically, the Chi-Square test was again employed (*see* section 2.3) The statistic clearly showed that land-use — farmland, woodland and moorland — exerts an important and significant influence upon the solute loads of streams.

## 4.2 PARTICULATE SEDIMENTS

Mineral grains and rock fragments, derived from the soils and superficial deposits of the drainage basin or from the channel bed and banks, are transported in suspension or as bed-load. The characteristics of the sediments not only reflect the process of sediment transport within the channel, but also the processes operating in the source areas.

### 4.2.1 Sediment characteristics

Individual grains of sediment may be described by three important characteristics – size, shape and degree of roundness. Some attempt at precision in the measurement of these basic descriptive measures is necessary because they may yield information about the physical processes acting during transport and deposition, and about the nature of the source materials. A more detailed discussion is presented by Briggs (1977).

Particle-size is a fundamental parameter, and several techniques are available for its determination. The objective is to allocate the particles to size classes (*Figure 4.3*) and to determine the proportion of the sample in each. For sedimentary deposits exposed in vertical sections, such as the river bank, useful information about particle-size can be obtained by visual estimation and with experience the Wentworth grade scale (Wentworth, 1922) can be accurately applied at least down to the silt grade. Silt and clay can be differentiated by rolling a small sample between the finger and thumb: a smooth feel and high plasticity are characteristic of clays. Coarse river sediments, which can be easily handled, may be measured directly in the field. Proportioning may be achieved either by counting the number of particles in each size class or, preferably, by weighing the particles in each of the different size fractions. The latter is more closely related to the processes of sediment transport.

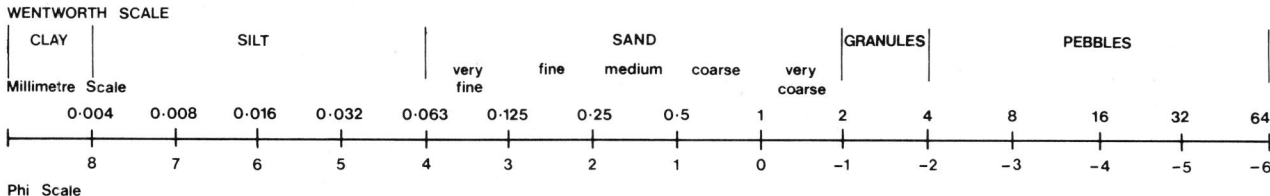

**Figure 4.3 Size classes for particulate sediments**

**Equipment:**

Ruler or calipers.

Scales or balance, readable to 0.5 g (optional).

Set of sieves.

Mechanical sieve shaker.

Drying oven.

Balance readable to 0.5 g.

**Sample:**

100—300 particles

Silt and fine sand — 0.5 g.

Coarse sand — 2 kg.

Pebbles — 5 kg (or more).

Measurement of particle size requires the determination of the mean diameter. This may be estimated by measuring the three primary axes of length (*a*-axis), breadth (*b*-axis) and depth (*c*-axis). Using a ruler or calipers, the longest axis is defined and measured; the particle is rotated about this *a*-axis and the longest axis at right-angles to it is recorded as the breadth; and the particle is rotated a further 90° to define the *c*-axis at right angles to both the '*a*' and '*b*' axes. All measurements should be recorded as millimetres. The mean diameter (*D*) is then estimated as:

$$D = \frac{a + b + c}{3}$$

An alternative, and even simpler method is to measure the *b*-axis alone. For most studies this measurement provides a rapid means of defining particle-size but if particle shape is also of interest then all three axial measurements will be required.

A third approach which is particularly useful for sand-sized sediments employs sieves formed of steel plate or wire mesh. The basic principle of his technique is to pass a sediment sample of known weight through a set of sieves having holes of known diameter and arranged in downward decreasing mesh diameters. The sieves are mechanically vibrated for a fixed period of time, normally twenty minutes, and the weight of sediment retained in each sieve is then measured and converted into a percentage of the total sediment sample. Some degree of sample preparation however is required before sieving.

All samples must be oven-dried (coarse sediments) or air-dried (fine sediments) and the latter, which tend to form hard clods, must be dispersed.

Dispersal is most easily achieved by mixing the air dried sample with a deflocculating agent such as a solution of Teepol (4 drops/litre), allowed to stand overnight and dried again. The sample will then be easily crushed with the fingers. Sieving does not provide a measure of size but some compound of size and shape; for most purposes, however, this problem can be (and is) ignored. Practically, the need is to standardise the procedure and to carry out that procedure with maximum precision. The major problem with sieving coarse particles is the large weight of sediment required to provide a representative sample. The analysis of gravels, for example, requires a sample of at least 5 kg.

It is commonly accepted that the metric scale of measurement is inadequate for the analysis of sediment size because, for example, an increase of particle size by 4 mm from 88 mm to 92 mm is obviously less significant than a change from 1 mm to 5 mm. The range of particle sizes within a deposit characteristically takes the form of a normal distribution only when the sizes are transformed into logarithmic values and the phi ($\phi$) scale introduced by Krumbein in 1934 has been generally adopted:

$\phi = -\log_2 d$, where $d$ = particle diameter in millimetres.

The phi units equivalent to the Wentworth grade divisions are given in *Figure 4.3*. The phi scale, by normalising the data, permits the use of arithmetic rather than logarithmic graph paper for plotting the results and considerably simplifies the calculation of descriptive statistics such as the mean and sorting coefficient. (Sorting provides a measure of the tendency for all the grains to be of one grain-size class). Also, because the scale is reversed with small particles having larger phi values, the scale satisfies the convention for plotting the larger sizes on the left of the graph so that particles decrease in size to the right.

Convention also requires that the particle-size distribution is plotted as a cumulative frequency curve on arithmetic probability paper. Such plots (e.g. *Figure 4.4*) have four advantages:

1.   Deviations from log-normality are represented by variation from a straight line.

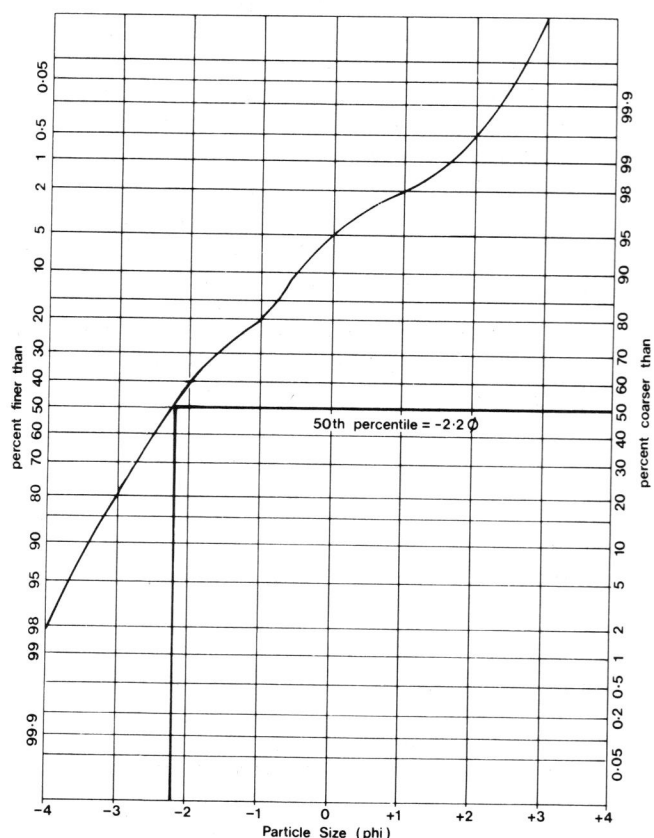

**Figure 4.4 The cumulative frequency curve** (*see Table 4.2*)

2.   The closer the curve to the vertical the better the sorting: a vertical line indicates that all particles fall into the same class.

3.   Significant proportions of coarse and fine end-members show up as near horizontal limbs at the ends of the curve.

4.   Many sample curves can be plotted on the same graph so that differences between samples are at once apparent.

To plot the curve, calculate the percentage of the total sample weight contained within each size class, then starting with the coarsest and proceeding to the finest, sum the percentage within successive classes (*Table 4.2*). The lower limit of each size class — and not the class mid-point — is plotted on the X-axis (arithmetic scale) against the sample percentage coarser than each size class.

**TABLE 4.2 PREPARATION FOR CUMULATIVE FREQUENCY CURVE**

| Size class (phi) | Percentage of total sample weight | Cumulative percentage coarser than size class |
|---|---|---|
| −5 | 0 | 0 |
| −4 | 2 | 2 |
| −3 | 18 | 20 |
| −2 | 38 | 58 |
| −1 | 22 | 80 |
| 0 | 15 | 95 |
| 1 | 3 | 98 |
| 2 | 1.5 | 99.5 |
| 3 | 0.49 | 99.99 |

The shape of the cumulative frequency curve may be described statistically in order to provide a measure of the median and mean particle sizes and a measure of sorting. Grain size of any cumulative percent is termed a percentile (i.e. the phi size corresponding to particular percentages on the Y-axis). Percentile values are used to determine three important measures:

1. Median     $\phi 50$

2. Mean     $\dfrac{\phi 75 + \phi 50 + \phi 25}{3}$

3. Sorting     $\dfrac{\phi 90 + \phi 80 + \phi 70 - \phi 30 - \phi 20 - \phi 10}{5.3}$

(a shorter alternative is $\dfrac{\phi 84 - \phi 16}{2}$ )

The sorting coefficient decreases as the level of sorting improves and ranges from less than 0.5 (well sorted), to between 0.5 and 1.0 (moderately sorted), to 4.0 or more (very poorly sorted).

Particle shape — the three-dimensional form of a particle — is conventionally described according to a scheme devised by Zingg (1935) which uses measurements of the ratios between the length (*a*-axis), breadth (*b*-axis) and thickness (*c*-axis) to define four different shape classes: spheres, rods, blades and discs. The scheme provides a quick but objective measure:

**Spheres**   $b/a > 0.67$; $c/b > 0.67$
**Rods**     $b/a < 0.67$; $c/b > 0.67$
**Discs**    $b/a > 0.67$; $c/b < 0.67$
**Blades**   $b/a < 0.67$; $c/b < 0.67$

Also of interest is the particle roundness which is completely independent of particle shape: it refers to the degree of curvature of the corners. A subjective but nonetheless meaningful classification of particle roundness may be usefully employed;

**Angular**     Little or no evidence of wear; edges and corners are sharp.
**Sub-angular**     Edges and corners slightly rounded but angles between faces still sharp and faces practically untouched.
**Sub-rounded**     Edges and corners rounded off to smooth curves but original shape of the grain is still distinct.
**Rounded**     Original faces almost completely destroyed, entire surface consists of broad, smooth curves.

For sand grains a hand lens will aid classification. Care must be taken, however, with classifying both broken and spherical particles. Grains with a freshly broken surface should be placed in the angular group regardless of the degree of rounding of the rest of the grain. In any classification roundness should be based primarily upon the wear shown by the edges of the particle, and those edges showing the most recent effect.

## 4.2.2 Sediment sources

The particulate sediment load of rivers is derived from the products of rock weathering that compose the soil. Sediment may be released to the stream system by surface erosion on hillslopes, by gully erosion or by the erosion of the channel banks. The material eroded may be derived directly from the products of the bed-rock or indirectly from the erosion of superficial slope deposits or river floodplain sediments. However, for most rivers, the largest part of the sediment load is derived from the headwater areas of high relief that comprise only a small proportion of a river's drainage area. In the Amazon River, for example, Gibbs (1967) revealed that 82% of the suspended sediment load is supplied from the 12% of the basin located in the Andes Mountains. At the global scale, some 80% of the sediment delivered by rivers to basins of deposition may be derived from only the 5–10% of the earth's surface that is mountainous. Rock-type too will play an important role, and considerable variations in the rates of erosion may occur within high relief areas: the annual sediment yield of streams draining basins underlain by mudstones may reach more than ten times those of streams draining resistant sandstones.

The potential for rain to cause erosion is a function of rainfall intensity and duration, and of the mass, diameter and velocity of the raindrops. Indeed, raindrops have the capacity to erode soil, that is to displace soil particles downslope on impact, and measurements of splash transport have shown that the amount of soil moved may exceed $5 \text{ kg m}^{-2} \text{ yr}^{-1}$ on unvegetated, moderate slopes. However, the character of a vegetation cover will exert an important control on the rate of soil erosion. A ground cover will intercept rain and reduce the effect of raindrop impact, root systems in the soil serve to bind sediment grains and to retard soil erosion and vegetation may reduce the rate of overland flow both by increasing the infiltration capacity of the soil and by increasing the surface roughness. Thus, it is not surprising to find a close relationship between rainfall, vegetation, runoff and the sediment loads of streams. This is clearly demonstrated in

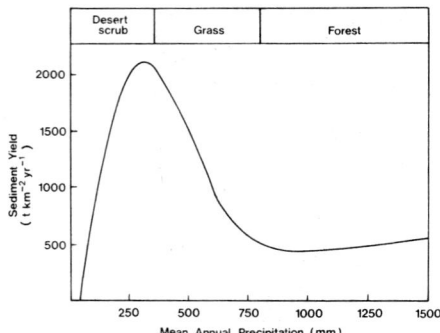

**Figure 4.5 Relationship between sediment yield, climate and vegetation. (After Langbein and Schumm, 1958)**

*Figure 4.5* which is derived from data for central USA. The highest sediment yields are observed for drainage basins receiving between 250 and 350 mm rain annually with a sparse 'desert' vegetation cover. At an annual rainfall of 750 mm grassland is replaced by forest vegetation and minimum values of sediment yield are found. Therefore, whilst for bare slopes soil erosion may be seen to increase with larger rainfall totals, at above 350 mm sediment yields decrease because of the stabilising effects of the vegetation cover.

The measurement of the sediment supplied from the hillslopes, gullies and channel banks may be achieved by using either traps and troughs which catch the eroded material as it is transported downslope, or erosion pins which provide an arbitrary datum from which the rate of ground surface lowering or river bank retreat may be recorded. Soil erosion on hillslopes occurs by rainsplash and overland flows and significant amounts of fine sediments may be delivered to streams; methods of assessing the significance of these sources are covered by Finlayson and Statham (1980).

In upland areas such diffuse sources of sediment are relatively insignificant because deep active gullies can supply large volumes of sediment to rivers. Often embryonic gullies occur where steep slopes of highly weathered material or of superficial deposits such as boulder clay have been undercut by the action of the stream (*Plate 4.1*). Gullies provide a major source of both fine sediments and coarse gravel and cobbles. Harvey (1974) has described gullies in the valley of Grains Gill located in the western part of the Howgill Fells, Cumbria, UK. Active gullies were found on slopes ranging from 35 to 55 degrees and sediment traps located at the foot of two small gullies yielded erosion rates of about 50 kg $m^{-2}$ $yr^{-1}$; erosion was observed to occur about thirty times per year on average.

The measurement of river bank erosion may provide the most interesting data for many reasons, not least because the process is relatively rapid and relatively widespread compared with many other geomorphological processes. Moreover, erosion is concentrated in well defined locations (*Plate 4.2*) so that measurement and the distribution of erosion pins in particular is less problematic. Erosion pins should be inserted horizontally into a river bank at two or three metre intervals; eroding sections are commonly observed around the outer bank of meander bends. The amount of erosion at each pin

Plate 4.1 Slope erosion on the upper Severn, Wales. During periods of low and moderate streamflow the slope is weathered and a cone of debris builds up at the base. The debris cone is an important sediment source for the channel. High streamflows remove the available sediment so that slope erosion is rejuvenated periodically

should be measured after each high flow. The mean rate of erosion within each section of bank may be calculated by summing the total amount of erosion during a given period of time and dividing by the number of pins. Field rates of erosion along rivers of south-east Devon, UK (Hooke, 1980) are comparable to those found in other British rivers. The data (e.g. **Table 4.3**) describe the mean erosion rate and the maximum rate measured on a single pin in each section. Over the 2.5 year measurement period, erosion was

**Plate 4.2 Bank erosion in a lowland stream: Grace Dieu Brook, Leicestershire**

**TABLE 4.3 FIELD RATES OF EROSION IN SOUTH-EAST DEVON, UK RIVERS (AFTER HOOKE, 1980)**

| River | River Exe | | | | River Axe | | | |
|---|---|---|---|---|---|---|---|---|
| Site | 1 | 2 | 3 | 4 | 1 | 2 | 3 | 4 |
| Mean (m.yr$^{-1}$) | 0.63 | 0.62 | 1.18 | 1.03 | 0.15 | 0.42 | 0.29 | 0.46 |
| Maximum (m.yr$^{-1}$) | 0.71 | 1.10 | 2.58 | 2.40 | 0.49 | 1.16 | 0.60 | 1.00 |

experienced on at least 15 occasions at all sites and a maximum erosion of 7 metres was recorded at one location.

## 4.2.3 Sediment transport

Particles lying on the bed of a stream will not begin to move until the flow of water achieves a certain 'power' which is related to the slope of the channel and the discharge. For a given flow power there will be a maximum size of particle that the flow can move; that is, each flow will have a particular competence. Consider *Figure 4.6*; Particles resting

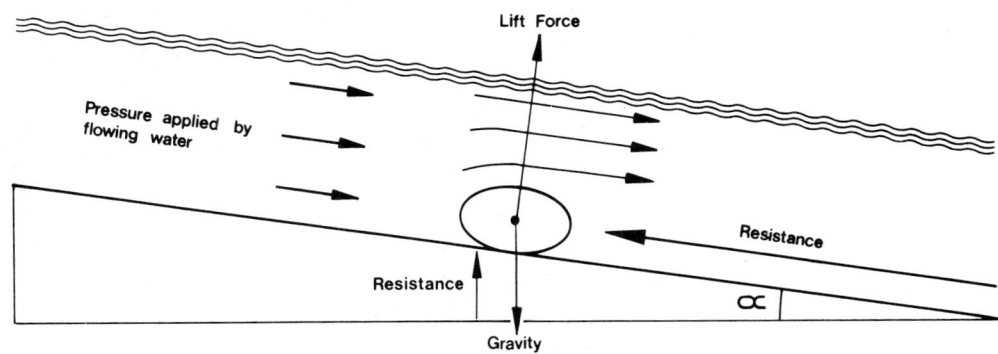

**Figure 4.6 Factors influencing grain movement**

on a surface are subject to the acceleration due to gravity ($g$). On a slope, the weight of the particle acts vertically in the direction of gravity but the resistance provided by the surface prevents movement in that direction. However, downslope movement is possible because the weight of the particle can also be resolved to a force which is parallel to the slope. The magnitude of this force ($F$) is related to the surface slope angle ($\alpha$) in the relationship

$$F = g \sin \alpha$$

so that the gravitational component increases as the slope steepens (the sine of an angle increases to reach a value of 1.0 for an angle of 90°). The gravity force could induce movement downslope but resisting forces operate to maintain the position of the particle. Resistance to movement is caused by the frictional force between the particle and the bed and is related to the size and weight of each individual grain. Fluid forces produced by the flow of water over the bed of the stream are therefore required to initiate sediment movement. Water flow past a particle on the stream bed will influence that particle in two ways. Firstly, flow will create a local zone of higher velocity and lower pressure above the particle so that a pressure gradient from the base to the upper surface develops; this acts as a lift force which may be capable of moving the particle off the bed. Secondly, the water will exert a shear stress or drag on an exposed particle which tends to roll it along the channel bed. Flow competence has been expressed as the shear stress imparted on a solid by the force of flowing water acting parallel to the surface, or as the critical velocity required for the movement of grains of given size.

The relationship between critical velocity and particle size is described by the "Hjulstrom diagram" as modified by Sundborg (1967) and shown in *Figure 4.7*. Strictly, this diagram applies only to flows having a depth of one metre and to homogeneous, (i.e. well-sorted), materials with a density equal to that of quartz (2.65). In reality, water flows over heterogeneous materials of mixed grain size so that the critical velocity may be considerably higher. The curve does describe, however, the fundamental characteristics of sediment transport (Briggs, 1977).

A linear relationship between critical velocity and grain size does not occur. The first grain sizes to be entrained with increasing velocity are not the smallest particles, the clays, but the sand grain sizes of between 3.0 and 1.0 $\phi$ (0.1—0.5 mm). At velocities above about 15 cm s$^{-1}$ the flows are capable of entraining progressively larger grain sizes so that at a velocity of 150 cm s$^{-1}$ gravels of over $-3.5$ $\phi$ (11 mm) can be moved. However, higher flow velocities also result in the progressive entrainment of smaller grain sizes. At a velocity of 100 cm s$^{-1}$ gravel particles of about $-3$ $\phi$ (c.8 mm) are entrained together with clay grains of 8.5 $\phi$ (0.00275 mm).

High velocities are required to move fine sediment due to the effect of compaction and cohesion which increases the resistance of clays and silts to movement. As velocity decreases, sediment is deposited. For all particle sizes, however, the critical erosion

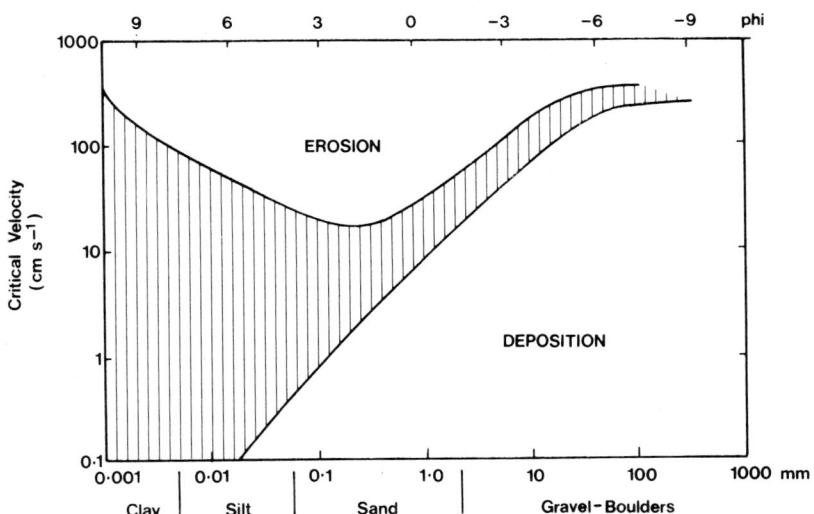

Figure 4.7 The 'Hjulstrom diagram' relating critical flow velocity and particle-size

velocity is greater than the minimum velocity required to maintain transport. For coarse particles the difference between the erosion velocity and settling velocity is negligible, but for clay and silt size fractions which are generally transported only in suspension it is particularly significant. Thus, sediments may be transported for considerable distances because lower velocities are required to sustain movement than for particle entrainment.

Once the power of the stream has been raised above the critical level, sediment of a certain grain size will begin to move. However, the rate at which it will move is limited. This limited rate of transport describes the flow *capacity*. Rivers have an almost unlimited capacity to transport clay and fine silt so that the rate of transport found in a river depends upon the rate of sediment production within the drainage basin, that is, upon the available supply.

The rate of movement of bed load, however, depends primarily upon the characteristics of the flow. If the rate of sediment supply to a river channel, say from a tributary, exceeds the transport capacity of that channel then the excess sediment will be deposited. Sediment will continue to accumulate until the morphology of the channel is so altered as to change the flow characteristics and to establish an equilibrium between the rate of

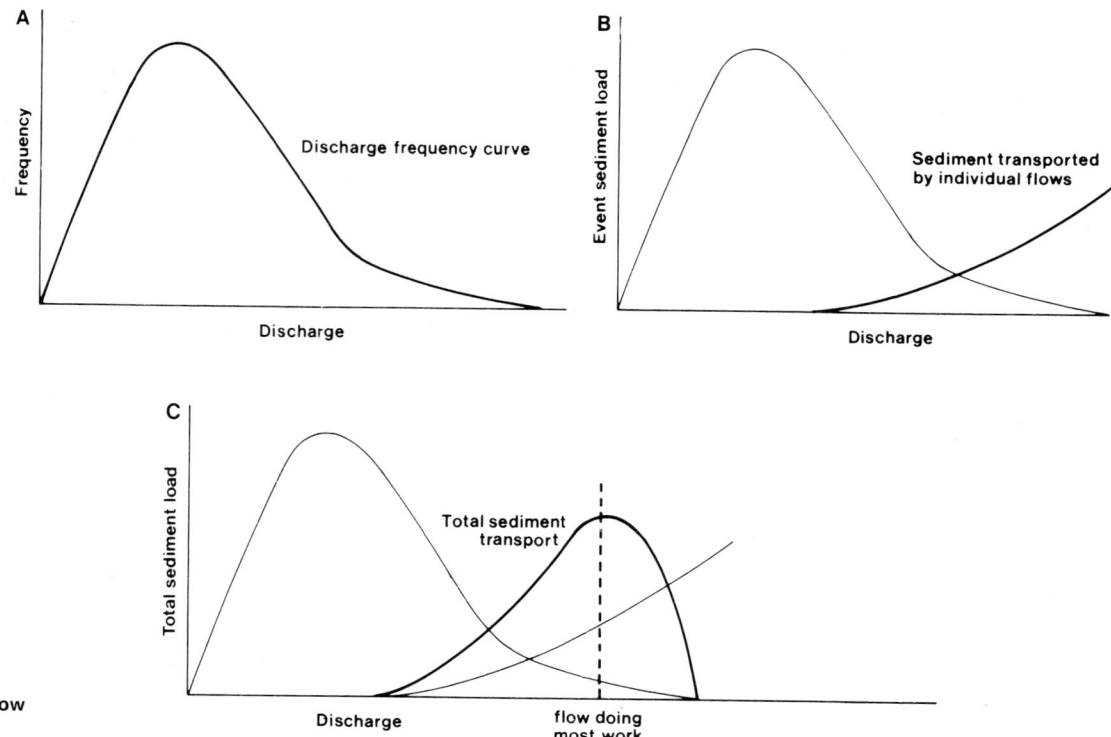

Figure 4.8 Derivation of the 'flow doing most work'

supply and rate of sediment transport by the river. For example, deposition of sediment on the stream bed will increase the slope of the channel until the flow velocity is increased to provide the required transport rate. This clearly demonstrates the relationship between the flows, sediment loads and channel morphology: the channel will adopt a form which will allow the downstream transport of all the sediment supplied from upstream (i.e. the form which will inhibit excessive erosion or deposition.

It has long been recognised that in the long-term it is not the rare, high-magnitude flood that transports the most sediment but an event of relatively high frequency. This may easily be visualised by constructing a sediment discharge frequency curve (*Figure 4.8*). First construct a frequency curve of discharge (A) and add a line which relates each discharge magnitude to its sediment load (B). Finally produce a collective sediment load curve by multiplying each discharge frequency by the respective load transported during one discharge event (C). It can be seen clearly that the discharge which collectively transports the most sediment (that does the most work) is characterised by a moderate magnitude and a moderate frequency. Rare, high magnitude flows may transport large quantities of sediment individually but they occur so infrequently that, compared to the more frequent smaller flows, they transport little in total. For low magnitude discharges, a large number of events will occur but little sediment will be transported.

**4.2.4 Data collection**

Sediment transport involves movement on or near the channel bed and in suspension, and the examination of each of these modes of transport requires a different approach. Sediment is generally supported in suspension by turbulence. Such eddying is highly variable within the channel and over time so that the concentration of suspended sediment (defined as the weight of sediment in each litre of water) may fluctuate between wide limits. Thus, the extraction of water samples for the determination of suspended sediment loads should aim to obtain a sample representative of the whole cross-section. This may be achieved either by taking a depth integrated sample or by bulk sampling. The former approach requires placing a slow-filling bottle sampler (*Figure 4.9*) into the river and slowly lowering, then raising the sampler from the bed to the surface until the bottle is filled.

A cheap sampler can be constructed by using a plastic bottle of about 0.5 litre

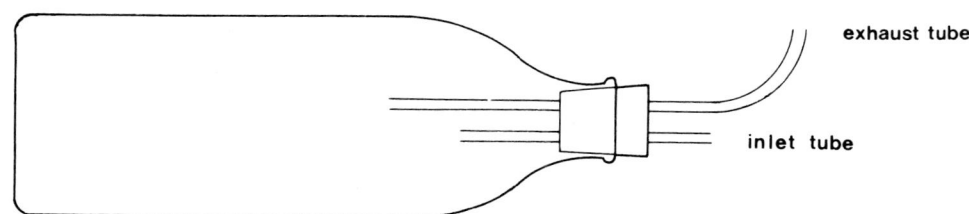

exhaust tube

inlet tube

**Figure 4.9 A slow filling bottle sampler for suspended solids**

which is sealed with a cap such as a rubber bung through which two holes have been drilled to take two tubes. The water-sediment mix enters the bottle through the inlet tube and air is expelled through the exhaust tube as the bottle fills. For convenience, the sampler may be attached to a rod to which a tail fin can be added in order to aid sampler alignment with the streamflow. The sample obtained will yield a sediment concentration which describes the average concentration of all depths between the bed and the surface. Ideally this should be undertaken at three or more verticals across the channel.

As for the determination of discharge (section 3.4.2) each vertical represents the centre of a sub-section for which the area, velocity and therefore discharge are known. The sediment load of each sub-section is the product of sediment concentration and discharge; the total load is then the sum of the individual sediment loads determined for each sub-section. The alternative approach simply requires the bulking of samples taken from different points within the cross-section using a sample bottle (milk bottles may be used for example) to give an estimate of the average concentration for the cross-section. This bulk sample is then multiplied by the total discharge for the cross-section at the time of measurement to give the suspended sediment load. Suspended sediment concentrations are usually determined by filtering the sediment-water samples:

**Equipment:**
Drying oven.
Filter funnel and flask; a flask which allows the use of a vacuum pump should be used where available to increase the efficiency of the procedure.

Filter papers; a pore size of 0.45 $\mu$m is commonly used; note that the pore size of the filter paper determines the minimum size of the sediment measured.

Measuring cylinder graduated in millimetres.

Balance readable to 0.001 g or 0.0001 g (the latter is preferable).

Desiccator.

**Sample:**

250 m$\ell$ (at least).

**Procedure:**

Dry the filter paper in the oven at 100 to 105 $^\circ$C for 15 minutes.

Remove to desiccator and allow to cool (c. 10 minutes).

Weigh the paper to 0.001 g ($W$1).

Shake sample bottle to disperse sediment and filter.

Measure the volume of water collected in the flask ($V$).

Dry the filter paper and sediment in the oven at 100 to 105 $^\circ$C for about 30 minutes.

Remove to desiccator and allow to cool (c. 20 minutes).

Weigh the filter paper and sediment ($W$2).

**Calculation:**

Suspended sediment concentration (SSC) in mg$\ell^{-1}$

$$\text{SSC}(\text{mg}\ell^{-1}) = (W2 - W1) \times \frac{1000}{V} \times 1000$$

Suspended sediments are normally analysed in terms of the concentration as opposed to total load. This is because a high correlation between sediment load and discharge is inevitable as sediment load is computed as a product of discharge (SSC $\times$ $Q$).

Suspended sediment concentrations typically vary with discharge and for any particular location it is possible to express the relationship as a straight line plot using a regression equation based upon logarithmic data, that is, as a rating curve. Variations also occur in the discharge-sediment concentration relationship during storm discharges (*Figure 4.10A*). Maximum suspended sediment concentrations generally precede the peak discharge, again because of the exhaustion of the sediment supply during the passage of a

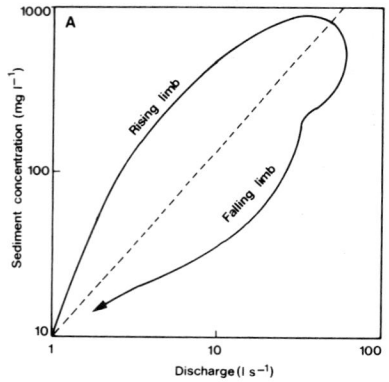

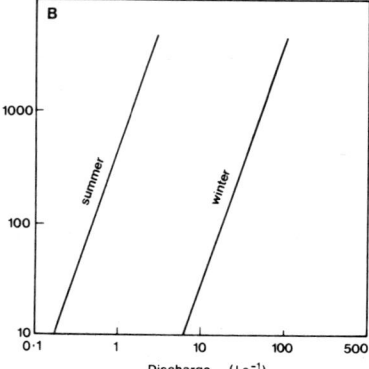

**Figure 4.10 Suspended sediment rating curves: the hysteretic loop (A) and seasonal differences (B)**

flood and because of the relatively high contribution of water from baseflow sources on the recession limb. If a long time period elapses between storms a large amount of sediment will be made available by weathering and mass movement. During a storm the supply of available sediment on the hillslopes is washed rapidly into the channel; fine sediments within the channel are picked up quickly; and as this readily available supply is depleted the sediment load is reduced, even though discharge continues to rise. As a result, the peak of water discharge is found to lag behind the sediment discharge peak, and for a given discharge the suspended sediment concentration will be higher on the rising stage than on the falling stage of the hydrograph: the relationship will be described by a hysteretic curve.

However, for most streams a distinction clearly exists between rating curves derived from samples taken during summer (April–September) and those taken during winter (*Figure 4.10B*). For a given discharge, the suspended sediment concentration is commonly higher for summer flows because of four seasonal factors. Firstly, storm runoff will dominate summer high flows whereas in winter baseflow makes a major contribution. Secondly, the summer period is often noted for the occurrence of intense short-duration rainfalls associated with thunderstorms and such rainfalls possess a high erosive capacity. Thirdly, the dry and dusty surface conditions in summer provide a greater availability of sediment; and fourthly, sediment sources may become exhausted during winter when the number of storms is highest and the time period between storm events is low in comparison to the summer 'dry' period.

The measurement of bed-load transport is notoriously difficult but two methods have commonly been used: traps and tracers. Bed-load traps are used to catch the sediment passing through a channel section during a pre-determined time period. The traps may be simple boxes or trays inserted into a trench dug in the stream bed. The sediment collected in a trap during a storm discharge is removed and weighed to provide an estimate of the bed-load movement. Data are normally expressed as weight per unit channel bed-width and may be related to discharge as a simple graph. It must be remembered that the bed-load generally represents only a small proportion of the total load transported.

Tracer analysis uses 'marked' sediment to track the paths and to monitor the timing of sediment movement. Particles are normally marked artificially with a durable, bright coloured paint. The tracers are then inserted in a relatively shallow and uniform channel section.

**Equipment:**
Calipers, or ruler.
Bright coloured and durable paint.

**Sample:**
100 pebbles with an intermediate axis of at least 25 mm should be collected from the stream bed.

**Procedure:**
Paint each of the pebbles and number to ease analysis.
Measure the three axes of the particle (see section 4.2.1).
Return the particles to the channel location from which they were extracted.
After a storm event a search is made for the pebbles, the distance moved is recorded and the particle identified.

A large number of particles are required because burial and transport over long distances may result in high losses: losses of 55% or more are not uncommon. An example of one such study is given in *Figure 4.11*. The data may be used to relate peak discharge to the size and shape of particles moved and to plot the path of movement. In the example, a maximum particle size of 48 mm was moved; the smaller sized particles tended to move furthest; and rod and sphere shaped particles in general moved further for a given grain size than the flatter disc and plate shapes. Also, note that particles tended to maintain their relative positions across the channel and did not move laterally, for example, from the outside of the channel to the inside of the bend.

**4.2.5 Sediment change along rivers**
During transport two sets of processes associated with particle *abrasion* and *sorting* operate so as to reduce the size of the bed-material, to reduce the range of particle sizes (i.e. to improve the degree of sorting), and to increase the degree of particle rounding with distance from the source in alluvial rivers (*Figure 4.12*). In 1875 Sternberg observed that the size of the largest particles in a river bed decreased semi-logarithmically with distance downstream and believed that the decrease in size was due wholly to abrasion,

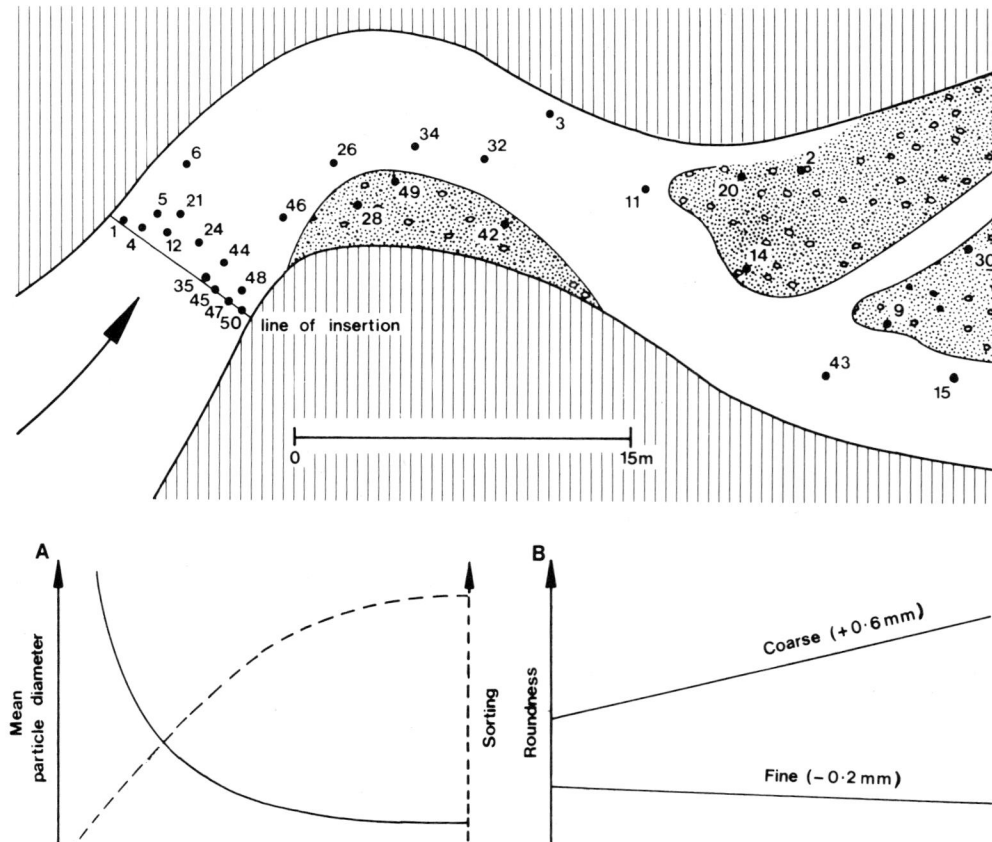

Figure 4.11 Movement of 'tracer' pebbles within a meander, Langedalen, Norway. Fifty tracers were inserted sequentially along the transect but only twenty-nine were recovered

Figure 4.12 Downstream changes of fluvial sediment character: size and sorting (A), and roundness for different size fractions (B)

that is to splitting, crushing, chipping and grinding. However, subsequent work has shown that selective erosion and deposition and chemical weathering are also important.

The size and shape of sedimentary particles depend initially on the nature of the source rock and the weathering processes to which it has been subjected. Laboratory studies have found that the rate of abrasion depends on the initial size, shape and mechanical resistance of the particle, as well as the intensity of the process, the size of the other particles within the bed-material load and the character of the floor over which transportation is taking place. Experiments have indicated that the mechanical abrasion of small pebbles is slight and becomes extremely slow for resistant grains less than 2 mm in diameter. Indeed, it has been suggested that to reduce a quartz cube 0.4 mm in diameter to a sphere would require transport of several million kilometres! But care must be taken in the extrapolation of such laboratory findings to the real world.

Two reasons have been put forward to explain why abrasion varies inversely with particle size: firstly, because the coarser particles tend to be less rounded than small ones and abrade more rapidly (particularly by chipping); secondly, because the coarse particles are commonly rock fragments — individual mineral grains within a relatively weak matrix which may be eroded relatively easily so that the fragments disintegrate. Therefore, large particles are reduced in size more rapidly than smaller particles and particle-size will decrease exponentially downstream. All abrasive processes are to some extent facilitated by weathering but the effect is most important with granular disintegration, that is with grain by grain disaggregation. The movement of the coarser particle sizes in streams is certainly intermittent. Gravels may spend long periods of time in temporary storage, for example as part of the river floodplain awaiting reworking. During these periods of temporary alluvial storage weathering processes alter the sediments. For some rock types, weathered clasts are especially vulnerable to abrasion when their transportation is resumed: the rate of abrasion may be five times faster for weathered material than for fresh rock. Granite fragments in particular may disintegrate on reworking because of weathering during storage.

Sorting by water movement involves the grouping together of particles that respond to the flow in a similar manner and, at the same time, the separation of such particles from those that respond differently to the flow. Hjulstom's diagram (*Figure 4.7*) shows that fine sand is the most easily moved particle size. Flows move larger particles such as pebbles and cobbles so that this coarser fraction accumulates as a lag deposit from which most of the sand has been removed. As the flow velocity increases so the maximum size of the particle transported and the range of sizes in transport increases. Coarser fractions are moved by flows that also carry finer materials; as flow competence decreases the coarser fraction is deposited but the finer materials are transported further downstream. Smaller grains will travel greater distances so that better sorting of the deposits results. In small headwater streams the bed-material is coarse and will move only by bed-traction and only during large floods, but downstream the bed-material may be sufficiently fine-grained for a substantial fraction to be held in intermittent suspension — even low flows may thus be competent to move most of the bed-material. In small streams, therefore, flow competence is the main control of bed-material sorting while the capacity of the flows plays an important role in large rivers.

During transport mechanical abrasion will operate on the exposed edges of angular particles so that an increase in particle roundness may be observed along a river channel. Well-rounded grains, however, may be inherited from temporary storages or from source bedrocks such as sandstones or conglomerates which commonly weather to release rounded fragments. Therefore, a true index of the degree of rounding is given, not by the most rounded grains but by the most angular grains. Improved roundness within sediments along a river is typically better observed for coarse particles which experience more rapid abrasion by fracturing and chipping; fine sediments of less than 0.2 mm commonly show little change — these are often composed of resistant quartz grains which undergo only slow abrasion; and particles between 0.2 and 0.6 mm may be seen to decrease in roundness due to the increasing dominance of resistant quartz at the expense of the less resistant, easily abraded minerals.

## 4.3 STREAM DEPOSITS

Although the bed-load component of the total sediment load is generally small, bed-load transport has an important influence upon the form of the channel itself and the character of other fluvial landforms such as alluvial fans and floodplains. The description of the sedimentary character of a deposit requires the measurement of three parameters: particle-size, particle-shape and particle arrangement.

**4.3.1 Field measurement**

River sediments may be easily examined on the stream bed or in vertical sections exposed in the river bank, the former will relate to the contemporary processes either because the sediments are being actively transported at the present time or because they affect the form of the channel, and in the latter evidence may be found of longer term channel movements (*see Figure 4.13*).

| **Equipment:** | **Procedure:** |
|---|---|
| Ruler or calipers. | Collect 100 particles at random. |
| Tape measure. | Measure the orientation and dip of each. |
| Compass. | Measure the *a*, *b* and *c* axes. |
| Clinometer. | Determine the mean axial length $\frac{(a + b + c)}{3}$ |
| **Sample:** | Estimate the degree of roundness. |
| 100 particles. | Determine the particle shape using the Zingg classes. |

Field sampling is easily undertaken for sediments on the stream bed by creating a grid over a deposit such as a point bar or the channel bed itself. For example, a 'grid' may be created by laying a tape across the deposit and each particle that lies immediately beneath a selected interval, say the 25 cm mark, is picked out for measurement. The tape is then moved a predetermined distance upstream and sampling repeated until 100 particles are collected. With this sampling procedure a tendency exists to bias the sample towards the larger sizes and care must be taken to ensure that the particle isolated by the tape mark or grid intersection is collected — no matter how small it may be! A workable lower limit of 0.5 cm is often employed. For deposits of finer sediments a bulk sample, or grab sample, should be taken from a location chosen at random; particle size analysis is then undertaken using sieving, and roundness determined using a hand lens. Before removing coarse particles it is of interest to note their arrangement in the deposit. In fact many deposits are composed of individual particles which display a preferred orientation related to the particle shape, the direction of transport, and the depositional

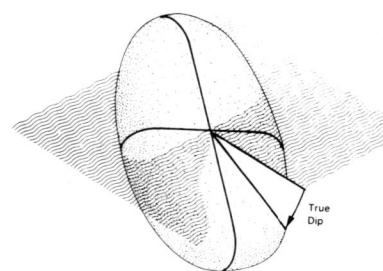

**Figure 4.13 Measurement of particle dip**

## 4.3.2 The character of channel sediments

**Plate 4.3 Imbricated gravel particles**

environment. The arrangement of all particles except spherical ones may be described by two characteristics, their orientation and inclination. The orientation of an elongate particle simply refers to the orientation of its longest axis, and the inclination or dip of the particle refers to the angle that the long axis makes with the horizontal (Briggs, 1977). Many particles have a plate- or disc-like shape; for such particles the orientation and dip are determined by reference to maximum projection area (*Figure 4.13*): the plane which gives the largest surface area, parallel to both the long and intermediate axes. The orientation here is the direction of the maximum dip of this plane — the maximum angle which it makes with the horizontal. In either case the orientation is measured as a compass bearing and the angle of dip recorded from a clinometer.

River channels provide temporary storages for sediment between phases of movement which is related to the occurrence of competent discharges. The arrangement and size distribution of particles on the stream bed will be related to the local flow pattern during and since the last major discharge. Gravel particles which form the bed materials of many rivers are often packed against each other, to form *imbrication* (*Plate 4.3*). Particles in discontinuous transport as part of the bed-load present greatest resistance to further movement when tilted upstream. Most particles will also tend to be orientated with their long axis parallel to the current, minimising the cross-section presented to the current and increasing stability. Thus, imbrication develops in response to the flow of water impinging on particles; orientation of the plane of maximum projection to dip upstream is the most stable position for closely packed particles because the force of the flow presses the particle to the bed.

River gravels commonly show a marked imbrication dipping steeply upstream at angles of between 15° and 40°. However, the stable resting position of a particle depends upon its shape and upon the concentration of gravels in the bed. Imbrication is particularly well developed by disc-shaped particles transported as bed-load and sufficiently well sorted to permit the particles to come into contact with each other. Rod-shaped pebbles commonly have their *a*-axis orientated perpendicular to streamflow because they move by rolling as well as sliding. In beds containing a large proportion of coarse materials such a tendency may be prohibited by interference between particles. A rod-shaped pebble may become lodged at one end so that it swings round to become orientated parallel to the current. Such particles in isolation in a mixed sand and gravel bed, however, will be rolled around their longer axis and arranged perpendicular to the flow direction. Once a pebble has come to rest on the stream bed a circular depression is excavated at its upstream end whilst the deposition of material on the downcurrent side supports the downstream end. Eventually the pebble becomes tilted at a low angle $< 20°$ and dips upstream in a position of equilibrium, with its *a*-axis remaining more-or-less

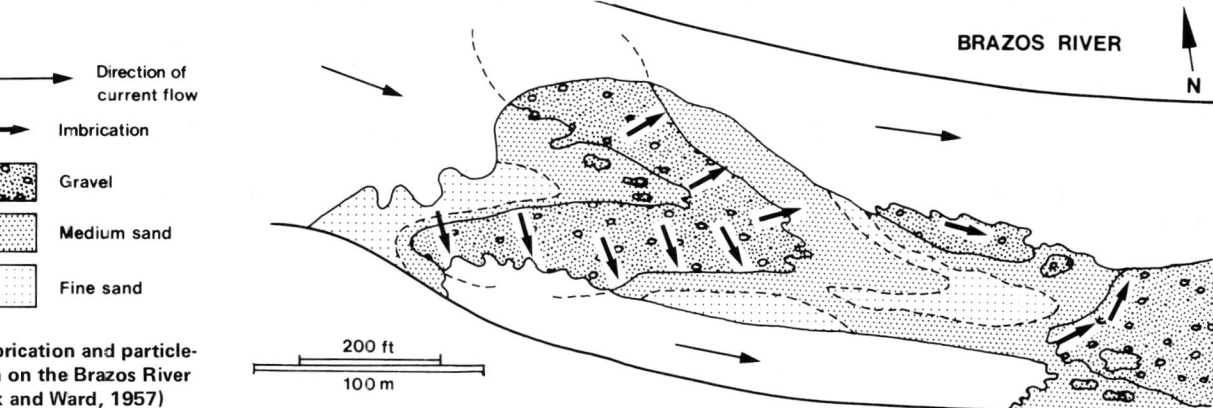

Direction of current flow

Imbrication

Gravel

Medium sand

Fine sand

**Figure 4.14 Imbrication and particle-size distribution on the Brazos River bar. (From Folk and Ward, 1957)**

BRAZOS RIVER

N

200 ft
100 m

horizontal. Nevertheless, the imbrication orientation on gravel deposits will describe the local water flow direction.

Folk and Ward (1957), for example, have examined the sediments which compose a bar in the Brazos River, Texas. The surface gravel was described as extremely discoidal, well-rounded limestone pebbles arranged to form a V-shaped outcrop pointing downstream and exposed at low flow (*Figure 4.14*). Measurements of pebble imbrication show that the particles had a characteristic dip of $20° - 30°$ in the upcurrent direction. The orientations, however, are complex and indicate the direction of water flow at the time the gravels were last activated. The data reveal that the water moved into the "trap" formed by the gravel V and then spread out over the limbs at about a 45° angle to the trend of the channel. Water flowing into the subordinate channel returned to the main flow at a sharp angle towards the downstream end of the bar.

This pattern of flow may be used to explain the distribution of the main sediment sizes found on the bar (gravel, medium sand and fine sand). The highest elevation of the bar was found to be at the point of the gravel V and each limb decreased in elevation upstream. Between the limbs of the V, a low area of relatively quiet water, the gravel is overlain by current rippled sand. a thick coating of sand flanks the outer edge of the V and tails out downstream, and this relates to the creation of a relatively slack water, low velocity zone where the flow was diverted laterally. At the downstream end of the bar the subordinate flow returns to the main channel and the increased velocity cleared the gravels of finer sediments. However, the character of the channel sediments at any location along a river will reflect not only the local flow conditions but also the quantity and character of the sediments supplied from upstream.

### 4.3.3 Major depositional landforms

Sediments within river channels may be stored for only short periods of time between competent discharges though deposition will occur at any location where the flow velocity is reduced or the capacity of a river is exceeded. For example, a heavily loaded stream emerging from a narrow channel confined within mountainous terrain and flowing out onto a gently sloping plain will experience a sudden slowing of velocity (associated with a marked increase in channel width in the unconfined location), and this will result in the immediate dumping of the coarser sediment to form a cone or fan-shaped accumulation, termed an *alluvial fan*. Such fans characteristically have a concave upwards profile being dominated by coarse materials, boulders and gravels on their steep upper slopes and finer materials on the lower, gentler slopes. This pattern of particle size variation directly reflects the ability of finer sediment to be transported at lower flows than the coarser material. On reaching the mountain-plain junction the channel divides to form a braided pattern, which tends to move by sweeps in a radial manner over the fan surface.

Alluvial fans are found as common elements of river systems in all latitudes, irrespective of climate conditions, and are particularly common in valleys which have been recently glaciated and in semi-arid regions, although the longer and best preserved forms are found in drier areas. Field surveys, particularly by Bull (1977), have shown that the size of the fans as described by their surface-area is related to the magnitude of the source from which materials are derived, that is the drainage area. Alluvial fans can

**Plate 4.4 Stages in the evolution of a model fan**

**Plate 4.5 Floodplain of the River Severn downstream from Shrewsbury showing an abandoned meander loop**

be studied in the laboratory by constructing a simple hardware model (*Figure 4.15*) which can be used to simulate fan evolution (*Plate 4.4*). At a slightly larger scale the development of alluvial fans may be studied in sand or clay pits where deposition on the flat floor may occur at the outflow from gullies cut into the steep walls.

A second important depositional landform, the river floodplain, is constructed by the river during the lateral migration of the channel. Floodplains are the relatively flat areas of the valley bottom bordering the river channel and at some time during their construction a river channel occupied each and every position within their limits (*Plate 4.5*). Characteristically, floodplains are inundated at times of high flows; these out-of-channel or overbank discharges should be expected to inundate the floodplain once in every 1.5 years on average within natural basins. Over time the

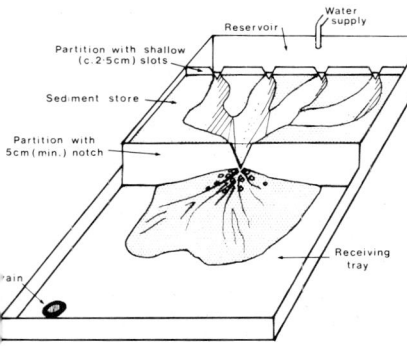

**Figure 4.15 A simple facility for examining alluvial fan development**

river channel moves laterally by the erosion of one bank and the subsequent accretion of sediment against the other. Floodplains are the product of channel migration within both meandering and braided rivers, but different deposits are associated with different channel forms. Each deposit is composed of a typical vertical sequence of sediments. These sediments are characterised by a particular grain-size distribution and particle arrangement.

Layers of sediment may be observed which have a relatively uniform range of particle size, and a characteristic arrangement of particles, distinguishable from the layers above and below. These beds may range from 1 cm to several metres in thickness; layers less than 1 cm thick are called *laminae*. A bed may be delimited by a gradational boundary but beds are frequently separated by sharp contacts which may be formed by either a period of erosion between two phases of deposition, or by a sudden change of the depositional conditions. Beds which display a clear internal arrangement of the particles are said to be *stratified*, and the term unstratified applies to those beds lacking any such arrangement. The nature of sedimentary structures that are formed within a deposit is determined, primarily, by the rate of deposition, the depth and velocity of flow, and the grain-size of the sediments.

A wide range of stratified beds may be observed but two contrasting types may be identified (*Figure 4.16*) — plane-beds characterised by a horizontal arrangement of particles, and cross-beds having strata inclined at an angle to the bed. The latter range in detail from small scale features produced by the movement of sand in the form of ripples to much larger forms associated with dunes, bars or small deltas. Some beds lack any internal arrangement or organisation of the particles. These "massive" beds may be formed in two ways. Firstly, by the very rapid deposition of sediment from suspension without any particle sorting or arrangement by bed-movement, or secondly, by the deposition — or "dumping" — of a very highly concentrated sediment load.

The classical model of floodplain formation describes the deposition of sediments by a meandering river flowing over a broad alluvial plain having a low slope and bordered on one side by the sea. Floodplains produced by such meandering rivers are composed of three main types of deposit: point-bars, overbank deposits (levées, crevasse-splay, and flood-basin deposits) and channel fills (*Figure 4.17*). Meander migration produces lateral

Common Sediment Structures

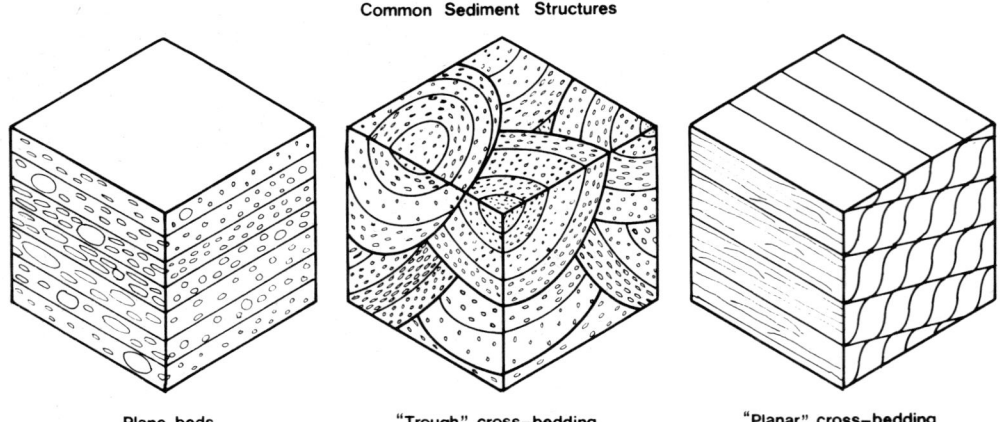

Figure 4.16 Common forms of
sediment stratification

Plane beds      "Trough" cross-bedding      "Planar" cross-bedding

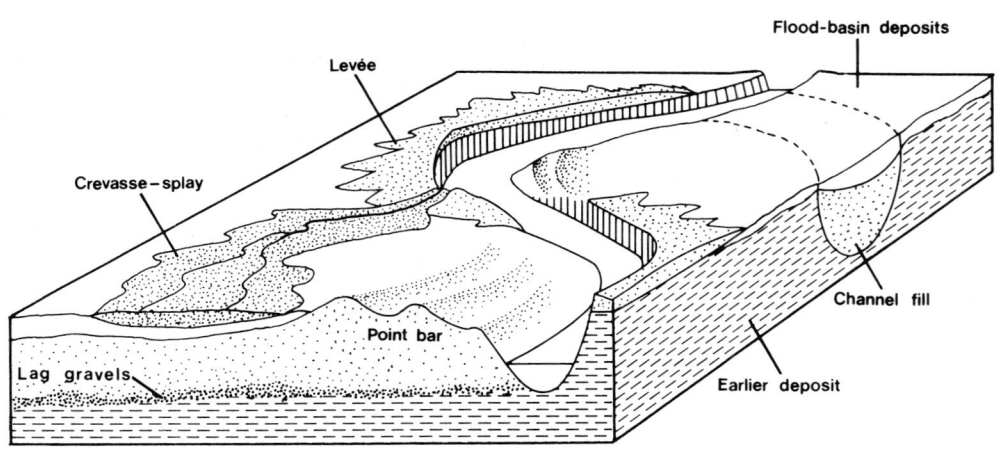

Figure 4.17 Floodplain deposits of
meandering rivers

**Plate 4.6 Point-bar on the Upper Severn, Wales**

accretion (*Plate 4.6*) through the formation of point-bar deposits in the form of curved, low ridges separated by intervening hollows (or swales) which give the characteristic appearance of meander scrolls — areas of gently curved ridges which are roughly conformable with the curve of the channel. Point-bars can account for up to 90% of floodplain deposits. Sediment is deposited in the low velocity and relatively shallow areas which are found close to the inner, convex bank and usually just downstream from the apex of the bend (*see* section 5.3.3). The crescent shaped bars form by accretion in the downstream direction and this migration produces a characteristic sequence of sediments and sedi-

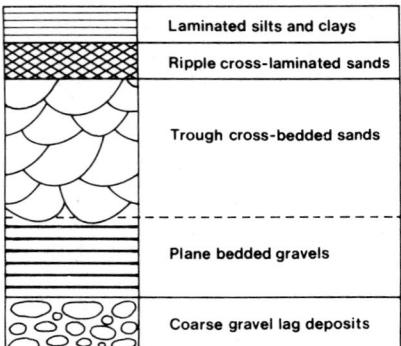

**A. MEANDERING CHANNELS**

| | Laminated silts and clays |
| | Ripple cross-laminated sands |
| | Trough cross-bedded sands |
| | Plane bedded gravels |
| | Coarse gravel lag deposits |

**B. BRAIDED CHANNELS**

| | Cross-bedded sands |
| | Massive, poorly sorted sands |
| | Large-scale cross-bedded sands and gravels |

**Figure 4.18 Sediment sequences within point-bar (A) and braid-bar (B) deposits**

mentary structures (*Figure 4.18A*); successively higher, and finer deposits correspond to sediments deposited successively higher on the point bar, under progressively lower flow conditions. The ideal sequence is one of progressively fining upward sediments which begins with coarse gravel and is then topped by silts and clays deposited by overbank flows.

Debris of gravel-size, or coarser, may be moved only during rare floods and these coarse materials can be left as a residual "lag" deposit which becomes concentrated into a thin sheet by the selective erosion of the finer material. In detail the coarse basal gravel is overlain by a plane-bedded deposit and then by large-scale cross-bedding. These are then overlain by fine ripple cross-bedding produced by the lower velocity flows across the higher parts of the point bar. In reality such ideal sequences rarely exist. Plane laminated sediments may be produced by higher velocity flows which can form locally over the point bar surface during floods. Also, rivers transporting large amounts of gravel may produce point bars of unstratified gravel and the floodplain will be formed predominantly as a single "massive" sheet. In such coarse grained deposits the normal 'fining upward sequences' may be absent or truncated and succeeded by sands which often display cross-bedding. These beds represent lobes of sediment built out on the downstream part of the point bar by floodwaters passing through a chute that is often found to cut across the convex bank of the meander.

In any case overbank deposits will be laid down on top of the channel sediments. Levées commonly develop along the channel margin (*Figure 4.17*). These deposits consist of fine sands and silts carried in suspension by turbulent flows and commonly display fine ripple cross-lamination. During floods these levées may be breached or crevassed with the formation of 'splays' of sediment across parts of the floodplain. More commonly, the fine suspended sediments, often containing large quantities of plant remains, are deposited over the low-lying areas. These fine deposits sometimes contain laminae of coarser silts and sands deposited during very high flows. This sequence may be interrupted by infilled channels: channels abandoned by the cutoff of meander loops — some may form 'ox-box lakes' — in which fine clays and silts accumulate. For some floodplains such channel-fill deposits are particularly important.

Braided streams with coarse loads are notorious for the rapidity with which their channels alter position and migrate across the floodplain. As a result, the floodplain relief is usually low, overbank flows maintain high velocities and overbank deposition is negligible. Floodplains produced by braided rivers generally show less internal organisation of the deposits (*Figure 4.18B*). Channel fill sediments are relatively uncommon and the deposits are dominated by the sediments of braid bars: high energy deposits characterised by generally poorly sorted gravels, and gravelly sands. Bedding is often crudely horizontal in coarse sediments or trough cross-stratified in finer materials. Fining-upward sequences are found rarely and then only as channel fill deposits. The ideal section is composed of horizontally stratified gravels representing longitudinal braid bars and cross-stratified gravelly sands deposited as transverse bar forms (*see* section 5.3.1). These high energy deposits are often overlaid by cross-stratified sands, representing the deposits of the bar surface.

# CHAPTER 5 RIVER CHANNELS

## 5.1 DRAINAGE NETWORKS

The initiation and establishment of a drainage network is controlled primarily by the tendency for water to flow along the line of steepest surface slope. The pattern of *consequent* streams so produced will be influenced, however, by geological factors such as rock type, and structure (folding, faulting, etc) and these factors will become particularly important as the drainage pattern evolves. Indeed, the pattern of the drainage network will become guided increasingly by the underlying geological characteristics as the channel system develops over time. Many of the major river courses in lowland England, for example, are guided by outcrops of relatively weak and easily erodible rocks. Such *subsequent* streams characteristically extend along lines of geological weakness, which include not only the outcrops of soft rock but also fold axes and fault lines, and it has been suggested that the degree of control that the geological structure is seen to exert on a drainage pattern may reflect the age of the river system. A highly adjusted system would then be inferred to have developed over a relatively long period of time.

Consequent streams often have a discordant relationship with the geological structure, whilst subsequent streams accord with these underlying controls. However, this is by no means always the case. Where the uplifted surface slopes in the same direction as the pattern of rock outcrops, consequent drainage will immediately develop an accordant relationship. The existence of an apparently 'abnormal' relationship between drainage pattern and underlying geology at the present time may also be explained by antecedent or superimposed drainage. The former refers to a case where slow and gradual earth movements affect an area after a drainage system has been established. The existing drainage pattern is maintained by incision into the newly formed structures as they develop. However, such conditions of long-term erosion rates exceeding rates of uplift appear rarely to exist and supporting evidence, for example, of warped river terraces is generally lacking.

More commonly, consequent streams initiated on one set of geological structures may be superimposed upon an older, and very different set of forms. Rocks of different ages are sometimes separated by an erosion surface, known as an unconformity, and the younger surface rocks may have a simple tilted structure whereas the older underlying rocks may be heavily folded. As the drainage pattern established on the younger rocks develops, erosion will eventually superimpose the surface pattern onto the folded older rocks. Superposition may also occur from marine cut planar surfaces or marine deposits, or even from ice-sheets. Much of Britain has experienced a marine transgression in geologically recent times and extensive surfaces cutting across geological structures have been formed. The discordance of the Hampshire Avon, for example, can be explained by the superposition of a drainage pattern developed on a southerly sloping sea floor.

All drainage networks branch in some way but the drainage patterns vary greatly from one kind of terrain to another, mainly in response to differences in rock-types or the structural pattern of folds and faults. A branching, tree-like or dendritic network is common to many streams and is typical of areas underlain by a relatively uniform rock-type. Within areas of contrasting rock types or of rocks affected significantly by jointing, fracturing and faulting the geological characteristics may control the surface drainage to produce more regular patterns. Alternating bands of resistant and weak rocks exposed at the surface by a series of folds may produce a trellis form and major joint systems in bedrock may produce a rectangular drainage pattern. It is apparent that the patterns produced under conditions of strong bedrock control are more ordered than the dendritic pattern which may be shown to reflect a random element in the arrangement of networks (*see* section 5.1.2).

### 5.1.1 Drainage network composition

Despite the variable character of the drainage pattern, each network has been found to have an ordered internal composition. Downstream, through a drainage basin, drainage area increases and the length of the main streams and the character of the network changes in a regular manner. One of the most significant advances in the numerical expression of landform has been in the field of *drainage basin morphometry* — the numerical analysis of landforms. Modern morphometry was founded by Horton in 1945. Horton's central concept was of *stream ordering* and this provided an objective means of subdividing drainage networks. This hierarchical concept allowed Horton to suggest "Laws of drainage composition" based upon four easily measured characteristics of stream networks — area, slope, length and number. Because of the need for large quantities of data, the time consuming nature of defining channels in the field and the difficulties attendant upon changes of channel length during storm runoff, drainage basin morphometry has been almost entirely based upon data derived from published maps (*see* section 2.3).

Within an area of homogeneous lithology and simple structure the character of the drainage network will reflect the minimum catchment area required to provide sufficient runoff for the maintenance of a channel form. Field and experimental observations have revealed that despite marked seasonal variations, and short-term changes during rainfall events, channel length tends to fluctuate about a constant value for a particular basin. Increased runoff leads to the extension of the channel headward but at the same time the area draining to the channel head will decline, the runoff supply will be reduced below the level required for channel maintenance and the channel length will shrink.
In Horton's ordering system (*Figure 5.1A*) each finger-tip tributary is designated a first order stream; two first-order channels meet to generate a second-order stream, and so on. However, Horton then projected the highest order stream back to the headwaters along the channel which involved least deviation from the mainstream direction. This second stage of the ordering procedure introduced a new complication not just in the subjective selection of the 'mainstream' but in the assignment of different orders to the smallest unbranched tributaries.

Subsequent to the work of Horton ordering methods have been refined. Strahler's modification of Horton's ordering system is the most useful general purpose ordering system and the one which has been most often used (*Figure 5.1B*). Strahler's system provides a completely objective and hierarchical approach: all basins of a given order contain at least one basin of all orders up to and including that order. The approach largely overcomes the objections to Horton's ordering procedure by designating all finger-tip tributaries as first order and omitting the second re-ordering part so that all unbranched channel segments are of the same order, and only one segment is designated the highest order — not the whole of the trunk system. Furthermore, using this modified ordering procedure Horton's laws may still be defined:

1.   The total number of streams of successively higher orders in a given drainage basin

**Figure 5.1 Common stream ordering systems**

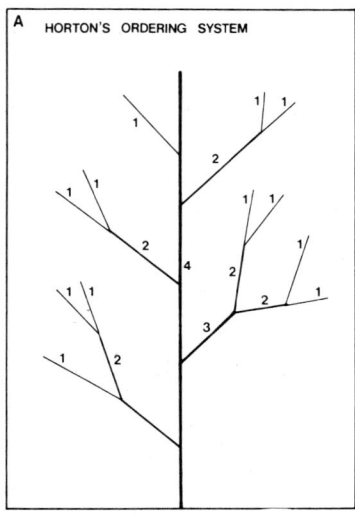

A   HORTON'S ORDERING SYSTEM

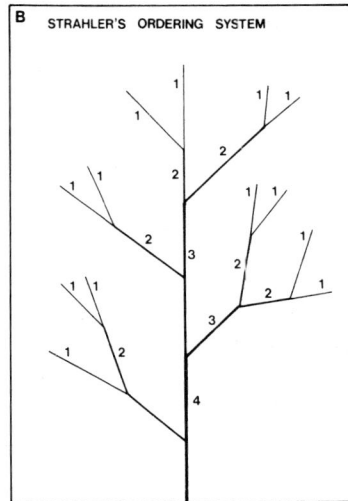

Figure 5.1 (continued)

**Figure 5.2 Geometric characteristics of drainage networks**

decreases as an inverse geometrical progression within which the ratio of the number of streams of one order to that of the next higher order, the bifurcation ratio, is commonly between 3 and 5;

2.    The cumulative mean channel length of each of the different orders in a given drainage basin increases as a direct geometrical series;

3.    The mean size of the drainage area for successively higher orders in a given drainage basin increases as a direct geometrical series.

All these geometric relationships are represented by straight lines on semi-logarithmic graph paper and may be demonstrated by plotting stream order on the arithmetic scale against stream number, mean channel length, or mean drainage area on the logarithmic scale (*Figure 5.2*).

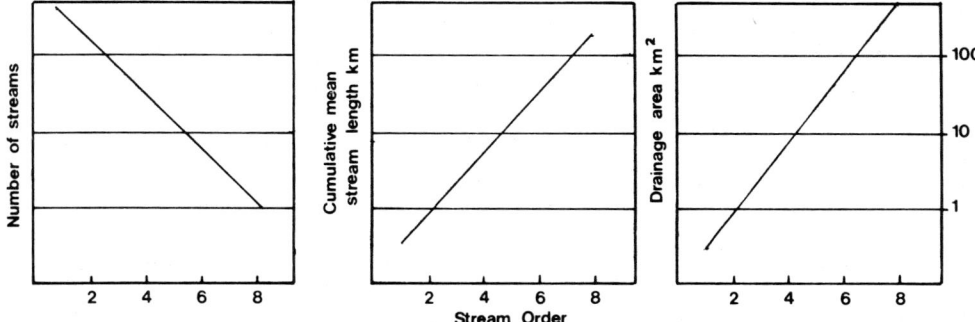

### 5.1.2 Order produced by chance

The recognition that stream networks have an ordered internal composition irrespective of the environmental conditions of climate and rocktype raises the question as to why this should be so? This section is concerned with exploring one hypothesis concerned with the fundamental reason behind the tree-like organisation of many networks: is the branching, tree-like structure of drainage networks a result of purely chance conditions?

Do Horton's "Laws of drainage composition" apply to networks produced by random movements of water over a slope? For practical purposes a hypothesis may be stated:

'drainage which develops freely from each of a series of unit areas in any of the four cardinal directions and directed by purely random (chance) processes, will produce an ordered dendritic network.'

Random statistical model networks are constructed and compared with natural drainage networks and one of three conditions will be observed:

1.    If the model matches all natural patterns then the hypothesis that drainage networks develop by pure chance is accepted. (If randomness is established then the problem of distortion and the factors responsible for that distortion can be examined);

2.    If the random model matches only some of the natural networks, then the hypothesis will be supported for those cases only and two further questions are raised — what controls the non-random patterns? and what conditions favour the establishment of random networks?

3.    If there is little similarity between the two then the hypothesis fails.

Methods known as 'random walk' are used to describe the path taken by successive moves on a surface: each move is a fixed distance and the direction of each move is determined by some random process although one constraint is normally placed on the direction of movement. Using the random walk a drainage network can be constructed, guided by one constraint — that water cannot flow uphill. Within each small unit area the direction of flow can be in only one of three of the four cardinal directions (i.e. north, south, east or west).

On a piece of graph paper outline an area of at least 6 X 10 squares: this delimits the model drainage basin. Then determine the direction of flow out of each square using a well shuffled deck of playing cards or a dice in the following manner:

|  | *cards* | *dice* |  |
|---|---|---|---|
| NORTH | hearts | 1 or 6 | FORWARD |
| SOUTH | diamonds | 2 or 5 | LEFT |
| EAST | clubs | 3 or 4 | RIGHT |
| WEST | spades |  |  |

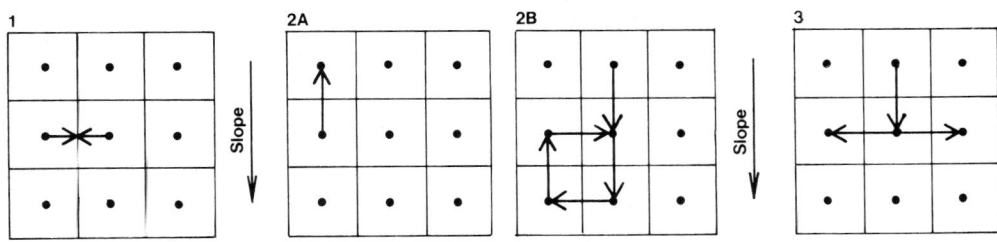

**Figure 5.3 Rules for the construction of random-walk networks**

Determine the first direction and place an arrow pointing in the direction of flow, beginning at the centre of one square and ending with an arrow-head at the centre of an adjacent square. Beginning in the top left hand square, this determines the flow out of this square. However, three rules must be obeyed (*Figure 5.3*).

1.   Each arrow starts in the centre of a square and joins with another arrow only at the centre of a neighbouring square;
2.   No streams can flow uphill (2A) and by the same token no stream can flow in a closed circuit (2B);
3.   Water must flow out of each square, but only in one direction.

If the direction obtained violates any of the rules a new direction is determined until a permissable flow direction is obtained.

Working from left to right along the top row determine a flow direction out of each square then continue on to the next row but in the opposite direction i.e. from right to left. Continue this procedure until all the squares have arrows pointing out of them, alternating the direction of working from row to row. Once the last square is filled the network should be inspected for hanging streams — squares with no outflow. The standard ordering procedures can then be applied to the simulated network, and the number of channels and cumulative mean channel lengths for each order can be compared with the geometric relationships found for natural streams. The stream generated in *Figure 5.4A* provides data when subjected to an analysis of the stream orders (e.g. *Figure 5.4B*) to suggest that the ordered internal structure of dendritic drainage networks is in fact

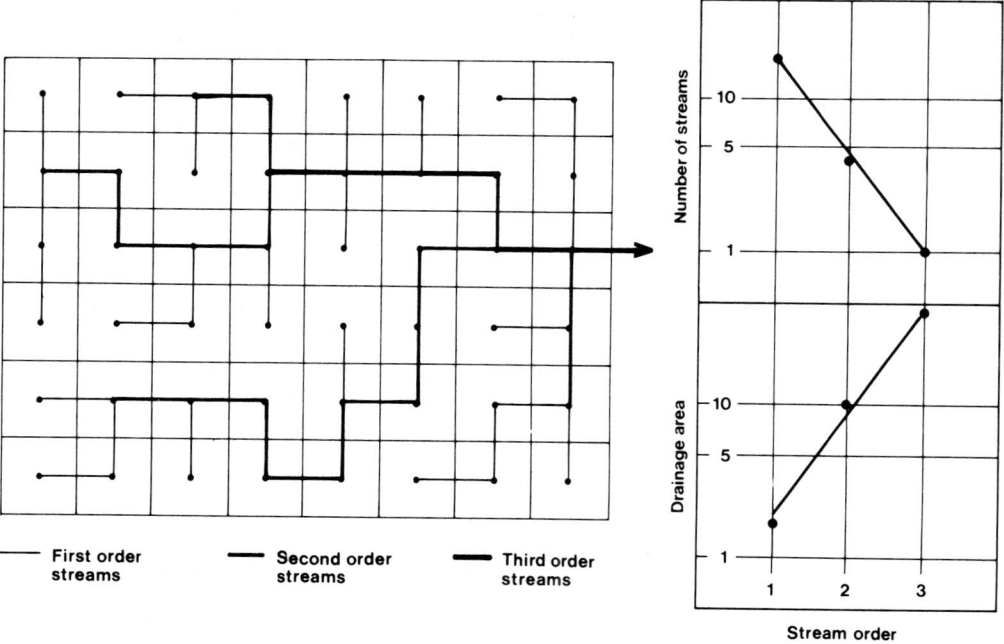

**Figure 5.4 A third-order random-walk network (A) and its geometric character (B)**

—— First order streams     —— Second order streams     —— Third order streams

the result of purely change processes: here there are 17 first-order, 4 second-order and 1 third-order streams.

### 5.1.3 Network variations between basins

In the above, the effect of scale was avoided so that major differences may be expected between the simulated and natural networks, related to the area required for channel maintenance. The constant of channel maintenance (*CM*) acts as a guide to the catchment area required to sustain a unit length of channel. It is defined thus:

$$CM = Da \div L, \text{ where } Da = \text{drainage area (km}^2) \text{ and } L = \text{total stream length (km)}$$

If a unit length is the distance taken by one move in the simulation then the constant of channel maintenance defines the area of each square for comparison with the natural network. Ordering is useful because it provides a quick way of quantitatively designating any stream or stream segment anywhere in the world, but a simple measure of the magnitude of a drainage network also provides interesting information.

Drainage density is an important characteristic of rivers because it reflects the combined effects of topographic, lithographic, pedological and vegetational controls on catchment hydrology. The density and extent of the channel network, therefore, provide a link between form and process within the drainage basin. Because channel flow is much more rapid than alternative pathways on or beneath slopes, the drainage density is an important hydrological parameter. The drainage density is defined as the total length of stream channel per unit area ($L \div Da$, the inverse of the constant of channel maintenance). In the UK drainage densities are commonly less than 5 km km$^{-2}$ but in semi-aird badlands drainage densities can reach 100 km km$^{-2}$. However, drainage density is dependent upon drainage basin area, being greater for small basins. Examination of the variability of total stream length, and in particular of how total stream length varies with drainage area, allows comparison to be made between basins by avoiding the problems of scale (*Table 5.1*).

**TABLE 5.1 DRAINAGE DENSITY AND ROCK-TYPE: RIVER DERWENT, DERBYSHIRE, UK**

| Sub-catchment | Rock-type | Mean annual precipitation (mm) | Total stream length | |
|---|---|---|---|---|
| | | | $Da = 5$ km$^2$ | $Da = 50$ km$^2$ |
| Derwent | Sandstone-shale | 1500 | 15.68 | 131.59 |
| Ashope | Sandstone-shale | 1500 | 15.73 | 112.31 |
| Wye | Limestone | 1100 | 6.46 | 27.36 |
| Amber | Coal measures | 800 | 6.36 | 67.03 |

Detailed examination of the way in which total stream length changes with drainage area also shows the effect of rock-type and mean annual precipitation. As expected, a large drainage area is required for channel maintenance by streams draining highly permeable rock-types and in impermeable basins with high precipitation totals the total stream length is relatively high and the rate of increase downstream is rapid.

Despite the random character of the channel arrangement within the network in most rivers, total stream length increases downstream with drainage area at a predictable rate; on double logarithmic graph paper the relationship yields a straight line. However, within a single catchment the increase of total stream length with distance downstream is stepped due to the addition of large increments of channel length (and drainage area) at tributary confluences. For drainage basins underlain by markedly different rock-types a more complex variation of total stream length is found along rivers. In the headwater area of the Derbyshire Derwent the relatively impermeable sandstone-shale formations produce a rapid increase of total stream length with drainage area, but the growth rate of the channel network is reduced as the proportion of the catchment underlain by permeable Carboniferous Limestone increases and particularly at the confluence with the River Wye.

For large drainage basins, ordering of the stream network and measurement of stream length and basin areas is extremely time-consuming and alternative approaches involving the measurement of drainage density for grid squares rather than for drainage basins have been adopted. For example, the number of junctions between channel network segments (or "links") may be counted within each 2 km by 2 km grid square defined on 1:25,000 maps. The variation in the number of junctions between grid square will reflect the spatial variation of drainage density. Junction counts can be transformed into an estimate of drainage density by a linear regression equation of the form:

$$Dd = a + bN$$

where $Dd$ = drainage density, $N$ = number of junctions and $b$ and $a$ are the regression coefficients.

The regression equation should be derived from a randomly drawn sample of not less than twenty-five grid squares within which the stream lengths are measured and the number of junctions counted. Using this method maps can be drawn showing the general

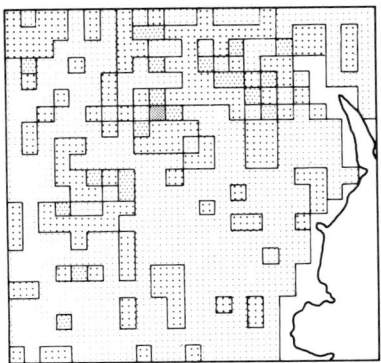

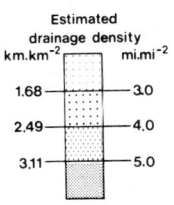

Estimated
drainage density

| km.km$^{-2}$ | | mi.mi$^{-2}$ |
|---|---|---|
| 1.68 | | 3.0 |
| 2.49 | | 4.0 |
| 3.11 | | 5.0 |

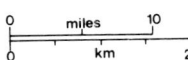

Figure 5.5 A drainage-density map
for part of S.W. England. (From
Gregory and Gardiner, 1975)

spatial pattern of drainage density variation over large areas. Such an approach has been used for a study of drainage density in south-west England (Gregory and Gardiner, 1975), and part of their map is redrawn as *Figure 5.5*. Urban areas and areas of extractive industry were omitted because of the artificially modified drainage courses, as were areas which included sea: the number of junctions on land areas of less than 4.0 km$^2$ could not be used as an estimate of drainage density because the linear regression equation was based upon a sample of grid squares having equal land area. Individual grid squares were then categorised according to the mean annual rainfall as depicted on the 1:62 500 map, using rainfall class intervals of 258 mm per year. A map of the same scale was also used to categorise the squares according to the major geological formations.

The mean number of junctions within each rainfall category was determined but no simple relationship was found. However, consideration of rock-type revealed interesting information: within grid squares of granite lithology drainage density increased within higher rainfall categories, whereas grid squares of sedimentary rock groups were characterised by lower values of estimated drainage density as rainfall increased. It was suggested that this variation reflected the different effects that the rocks have upon the movement of water within the catchment during periods of storm rainfall.

As shown above, the influence of rock-type is an important factor for the explanation of drainage density variations between basins within relatively uniform climatic regions although the effect of altitude, through its control on rainfall, is also significant. At the world scale climate combined with vegetation exercises an important control over drainage networks. Indeed, drainage networks possess a distinctive character in different climatic zones. The highest values of drainage density are derived from semi-arid areas or from areas of marked seasonal precipitation, characterised by high intensity rains and sparse vegetation cover. Areas with sparse vegetation cover are more susceptible to the erosional effects of high intensity rains whereas in humid areas with a good vegetation cover, and where rainfall intensity is lower, drainage densities are reduced. Thus, whilst the world pattern of drainage density values conform broadly to the major climatic zones, this is only indirectly the result of variations of mean annual rainfall — through its effect upon vegetation — and more directly relates to regional differences in rainfall intensity.

## 5.2 CHANNEL MORPHOLOGY

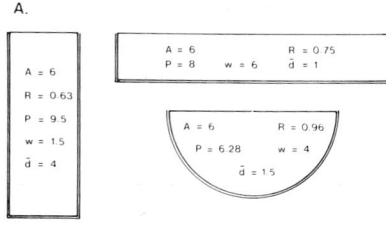

A.

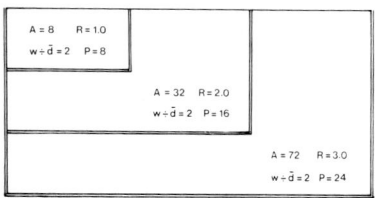

B.

**Figure 5.6 Relationships between hydraulic radius (R) and channel shape (A) and channel size (B) (A = cross-sectional area, P = wetted perimeter, W = width, d = mean depth)**

The morphology of a river channel may be described by its dimensions in plan (the channel pattern) and in cross-section. For convenience, these two characteristics are commonly considered in isolation but it must be remembered that they are strongly inter-related. The character of the channel form produced by flowing water is related to the 'power' of the stream to transport sediment — a function of discharge and slope — and to the quantity and size of material supplied.

Water flowing down a slope under gravity will follow the path of least resistance: the path which allows maximum flow rate and minimum energy loss due to friction. Frictional energy loss occurs predominantly because of the resistance to water flow of the surface or boundary materials, so that the path of minimum energy loss will be the one which keeps the ground-water contact (the wetted perimeter) as short as possible. Thus, flow within a channel provides a more efficient path than flow as a sheet over a slope. The efficiency of the stream for transmitting water improves by reducing the wetted perimeter to a minimum whilst maximising the channel size in cross-section (the cross-sectional area). These changes of channel form are produced by adjustments of channel shape. Efficiency may be described in terms of channel shape by the ratio of the wetted perimeter to its cross-sectional area (*hydraulic radius*). As the hydraulic radius decreases, the length of water-boundary contact increases, and the efficiency of the stream decreases. If streams carried only water then the channel shape would tend towards a semi-circle, the shape of greatest hydraulic radius, and the shape which reduces the frictional resistance to a minimum (*Figure 5.6A*). Channel efficiency may be expected to change downstream because the hydraulic radius is significantly influenced by the size of the channel: a large channel is twice as efficient for a given shape than one half the size (*Figure 5.6B*).

Rivers, however, also transport large quantities of sediment and it is the coarser material carried as bed-load which has the dominant effect upon the channel dimensions. Rivers transporting large quantities of coarse bed-load require wide bed-widths and high velocities in order to maximise sediment transport. They will therefore tend to produce a wide and shallow channel form in contrast to the relatively narrow and deep channels of streams carrying finer sediments. These variations of cross-sectional shape are also related to different channel patterns. Rivers carrying large bed-loads commonly exhibit a *braided* planform within which the river channel splits into several separate sub-channels. The result of this subdivision is an increase in the length of the wetted perimeter and a reduction of the hydraulic radius within the cross-section. Rivers carrying smaller amounts of bed material load will commonly have a well-defined, *straight* or *meandering* planform, and a narrower and deeper cross-section with a higher hydraulic radius.

The form of a river channel represents a compromise between two opposing tendencies to maximise the efficiency of water transmission and to maximise the efficiency of bed-material transport. Downstream, however, river channels also tend to minimise the variation in the rate of energy loss between successive unit lengths of channel (i.e. to produce a smooth distribution of energy loss with distance downstream). Along a river the characteristics of the major variables progressively change in a predictable manner, *Table 5.2*. Constrained by base-level and as a result of the tendency to maintain uniformity in

**TABLE 5.2 FACTORS ENCOURAGING CONCAVITY OF CHANNEL SLOPE**

| Variable | Downstream direction of change* | Comment |
|---|---|---|
| Discharge | Increases | Rate of increase is |
| Sediment load | Increases | normally slower than |
| Particle-size of load | Decreases | that of discharge |
| Cross-sectional area of channel | Increases | |
| Hydraulic radius of channel | Increases | |
| Channel boundary roughness | Decreases | |

*Not necessarily applicable to semi-arid, ephemeral streams.

the rate of energy loss per unit channel length, channel slope is reduced in the downstream direction. The cross-sectional area of the channel also increases in size, and the particle-size of the material in transport is commonly reduced, so that the channel is able to achieve a higher hydraulic radius. Despite the downstream reduction of channel slope, flow velocity can increase or at least remain constant because of the increase in channel size and the associated increase in efficiency. Within downstream locations, however, further adjustments of channel efficiency may be achieved by changing channel pattern. Bends in a river's course produce a high rate of energy loss because energy is used to deflect the direction of water flow. Nevertheless, the meandering pattern provides the planform shape which most closely approaches a minimum and uniform distribution of work.

Two general cases may then be identified. In the headwater area channels are lined by coarse sediments; they adopt a relatively wide and shallow cross-section; and are characterised by steep slopes. At downstream locations narrower and deeper channels, with smoother boundaries, are characterised by low rates of energy conversion and possess a much more gentle slope. Several factors operate, however, to modify these general cases. It has already been noted that a relationship exists between the particle-size of the bed-material and the channel form and that the bed-materials commonly decrease in size downstream. In some areas, particularly those which have experienced glaciation in the recent past, the channels may contain immobile residual bed-material inherited from an environment characterised by higher discharges than at the present time, or representing a lag deposit derived from the weathered bedrock. Under such conditions the channel will tend to be wider and shallower, with a higher width-depth ratio, and with a locally higher slope than expected. The channel bank materials are produced in many cases by the contemporary river but in some instances the channel may cut into older deposits. If these materials have a high degree of cohesion then a narrower channel form will result, because higher flows will be required to erode the bank sediments. In humid areas the resistance of the bank materials to erosion is often markedly increased by vegetation such that in very small catchments, of less than about 2 km$^2$, vegetation may provide the dominant control on channel form.

The morphology of a river channel is directly related to the discharges and sediment loads experienced under stable climatic and drainage basin conditions such that a balance exists between the fluvial processes and channel form. The stable form of a river channel is said to be in *"quasi-equilibrium"* with the processes operating, but this may vary locally depending upon the type of materials which compose the channel bed and banks. However, stable channels do not have a constant form. Because the flows and sediment loads are continuously changing the actual channel form at each location will respond to these changes by adjusting its shape, size and pattern. These adjustments will merely cause the channel form to fluctuate about a mean condition: it is this mean condition which represents the "equilibrium form". To maintain this equilibrium the channel may adjust its cross-sectional size and shape (width, depth, wetted perimeter, hydraulic radius) slope, planform (sinuosity, meander wavelength) or bed roundness. Commonly, equilibrium will be maintained by slight changes of all the parameters rather than of a single variable alone, and the changes will be uniformly distributed among the variables as is permitted by the local constraints.

The *dominant discharge* with which the channel form is in "equilibrium" has been a major topic for research because of its obvious importance for the river channel. However, because of the conflicting tendencies for rivers to adopt the form which maximises the efficiency for sediment and water transport no simple "control" discharge can be defined. Nevertheless, the recognition of the existence of causal relationships between fluvial processes and channel morphology implies that a discharge frequency for explaining channel form should be definable. In the late 1950s and 1960s studies of the relationship between channel form parameters and specific discharge frequencies suggested that the frequency of discharge at *channel bankful stage* was markedly similar for a variety of rivers of various scales and for a range of environments.

On hydrological grounds the significance of the channel bankfull stage was explained because flow resistance decreases as water depth within the channel increases; reaches a minimum at bankfull stage; and increases again as the water flows out of the channel and onto the adjacent floodplain. Thus, the channel operates most efficiently with regard to water conveyance when the flow is at the bankfull stage. However, in terms of sediment transport — and specifically of bed-load transport — studies from different rivers have demonstrated that the dominant discharge (the most effective discharge) for bed-load transport is not the same as the bankfull discharge. Indeed, it is increasingly becoming apparent that channel morphology is the product of the whole series of discharge experiences. Therefore, the discharge at the bankfull stage should not be thought of as the formative discharge. Nevertheless, it does provide a working approximation of the dominant formative discharges for the examination of channel form variation. Many studies have used a discharge with a frequency of 1.5 years as derived from the annual series, and this may be used as a standard for comparison between channels.

## 5.2.1 Criteria for the identification of the bankfull stage

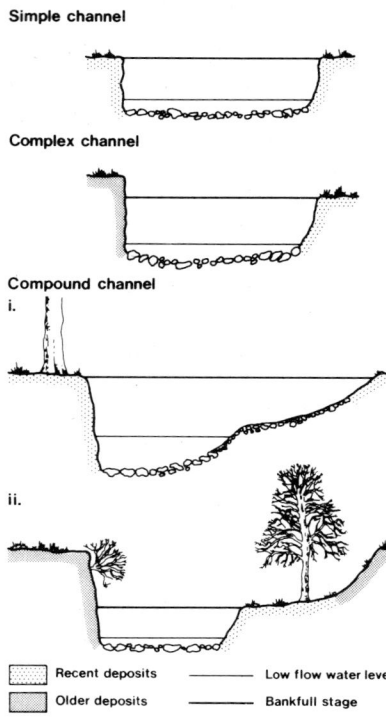

**Simple channel**

**Complex channel**

**Compound channel**

i.

ii.

| | |
|---|---|
| ▢ Recent deposits | —— Low flow water level |
| ▨ Older deposits | —— Bankfull stage |

**Figure 5.7 Definition of channel 'bankfull' stage**

It is important that a consistent method is adopted for the identification of 'the active channel' in order to allow the examination of channel form variations downstream along a single river and between rivers. The task of defining the river channel is not as simple as it may appear at first. A simple, uniform channel cross-sectional form with a flat bed bounded by two straight banks which intersect a floodplain at a sharp angle (*Figure 5.7*) is uncommon in natural channels. The valley floor may be of different elevations on either side of the channel, the banks may be convex upwards so that the contact between the channel banks and the valley floor may not be sharply defined, or levées may occur raising the observed bankfull stage above the level of the floodplain. Compound channel cross-sections introduce irregularities into the cross-section which render the definition of a consistent bankfull level problematic, particularly where a well developed floodplain is absent. The irregularities may be the result of different types of materials occurring in the channel banks, of channel incision into its bed materials, or of depostion along the channel margins to form benches. The problem lies in identifying the outer limits of the active channel, that is the channel floodplain junction. Several techniques have been devised in an attempt to provide a truly objective approach to the delimitation of 'the active channel' but all introduce a degree of subjectivity.

If sites of compound section divide two clearly defined reaches, the delimitation of bankfull stage within the compound reach may be achieved by looking for debris lines left by a high discharge: the tracing of such debris lines can provide a useful aid in standardising the determination of channel capacity over short distances. Vegetation limits also aid in the determination of contemporary bankfull levels. The establishment and maturation of plant species on a floodplain are the result of an interrelated sequence in the timing of seed dissemination and germination, environmental conditions, the magnitude and frequency of flood events and the sediment content and quality of the flood water. The variation of vegetation type within different parts of the cross-section may reflect different rates of colonisation by species demonstrating different tolerance levels to a particular frequency of inundation. Perennial woody plants commonly grow on surfaces down to the level of the maximum discharge during extended periods of low flow, and similar limits have been related to the distribution of herbs and forbs. Grasses are very rapid colonisers and may be seen to grow over immature point bars, for example, during summer.

Deposition of sediments along the sides of a channel typically occurs up to a particular elevation — the level of the floodplain — and it is this process which in part serves to maintain the stream channel in a state of quasi-equilibrium. Indeed, the surface of point bars within actively meandering rivers will be built up until they reach an elevation in equilibrium with the existing conditions of discharge and sediment load.

The newly formed point bar or channel side bench appears to undergo a sharp reduction in its rate of aggradation once its surface has been elevated to a level which can no longer sustain the transport of coarse channel sediments. The surface deposits of a mature point bar or bench are commonly composed of sands and silts — contrasting with the underlying floodplain gravels of many rivers (*see* section 4.3.3). Thus, floodplain construction, or point-bar or berm aggradation will continue until a channel is formed which has such a cross-sectional area (or capacity) that will be exceeded only by relatively infrequent discharges. In many rivers the bankfull capacity of the channel is equalled or exceeded once every one to three years on average. Also, by definition, the *active floodplain* will itself be inundated every few years. Terraces (old floodplains), however, will be above the level of frequent inundation and will have a more mature character. The soil, for example, may be used as a guide to separate the contemporary floodplain from older terraces because alluvial soils have unique properties due to the fact that they are periodically inundated by flood waters. Because they receive periodic deposits of fresh sediment from overbank discharge, alluvial soils lack the distinctive horizon sequence characteristic of stable land surfaces and are themselves characterised by relatively fine layering.

For all studies the bankfull level should be determined in the field, and most importantly the criteria adopted should be strictly and consistently applied. Bankfull capacity should be observed as a major break of slope separating a well-defined channel from a floodplain or floodplain bench which may be as little as 1 m in width. For compound sections reference should be made to the evidence identified above in order to gain an appreciation of the relative ages of the different surfaces, and the relative significance of these surfaces for the contemporary channel.

## 5.2.2 Measurement of the channel cross-section

### A.

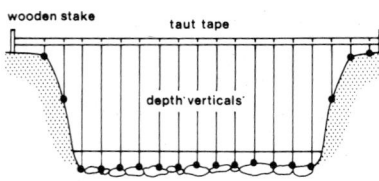

wooden stake   taut tape

depth verticals

### B. Simple depth gauge

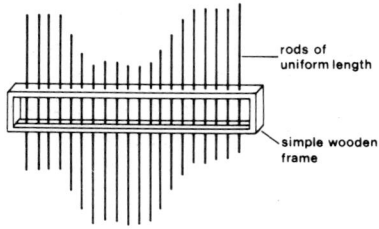

rods of uniform length

simple wooden frame

### C.

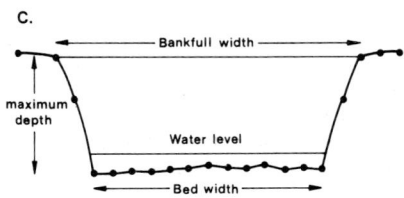

Bankfull width

maximum depth

Water level

Bed width

**Figure 5.8 Measurement of channel form in cross-section**

The detailed definition of the channel cross-section involves field surveying based upon the recording of depths to the floodplain surface or channel bed from an arbitrary horizontal datum line.

### Equipment:

Tape and calibrated staff or rule.
*or* Simple depth recorder.
*or* Surveyor's level and calibrated staff.

For channels less than about 5 m wide, a tape stretched taut across the channel or a calibrated staff laid horizontally, and at right angles to the main channel orientation, is adequate. Depths are measured vertically down from this datum (*Figure 5.8A*) to the channel perimeter or floodplain surface. It is desirable to extend the survey either side of the channel itself as the final definition of bankfull stage is best achieved during the survey and after the detailed shape of the section has been examined. The field measurements of channel width and depth (recorded to the nearest centimeter) are then plotted on graph paper and the cross-profile drawn so that the channel dimensions can be measured. The accuracy of these measurements is not only dependent upon the scale chosen for plotting the profile and the care taken in abstracting the data but also upon the number of depth measurements taken in the field: at least twenty measurements of depth should normally be taken at each site.

For profiles of about 1 m wide, improved detail can be obtained by constructing a simple depth recorder (*Figure 5.8B*) which uses vertical wooden rods each between 30 cm and 50 cm long, located at regular intervals, normally between 3 cm and 5 cm, and set in a wooden frame. The frame is laid horizontally across the channel and the rods pushed down until they touch the perimeter of the channel or the floodplain surface. The length of each rod below the horizontal datum provided by the base of the frame is then recorded as the point depth. For each of the methods, care must be taken to ensure that the datum line is truly horizontal and a spirit level or clinometer may be employed as a check.

Channels greater than 5 m wide require more sophisticated techniques for their survey because tape sag and the effects of wind reduce the accuracy of measurements made with a stretched tape. Accurate results can be obtained by using a level to determine the changes of surface elevation across a river channel but the technique needs two people, one to use the level and to record the data and an assistant to hold a calibrated staff and to record the water depth where required. A standard quickset level can be used for sights up to 50 m; at greater distances the reading of staff graduations becomes increasingly more difficult (*see* Pugh, 1975 for instruction in the use of levels).

Once the cross-profile has been drawn the bankfull capacity of the cross-section should be delimited by a horizontal line joining the two banks (*see Figure 5.8C*). The cross-sectional area (*Cc*) can then be determined either by using a planimeter or by counting the total number of graph paper squares enclosed by the channel up to the bankfull level. Obviously the accuracy of this latter method is dependent upon the type of graph paper used and the scale selected for drawing the profile. The bankfull channel width (*W*), maximum depth (*D*) and the length of the wetted perimeter (*P*) can be measured directly using an opisometer, pair of compasses or piece of string. Bed-width (*BW*), the total channel width between the banks at the bed including that part exposed at low flow, may also be usefully measured because it relates to the process of sediment transport. Bed-width also avoids the common problem of defining the bankfull width where the channel bank-floodplain boundary is curved. Other important variables are then computed from the primary measurements above:

Mean channel bankfull depth $(\bar{d}) = Cc \div W$
Hydraulic radius $(R) = Cc \div P$
Width-depth ratio $(w/d) = W \div d$

### 5.2.3 Measurement of channel slope

Channel slope may be determined from 1:25 000 maps by reference to the distance along the 'blue line' stream between two 25 ft contours, one located upstream and the other downstream of the survey cross-section selected for study. This method is suitable for most studies but where detailed variations of channel morphology are to be studied the local channel slope associated with each measurement site should be surveyed in the field using a clinometer or level. Rivers are often characterised by alternating shallows (riffles) and deeps (pools). These must be allowed for when carrying out field surveys.

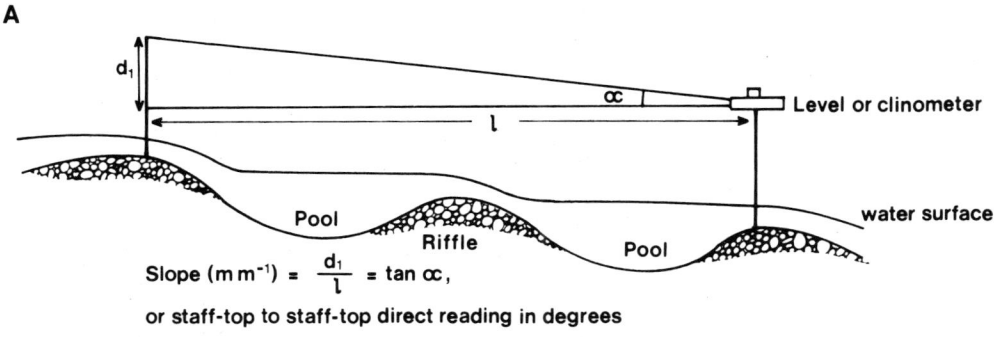

**A**

Slope $(m\,m^{-1}) = \dfrac{d_1}{l} = \tan \alpha,$

**or staff-top to staff-top direct reading in degrees**

**B**

Slope $(m\,m^{-1}) = \dfrac{d_1 - d_2}{l}$

**Figure 5.9 Channel slope measurement with a level or clinometer (A) or hose-and-staff (B)**

Field survey requires two people and involves the measurement of the slope over a channel reach normally between three riffle crests, the middle riffle being used as the site for the surveyed cross-section (*Figure 5.9*). Two calibrated staffs, two ranging poles or two people of the same height(!) are needed to determine the angle between two points each of the same height above the ground surface. Ranging poles are wooden or light-metal rods commonly 2 m in length with a pointed strengthened shoe at one end, and painted in sections, often of red and white, which are either 200 or 250 mm long.

The measurements may be made with the level (**see** Pugh, 1975) but a clinometer is more commonly used. In this case the distance between the two points is measured in metres with a tape and the angle measured in degrees. This must then be converted to a record in metres per metre: this is simply achieved by finding the value of the natural tangent of the measured angle from mathematical tables. If two clinometers are available then the second person should also take a backsight to provide a check measurement.

In practice, the levelling techniques described above can produce large errors, particularly if used by inexperienced operators to measure low angled slopes or slopes over short distances. Moreover, the equipment can be expensive. One simple and inexpensive technique that can give an instant, accurate reading uses a length of plastic tube and two calibrated staffs (*Figure 5.9B*). The hose-and-staff technique is robust; it is practicable for slope measurements over short distances (of about 10 m); and it may be used even if the two ends are not intervisible. The clear plastic tube is laid out between two staffs on the survey line and of known distance apart. The tube is filled with water and the ends are held vertically so that the height of the water level within the tube can be measured at each end. The difference between the two measurements then gives the fall of the surface between two points.

**5.2.4 The downstream variation of channel form**

A longitudinal zonation of channel forms may be recognised from the headwaters downstream to the river mouth. Such changes reflect the common tendency for rivers to have a progressively lower slope and an increase in total discharge (reflected by the continuous addition of tributaries and increasing drainage area) downstream. The downstream variation of channel form may be described by using regression analysis to relate a dependent variable (e.g. channel capacity, channel width, etc) with either a representative discharge or a surrogate variable such as drainage area. Both sets of data are transformed into logarithmic values before analysis.

The selection of suitable channel reaches for field survey is one of the most important elements in the collection of channel form data. Obviously it is expedient to examine the total stream network. Therefore it is necessary to observe the fundamental sampling requirement that the channel sections analysed are representative and are selected so as to provide an unbiased estimate of the parameters required. An 'ideal' channel reach is virtually non-existent and consequently the problem is one of selecting the best reach available. The need to ensure that the data being analysed are sufficiently accurate, and conform to the assumption made in the analysis, requires that the investigation procedure is standardised. At least fifteen measurement sites are required for analysis; each being a riffle section. The sites should be relatively straight and uniform in character. Sharp bends and sites affected by major obstructions, such as rocks or fallen trees, should be avoided where possible as should sites immediately below tributary confluences because complex flow conditions may produce unstable channel forms at these locations. Similarly, locations on mountain streams should be free of abrupt drops in the water-surface elevation caused by waterfalls, rapids or constrictions.

Discharge records of sufficient quality or length to justify analysis are rarely available for all the survey locations along the river. However, once the channel dimensions have been determined it is possible to estimate the bankfull discharge using the Manning equation which requires measurements of channel slope, hydraulic radius and boundary roughness (*see* section 3.4.2). The bankfull discharge is simply the product of the channel capacity and the estimated bankfull velocity:

$$Q^{bk} = Cc \ (\text{m}^2) \times V \ (\text{ms}^{-1})$$

where $Q^{bk}$ is the bankfull discharge, $Cc$ is the channel capacity and $V$ is the estimated mean velocity:

$$V = \frac{R^{0.67} \times S^{0.5}}{n}$$

where  $R$ = hydraulic radius;
   $S$ = channel slope;
   $n$ = roughness coefficient.

The data can be used to examine the manner in which the channel dimensions vary along a river (as well as the variation of discharge and velocity with increasing drainage area). This approach is known as the '**Downstream Hydraulic Geometry**' and was developed by Leopold and Maddock (1953). The relationships again have the form:

Width $(W) = aQ^b$

Depth $(D) = cQ^f$

Velocity $(V) = kQ^m$

$b + f + m = 1.0$, and channel capacity $= (axc)Q^{(b + f)}$ in compliance with the concept of continuity (Section 3.4).

The downstream hydraulic geometry of the River Hodder, UK, for example, is given below:

$$W = 0.284Q^{0.55} : D = -0.491Q^{0.34} : V = 0.207Q^{0.11}$$

Here it can be seen that velocity in fact changes very little along the river as demonstrated by a low exponent of 0.11, and that the increase of channel capacity downstream is primarily associated with an increase of channel width as shown by the relatively large exponent of 0.55. Also, the anti-logarithms of the regression constants describe the parameter dimension at a discharge of 1 m$^3$ s$^{-1}$: width = 1.92 m, depth = 0.32 m, velocity = 1.61 ms$^{-1}$.

In the absence of adequate flow records a variety of surrogate variables may be used. Drainage area has been the most frequently employed because it is a scale variable and is directly correlated with discharge. The total stream length of the channel network upstream from the measurement location has proved successful, particularly for the comparison of rivers within catchments of different rock-type, because it may be viewed in its simplest form as a measure of the basin efficiency for removing excess rainfall inputs. Simple relationships have also been found to exist between the channel form parameters and drainage area, and within uniform basins channel form is seen to vary systematically along the river.

However, within large basins containing discrete areas of very different rock-type a simple straight-line graph on logarithmic paper may not satisfactorily describe the downstream variation of channel form. The application of the approach is clearly shown by the example of the River Derwent, Derbyshire, UK. In the headwaters, the Upper Derwent and Ashope rivers drain basins underlain by alternating sandstones and shales. Although the sandstones are often permeable the frequent beds of shale ensure that the rocks act as a relatively impermeable unit. In contrast, the River Wye tributary is dominated by the Carboniferous Limestone Series which acts as a pervious unit characterised by low drainage density.

Clear relationships exist between channel capacity and drainage area for the rivers (*Figure 5.10*) but different relationships relate to the different rock-types: larger drainage areas are required to maintain a channel of given dimensions for rivers draining permeable

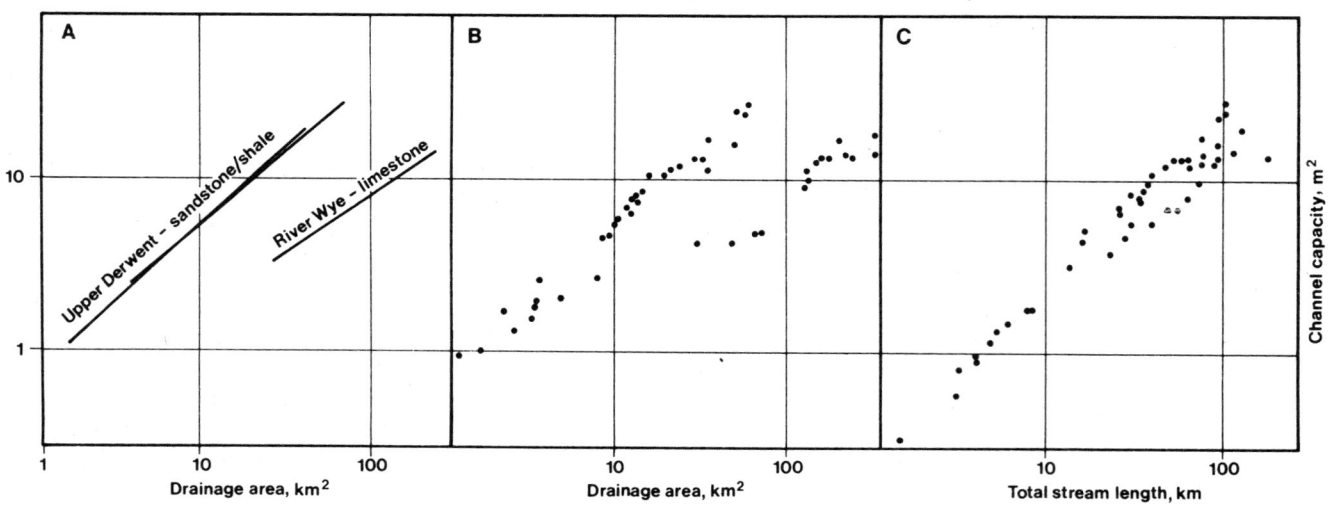

Figure 5.10 Channel capacity variation along rivers draining different rock-types: regressions (A) and scattergram (B) for drainage area and (C) for total stream length as the independent variable

basins. When considering the other channel form variables, strong downstream trends are also derived. Examination of the whole drainage network (*Figure 5.10B*), however, shows that the relationship between channel capacity and drainage area is weaker than for the individual tributary sub-basins with the degree of explanation, indicated by the square of the correlation coefficient, having a value of 60%. In large catchments of varied lithology total stream length may provide a more pertinent independent variable than drainage area, despite the problems of its derivation from topographic maps. Measurements of total stream length from 1:25 000 Ordnance Survey maps for the River Derwent improves the degree of explanation ($r^2 = 88\%$).

### 5.2.5 Relationships between channel form variables

In the previous section regression equations were used to examine trends relating to the downstream variation of the channel form parameters. Relationships between the form variables may be examined by determining the strength of the correlation.

It has been established that river channels maintain a quasi-equilibrium relationship with the fluvial processes through the inter-adjustment of channel slope, cross-sectional form and the size of the channel bed-materials. Characteristically, negative correlation coefficients are found between channel slope and drainage area, channel slope decreasing in the downstream direction. The particle-size of the bed-materials also decreases downstream so that a positive, although generally weak, correlation is commonly found with channel slope. Channel shape (e.g. channel width) is also characteristically related to the size of the bed-material, the coarser bed-materials being associated with the wider channel forms. However, the strength of the relationships may be expected to vary as the spatial scale under consideration changes: that is, the degree of explanation provided by one parameter for the variation of a dependent variable will differ as the spatial scale changes.

The use of correlation analysis and the influence of spatial scale upon the results obtained is exemplified by a study of streams within south-east England and south-east Scotland undertaken by Penning-Rowsell and Townshend (1978). The former region lies outside the area covered by Quaternary ice-sheets whereas the latter has been glaciated and the channel bed-materials contain coarse lag deposits inherited from processes operating under glacial conditions. Measurements of local channel slope, bed-material size and cross-sectional form were made at riffle sites, and the contributary drainage area (used as an index of discharge) and reach slope were obtained from 1:25 000 maps. Channel shape at the riffle sites was described as:

$$I = Cc \div P^2$$

where  $I$ = channel shape index;
$Cc$ = channel capacity;
$P$ = wetted perimeter.

Unlike the hydraulic radius ($Cc \div P$), this ratio does not vary with channel size. The ratio reaches a maximum for a semi-circular channel and gives low values for wide and shallow, rectangular forms. Some of their data are shown in *Table 5.3*.

The relationship between reach slope and drainage area clearly shows the expected downstream decrease, indicated by a strong negative correlation. At this scale drainage area is the dominant variable in explaining the downstream change of channel slope, accounting for 70% of the variance along both the Ashdown Sand and the glaciated Birkhill Shale channels. In contrast, the bed-material size shows only a relatively weak correlation with the reach slope for the Ashdown Sand streams. The data for all the sites in south-east England ($N$ = 96) supports the observation that the bed-material size is relatively unimportant at this scale ($r$ = 0.28) as an influence upon channel slope. However, a moderately strong correlation was found between bed-material size and reach slope for the glaciated sites. Despite the higher correlation coefficient for bed-material size the variation of channel slope at this scale is again explained primarily by the variation of discharge as indexed by drainage area.

Reduction of the scale of observation to examine the local slope variations within areas of uniform lithology reveals important differences in the strength of the correlations: the strength of the relationship between drainage area and channel slope is markedly weakened but the significance of the bed-material size is increased. For all the south-east England data the correlation coefficient for the relationship between drainage area and local slope is only −0.29, whereas for bed-material size the correlation coefficient is

**TABLE 5.3 CORRELATION COEFFICIENTS FOR RELATIONSHIPS BETWEEN STREAM CHANNEL FORM VARIABLES**

*(Data is given for the Ashdown Sand streams in south-east England and for the glaciated Birkhill Shale streams in Scotland (in brackets), N = 27 for both areas.)*

|  | Drainage area | Bed-material size | Channel form |
|---|---|---|---|
| Macro-scale REACH SLOPE | −0.88 (−0.84) | 0.12 (0.53) | − |
| Meso-scale LOCAL SLOPE | −0.68 (−0.48) | 0.22 (0.57) | −0.07 |
| Micro-scale LOCAL SLOPE | − | 0.63 | −0.75 |

*Notes*: The macro- and meso-scales refer to variations within areas of uniform rock-type. The micro-scale refers to variations between cross-sections located along a short channel reach.

REACH SLOPE was determined as the average gradient between adjacent contours over a distance of about 1 km as shown on the 1:25 000 maps.

LOCAL SLOPE was surveyed in the field over a distance of about 6 m.

BED-MATERIAL SIZE was determined as the mean *b*-axis of a sample of between 50 and 150 particles, selected using the grid method.

0.41 — and within individual areas reaches a maximum of 0.48. Stronger correlations are also shown for the Birkhill shale sites which have a wider range of particle-sizes derived from the deposits within the glaciated valleys. Thus, bed-material size is seen to become increasingly important in explaining the variation of channel slope as the scale of observation is reduced from the reach to the individual cross-section.

At the micro-scale, consideration of the factors influencing local channel slope variations within a reach reveals the significance of another variable — channel shape. Within a single reach between tributaries, discharge can be assumed to be constant along the channel so that the interactions between other variables can be studied more closely. Twenty-three riffle sites were surveyed within a 1.1 km reach of a stream on the Ashdown sand having a drainage area of 9.6 km$^2$. Local slope at the riffle sites was found to be moderately related to the bed-material size, steeper slopes being associated with coarser bed-materials. More important is the relationship between channel slope and the index of channel shape. Higher slopes are associated with wide and relatively shallow channels (which commonly have coarser bed-materials).

Thus, the interrelationships between the channel form variables must be considered with due reference to spatial scale: at the macro-scale variations of channel slope between 1 km channel reaches are explained primarily by the downstream variation of discharge (here as indexed by drainage area), at the meso-scale bed-material size becomes discernible as a significant control of local channel slope within areas of uniform geology, and at the micro-scale, variations of local channel slope within a channel reach are strongly related to the cross-sectional shape of the channel.

---

## 5.3 CHANNEL PATTERN

The pattern or planform of the channel is an important indicator of a river's general character. Traditionally, channel patterns have been divided into three types, namely — braided (or divided), meandering and straight.

As suggested in the preceding section, these different patterns may be differentiated by certain combinations of discharge, sediment character, slope and cross-sectional form (*Figure 5.11*). For a given discharge, braided channels with wide, shallow cross-sections will occur on steeper slopes with coarser sediments than meandering ones. At the same slope, meandering channels commonly have a lower discharge. Also, braided channels tend to occur in association with easily erodible floodplain deposits of loose sand and gravel; straight channels commonly occur in resistant materials — bedrock or cohesive sediments; and meandering patterns exist as an intermediate group.

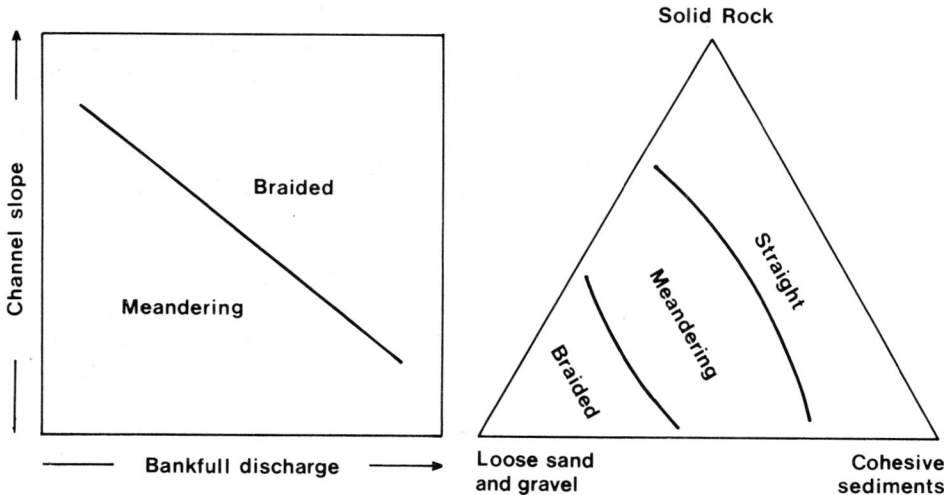

**Figure 5.11 Distribution of channel patterns. (After Leopold and Wolman, 1957:A; and Tanner, 1968:B)**

Many British rivers, however, are relatively inactive at the present time and their channel patterns contain evidence of Postglacial environmental change so that the conventional relationships are not universally applicable. Many rivers are confined within narrow valleys that restrict the development of channel patterns and others are lined by trees that can have an important stabilising effect upon the channel banks and their protective influence may have inhibited the adjustment of channel pattern, in some cases for several centuries. Nevertheless, the above relationships do provide a general framework for the examination of channel planform.

## 5.3.1 Braided Channels

Braided rivers are characterised by a seemingly chaotic array of channels divided by bars of sediment and have been found to exist in a wide range of environments. In proglacial areas (*Plate 5.1*) complex braid systems occur on broad gravel floodplains (known as sandurs), whereas in semi-arid environments wide braid systems are often associated with large loads of sand-sized sediments. In humid environments wide gravel floodplains and high channel slopes are often associated with braiding. Local channel division

**Plate 5.1 A braided glacial outwash channel: Glacier du Mont Mine, Valais, Switzerland**

is also quite common, particularly in upland areas, and small streams form braids where the channel is choked by gravel derived from the erosion, for example, of adjacent mine waste tips (*Plate 5.2*). Various factors have been identified as important for the development of divided channel patterns such as high regional slopes, variable discharges and easily erodible bank materials, but the availability of an abundant supply of sediment has generally been recognised as the dominant factor. In detail the braided channel is an unstable form and the size, shape and distribution of channels and bars constantly vary, but equilibrium is again maintained through the interaction between the planform, cross-sectional form and slope.

Plate 5.2 A braided channel
associated with an important source
of coarse sediment — mine waste:
Upper Wye, Wales

Braiding commonly is initiated by lateral channel bank erosion. Channel width becomes excessive and a short, narrow bar of sediment is deposited in the centre of the channel. These bars are commonly submerged at times of high flow so that the channel may appear undivided. Once initiated the bar grows vertically up to the general level of the floodplain, and downstream through the deposition of further material in the slack water created behind the initial bar form. As the bar grows the flow is increasingly diverted outwards into the channel banks and lateral erosion ensues. Eventually the bar may become stabilised, and vegetated if its development is unimpeded, and a complex channel system may evolve (*Figure 5.12A*). In reality two different types of channel bar may be

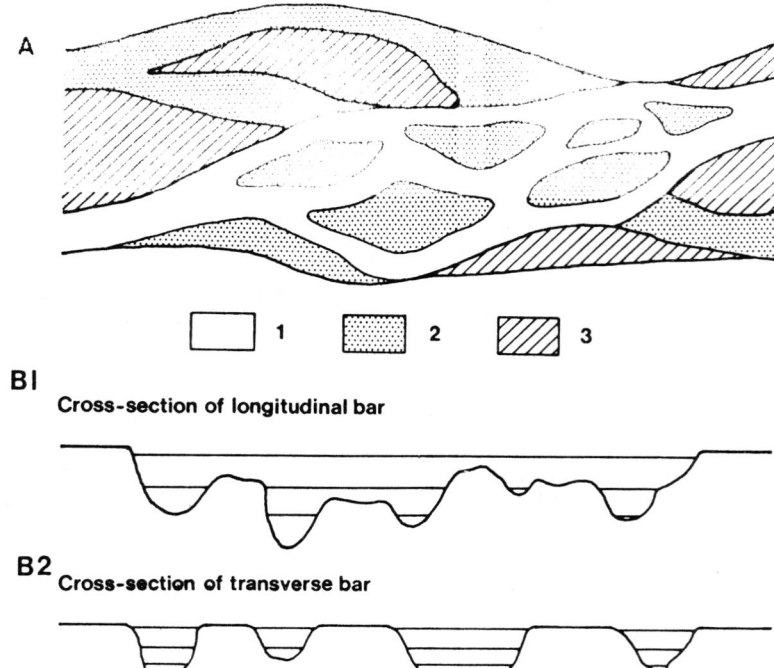

**A**

1    2    3

**BI**
**Cross-section of longitudinal bar**

**B2**
**Cross-section of transverse bar**

Figure 5.12 Braided channels can be viewed as composite features: in A first-order components (1) contain water flow even at low discharges, second-order components (2) are inundated at moderate flows and third-order components (3) at very high flows. The bars may be longitudinal or transverse, associated with gravel- and sand-sized sediments respectively, and each produces a different type of cross-section

identified (*Figure 5.12B*). In high energy, coarse bedload areas, as found in upstream locations, longitudinal bars develop parallel to the main channel orientation, are elongate downstream, and give the channel an irregular cross-section. At downstream locations, transverse bars commonly develop across the channel and these give the channel a more uniform cross-section. However, the pattern of bars and channels observed at any time will be dependent upon the water level because additional channels may be utilised or bars may be drowned with increasing discharge.

## 5.3.2 Undivided channels

One way of expressing the pattern of undivided channels is in terms of the sinuosity, that is the ratio of the length of the river between two defined points to the length of valley between these points. Rivers display a continuum of sinuosities. At one extreme, straight channels are defined as having a sinuosity of less than 1.5 for a distance which is at least ten times longer than the width of the channel. A channel is said to meander when its sinuosity exceeds a value of 1.5. Straight channels are in fact very uncommon (except when man-made) and such channels exceeding 10 channel widths are rarely found. However, any division between straight and meandering channels is purely arbitrary and closer examination reveals that all undivided channels share several common characteristics.

At low flow it may be clearly seen that the thalweg — the main streamline of the water flow — follows a sinuous course even within straight channels (*Figure 5.13*). This pattern is related to the presence of pools and riffles which are characteristic of undivided gravel-bed rivers. The terms riffle and pool describe the shallows and deeps in the bed profile which can be observed during periods of low flow. Riffles and pools differ also in terms of their sediment sizes: the bed of the pool may be predominantly sand sometimes with a few very large particles (a lag deposit), in contrast to riffles which represent lobate deposits of gravel-sized sediments. In straight reaches the pools occur cn alternate sides of the channel opposite to bars linked by riffles. Within sinuous reaches,

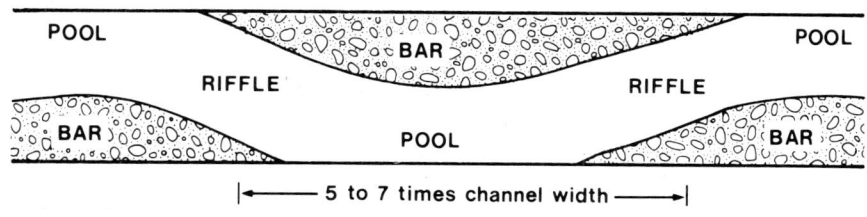

**Figure 5.13 The characteristics of straight channels**

**Plate 5.3 The meandering Afon Heulog, N. Wales, at a scale of 1:10 000. Point bars are well-developed and former meander courses are seen clearly on the floodplain**

riffles are found at the cross-over or point of inflection where the curvature changes, and the pools are located near the concave bank at the place of maximum curvature and opposite to the point bar on the convex bank.

The meandering pattern (*Plate 5.3*) refers to channels which exhibit rounded curves of repetitive and uniform shape; pools are found at the bend and riffles at the inflection points; and the thalweg is close to the outside of the bend and crosses over near the point of inflection so that it is seen to change from one side of the channel to the other. Deposition occurs on the inside of bends where velocities are relatively low to form point bars (section 4.3.2) and erosion along the outside produces vertical or undercut banks (section 4.2.2).

The winding flow of water in channels produces a characteristically helicoidal or spiral pattern. However, a more detailed examination of water movement reveals that two distinct patterns may be observed: surface flow is *divergent* at riffles and *convergent* at pools. These secondary flow circulations may be demonstrated simply by mapping the path taken by floats, weighted so as to be partly submerged to reduce wind interference, and inserted at intervals along transects across the channel (*Figure 5.14B*). In pools the floats converge along a zone where the flow plunges and at riffles the floats diverge,

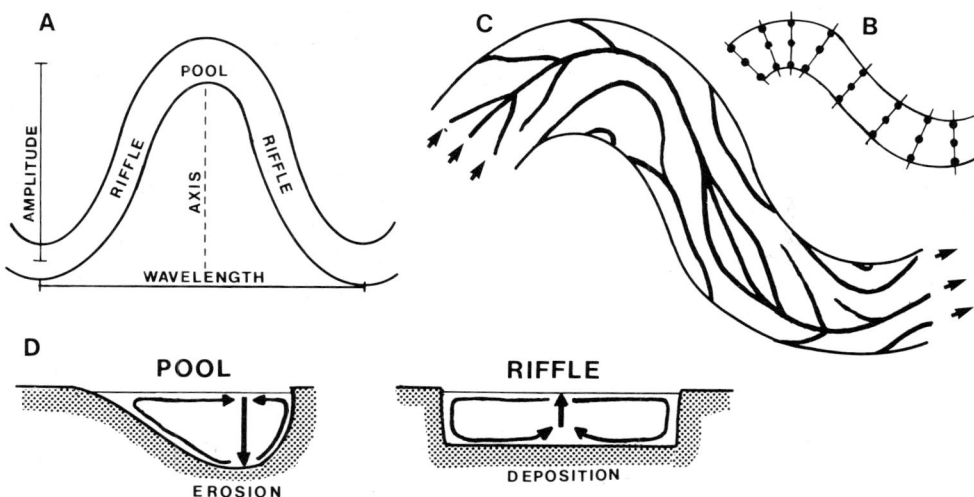

Figure 5.14 Meander characteristics and dimensions (A) and the pattern of water flow: the points of float insertion (B) and the flow pattern described by float pathways (C) within a small meander, Burleigh Brook, Leicestershire, which demonstrate the expected secondary circulations at pools and riffles (D)

moving away from the mid-channel zone of rising current (*Figure 5.14C*), and this flow pattern is maintained by opposite movements at the bed (*Figure 5.14D*). Secondary circulation cells are superimposed upon the general downstream flow to produce a regular pattern of scour (pools) and fill (riffles). Flow convergence at the bed is associated with ascending currents, favouring deposition, and flow divergence at the bed is associated with descending currents which encourage scour. Thus, the pattern of flow within the confines of the gross channel morphology (e.g. channel width) clearly contributes to creating the form of the channel bed.

The riffle-to-riffle and pool-to-pool spacing is regular and is, on average, between five and seven times the channel width. As channel width increases downstream so the pool and riffle spacing also increases. The tendency for streams to develop regularly spaced pools and riffles is a fundamental characteristic of many rivers and is independent of the boundary materials. Pools and riffles are found in bedrock, alluvial and supraglacial channels and tend to be relatively stable features. The riffle-to-riffle spacing is approximately one-half the meander wavelength, and this relationship is common to all meander forms. Other relationships commonly apply also: a nearly constant radius of curvature is found for a particular meander wavelength, meander wavelength is usually 6 to 10 times the channel width, and meander wavelength has a strong positive correlation with discharge and drainage area. Such relationships emphasise the regularity of meandering channel forms and also highlight the interrelated character of the channel form parameters. However, different planforms are not related to discharge alone and relationships may be derived which incorporate two or more control variables: the use of slope is particularly common. Also, channel pattern is related to the type and quantity of sediment supplied. In general, the meander wavelengths of rivers transporting a high proportion of bed-material load will tend to be greater than those in channels of similar discharge but transporting mainly fine sediment loads.

### 5.3.3 Field survey of channel pattern

Field surveys provide valuable data describing the characteristics of the channel pattern particularly when integrated with measurements of the cross-section form, sediment type and distribution, and flow pattern. Furthermore, field surveys direct attention towards the interrelationships between the different attributes of the channel form.

Two techniques are commonly employed for the survey of channel pattern: the compass traverse and the plane table survey.

The **compass traverse** provides a quick method for mapping channel pattern but its application to more detailed work is limited because of a low standard of accuracy. The term 'traverse' simply refers to a line survey. The compass allows the determination of the arrangement of points in space by reading bearings from north in a clockwise manner. Distance between the points is measured to the nearest 10 mm using a tape of 20 m or longer. The ranging poles are used as the target onto which bearings are taken.

### Equipment:
Compass.
2 tape measures.
2 ranging poles.

Two people are required, one person at each end of the tape and each with a ranging pole. Starting at point A on **Figure 5.15** the leading person moves to a point of interest, identified as station B and stands sideways to the follower so that the latter's view is not obstructed. The ranging pole is held so that it hangs vertically from the hand and is then placed firmly on the ground. A forward bearing is then taken to station B and this should be recorded to the nearest half degree in a field note book (**Table 5.4**). The follower then concentrates on holding the zero of the tape against the first station's pole whilst the leader pulls the tape taut alongside the pole at station B: the distance between the stations is then measured and recorded. Leaving the pole at station B in place the follower moves to the third station and the procedure is repeated. Note that the distance between each station should be smaller for tightly curved sections than for relatively straight reaches. At each station or at any measured interval between stations offsets may be taken to locate points of detail such as the channel banks, the water edge, or the limit of a particular type of deposit. Offsets can be taken at right angles to the tape-measure which forms a base-line joining the two stations, or as a compass bearing. The zero of a second tape is taken to the point of detail being located and the distance to the baseline recorded. For smaller scale surveys requiring more detailed information a single straight line traverse may be used with a large number of offsets. Care should be

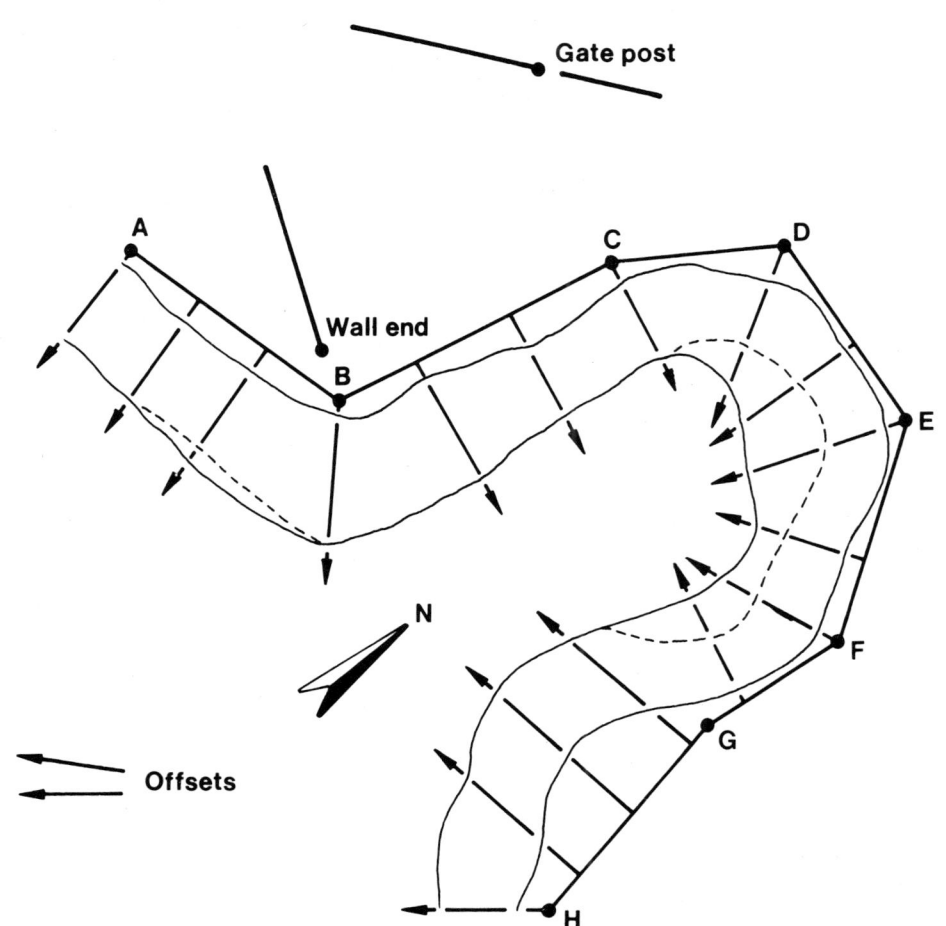

Gate post

Wall end

A

C

D

E

B

N

F

G

Offsets

H

Figure 5.15 A large-scale compass
traverse of a meandering channel

taken to select a scale appropriate to the area of survey and the detail required.

For most surveys the *plane table* method using a network of fixed points to minimise the error of measurement provides a rapid and more accurate procedure.

### Equipment:

*Wooden board (the 'table')*, 0.6 X 0.45 m is suitable for most operations; it must have a very smooth upper surface which must not be chipped or marked.

*Tripod*. The board is fixed to a broad-topped frame tripod by a wing-nut on its underside,

**TABLE 5.4 PART OF A FIELD NOTE-BOOK RECORD FOR A COMPASS TRAVERSE OF A SINUOUS CHANNEL**

| Station | BEARINGS (°) | | | | LENGTH (m) | BASELINE DISTANCE (m) | OFFSETS | | |
| | Forward | Backward | Backward ± 180° | Average | | | Angle (°) | Distance (m) | Notes |
|---|---|---|---|---|---|---|---|---|---|
| A | | | | | | 0 | Rt | 6.2 | Far bank (FB) |
| | | | | | | 0 | Rt | 0.4 | Near bank (NB) |
| | 056 | 237.5 | 57.5 | 56.75 | 15.4 | 5 | Rt | 6.8 | FB |
| | | | | | | 5 | Rt | 1.3 | NB |
| | | | | | | 10 | Rt | 7.7 | FB |
| | | | | | | 10 | Rt | 7.0 | edge of gravel bar |
| B | | | | | | 10 | Rt | 1.5 | NB |
| | | | | | | 15.4 | 262 | 13.6 | End of wall |
| | | | | | | 15.4 | 136 | 8.1 | FB |
| | | | | | | 21 | Rt | 7.6 | FB |
| | 013 | 192 | 12 | 12.5 | 18.5 | 21 | Rt | 0.8 | NB |
| | | | | | | 27 | Rt | 6.7 | FB |
| | | | | | | 27 | Rt | 2.4 | NB |
| C | | | | | | 33.9 | 290 | 12.1 | Left gatepost |
| | | | | | | 33.9 | 104 | 6.2 | FB |
| | | | | | | 33.9 | 104 | 1.2 | NB |

*Note: Narrow deep section

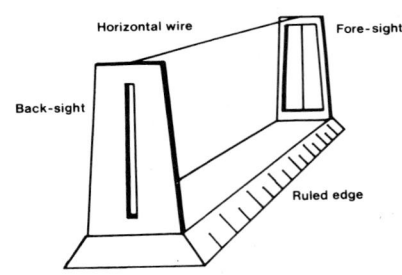

**Figure 5.16 The alidade**

if only partially tightened the board will be held to the tripod but can be rotated in a horizontal plane.

*Alidade*. In its simplest form the alidade is a wooden straight edge marked in centimetres with a slit back-sight and a hair fore-sight arranged so that the line of sight is parallel to the ruled edge; a horizontal wire joins the centre of the two sights so that the targets above and below the line of normal sight can be sighted using the backsight (if above) or the wire and fore-sight (if below) (*Figure 5.16*).

*Ranging poles*. The number of targets depends upon the area to be surveyed and the number of assistants available.

*Paper*. Paper is fixed to the table and the measurements are plotted directly; the paper should be at least 10 cm wider and longer than the table because the paper is to be fixed on the UNDERSIDE so as to avoid marking the table surface and to maximise the work area; adhesive tape is preferable to pins as the latter allows the paper to work loose as the pinholes enlarge; the paper should be stretched as tightly as possible and any irregularities on the paper pressed out.

*Tape-measure*. A tape of at least 20 m is required.

In any survey the stations should be 'fixed' as precisely as possible. For most channel surveys with good visibility the number of stations can be small but it must be remembered that each station may be identified at best only by a vertical ranging pole and that at least three stations must be visible from every part of the area to be mapped. Particular care must obviously be taken in well vegetated areas or areas of high relief. Thus, stations must be located so that they are visible from as much of the area as possible. Also, the 'fixed' sites may need to be used on a subsequent occasion and they should be able to be relocated. Vegetation growth in particular can rapidly conceal pegs or painted stones. A description and field sketch made for each station and including sitings onto readily identifiable objects (walls, fences, trees etc) provide an unobtrusive yet effective approach.

First, two 'fixed' stations should be identified and the distance between the stations measured with a taut tape measure, and recorded to the nearest 10 mm. Using this measurement as a guide an appropriate scale is chosen (three common scales are: 10 mm = 1 m, 2 m or 5 m) and the two stations are marked on the paper (*Figure 5.17*) and joined by a

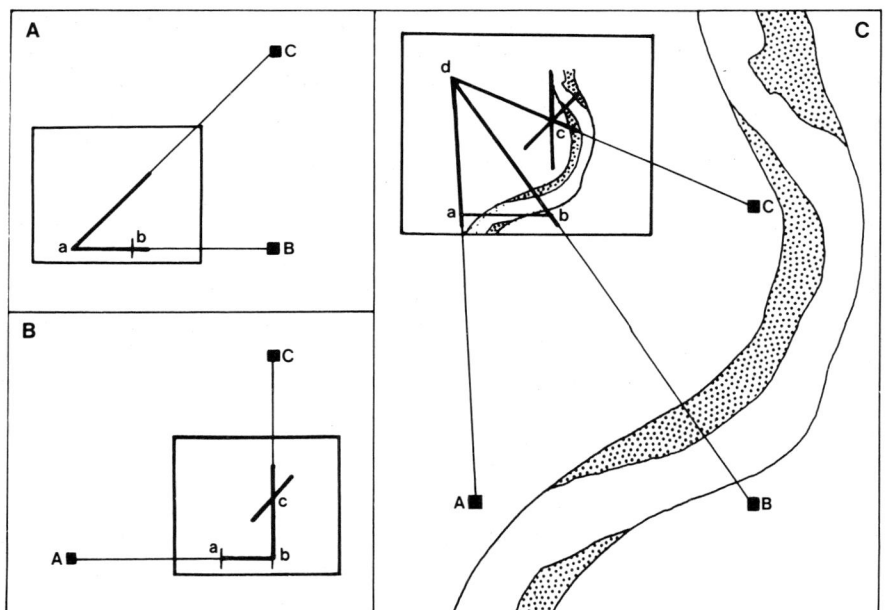

Figure 5.17 A plane-table survey. The location of three primary stations is shown in A and B, and the location of subsidiary stations using semi-resection is illustrated in C

line (ab). The plane table is then set up at station A, and oriented onto station B by placing the alidade along the line ab and rotating the table until station B is sighted through the alidade when the table is clamped tight. After clamping it is important to check that the correct orientation is still maintained. The table is now established in a position for the fixing of other stations. When establishing a station the plane table should be set up so that the station mark on the paper is directly over the mark on the ground. If the table is not centred over the ground mark small errors of orientation will result. This is a common source of error, especially in large scale (say 1:100) surveys within which the distance between stations is relatively short. Note that work on the plane-table should be done without excess pressure on the table so as to avoid accidental movement.

A third station is set up, for example at C of *Figure 5.17A*. The alidade is then rotated about position 'a' until the station C ranging pole is sighted and a ray is drawn from 'a' along this orientation. The distance from A to C measured with a tape is then scaled down and point C located on the ray 'ac'. Although this linear measurement can be avoided, and all the remaining stations will be located by angular measurement alone, at least two accurately measured distances should be obtained so that subsequent locations can be checked.

Once the three main survey points are fixed, detail around station A can be added by radiating out to points of interest. An assistant takes a ranging pole and the zero end of a tape to the feature of interest, such as the stream bank; the observer then reads the distance to the station mark, draws a ray from the station to the ranging pole using the alidade, and locates the point on the map. The procedure is straightforward but several points should be noted: firstly, the measured lengths using the radiating method can conveniently be as much as 60 m but for small scale surveys lengths of up to 20 m (i.e. one tape length) will minimise the risk of error; secondly, the rays to points of detail should not be drawn all the way from the station but only for a short distance either side of the estimated location of the point so as not to obscure the map unnecessarily; thirdly, a carefully selected number of prominent features should also be included in the survey so as to aid relocation of the stations on future surveys.

Having mapped all the required detail about station A the plane table is moved and re-established over station B. The table is levelled and the alidade is set along the line 'ab' and the table is rotated until the observer sights onto the ranging pole replaced at station A. The table is then clamped. The alidade is then rotated around 'b' to sight onto station C — the ray drawn should meet the point 'c'; if not primary measurements ('ab' and 'ac') and the orientations of these primary rays should be checked. Detail about station B is then mapped as before by radiating to points of interest and including rays to a few prominent features.

After the survey around the three primary stations has been completed the plane table may be moved to other areas not yet visited in order to map surrounding detail by the radiating method. However, the location of the new subsidiary stations must first be established. The quickest and simplest method to locate the plane table is to use a semi-resection. Before moving from station C set up a ranging pole at a new station (D) around which information is required, and a ray is drawn using the alidade from C towards D. The plane-table is then moved to the new location, centred and levelled, and a ranging pole set up at C. The alidade is then laid along the line just drawn (cd) but oriented in the opposite direction and the table rotated until the foresight intersects the ranging pole at C. The table is now correctly oriented so it can be firmly clamped. In order to 'fix' the new point, pivot the alidade around the marked position of 'a' on the paper, sight onto the pole at station A and draw a line back from 'a' to intersect the ray drawn from 'c'. This is the position of 'd' which can be confirmed by making a similar sighting onto B; the ray drawn back from 'b' will pass through the same point. A general rule is to repeatedly back check from new stations onto the primary stations, and note that because of error at low angles, rays to prominent features or subsidiary stations should have an angle of between 30 ° and 150 °. The last station employed in a survey must be sited so as to allow sighting onto at least two of the primary points so that a check may be made on the accuracy of the overall survey using the above method.

# CHAPTER 6  CHANNEL CHANGE

River channel change refers to the changes of channel form within the context of the cross-section, the pattern or network in a drainage basin, and the measurement of change has been an important focus for study during the past thirty years (Gregory, 1976b). However, the recognition that channels change is itself not new. In the late fifteenth century Leonardo da Vinci observed channel migration within meandering rivers and, more significantly, he reported that human activity would cause channel change and specifically that dams would induce deposition upstream and erosion downstream:

*"The windings which the rivers make through their valleys . . . cause the bank to form curves, and these curves move . . . and in the course of time seek out the whole valley"*
*(Volume 1, p. 310)*

*"I find that the water, that falls at the foot of the dams of rivers, places material towards the approach of the water, and carries away from the foot of the dam all the material on which it strikes as it falls."*
*(Volume 11, p. 145)*
*'The Notebooks of Leonardo da Vinci', MacCurdy, 1938*

These observations provide examples of the two kinds of channel change which can be distinguished:

1.  **Fluctuations of channel form about a mean or equilibrium condition** — *autogenic* change. These changes are a fundamental characteristic of rivers and include short-term changes of drainage network or cross-sectional form, and channel migration;
2.  **Adjustments of channel form in response to changes of sediment load and/or discharge** — *allogenic* change. Longer term changes of drainage networks, channel planform and cross-section may result from modifications to both sediment and water discharges produced by climatic change or human activity.

Several sources of information are available for the examination of channel changes.

*Field survey* or *photography* may be used repeatedly to record changes that occur during periods of a few years or less, for example, measurements of channel bank erosion (*see* section 4.2.2). Such methods can provide useful data on the rate and characteristics of channel change at particular locations. However, the data generally relate to only short periods of observation and these cannot be confidently applied to longer time periods. Consequently, *historical data sources* are employed. These may be in the form of topographic surveys and maps, photographs or documentary records. Two-dimensional information only may be available and the information relates to a specific time. Nevertheless, historical data sources provide valuable information on the general direction and rate of channel change which cannot be obtained in any other way.

In some areas the above sources may be usefully complemented by *dating techniques* which can provide information on the age of land surfaces exposed by erosion or created by deposition. Also, the analysis of sediment sequences together with the dating of defined layers (horizons) within the sequence may provide a record of the environmental conditions to which channel changes can be related. In particular, rates of sediment deposition in lakes have been used to examine the effects of land-use change upon the fluvial processes within the contributary drainage area. Additionally, local changes — changes within a single river — may be identified by the comparison of channel form between rivers or between 'natural' and 'changed' sections along individual rivers. This method has been termed *space-time substitution*.

Channel form has been shown to vary in a predictable manner along a river and this provides a basis for the evaluation of change particularly where drainage basins have been affected by human activity: land-use change, urbanisation or dam construction for example. But again the information needs to be complemented by dating techniques if an apparent cause of channel change is to be confirmed.

---

## 6.1 HISTORICAL METHODS

A considerable amount of valuable information about river channel change can be obtained from topographic surveys and maps, documentary records, and photographic sources. Historical data sources may be used to study channel change over two different time-scales — short-term changes over periods from a year to a few hundred years, and long-term changes that have occurred over several thousand years.

Short-term studies frequently use the method of comparing present field surveys of channel cross-sections, channel pattern or drainage networks with earlier surveys, maps, documents or photographs. This approach uses historic evidence which contains information relating to a specific point in time and differences between surveys of different date are interpreted assuming a uniform change over the intervening period. Historic data sources also contain evidence of long-term channel changes associated with drainage contraction, recorded in the form of the valleys and described by the pattern of contours on topographic maps.

## 6.1.1 Long-term channel changes

**A.  *Drainage network contraction.*** In humid temperate landscapes dry valleys are a common feature of many river systems. Dry valleys have been visualised as landforms of permeable rocks, particularly limestone, but in fact they occur on a wide range of rock types. Even in the case of permeable rocks, some of the dry valleys may be ascribable to percolation but many appear to be unrelated to contemporary processes.

Often, a dry valley occurs as a simple headward extension of the main valley which is occupied by a stream but dry valleys also occur as independent tributaries which are dry along their entire length. Valley networks — which incorporate both the present-day channel network and dry valleys — may represent expanded river systems which existed during former climates and which relate to periods of higher surface runoff. Certainly drainage network contraction appears to be a feature of mid-latitude areas.

The reconstruction and analysis of former stream networks utilise the morphometric techniques described for the study of present-day drainage systems but using data obtained from measurements of the valley network instead of the channel system. Examination of the contour configuration on 1:25 000 maps may be undertaken to delimit the character of the valley network (*Figure 6.1*). However, a field survey is also required because the 'blue line' stream depicted on the map may be a simplification of the real stream network: the mapped stream is found often to be only one-half to one-third of the real stream channel length within small drainage basins. Also, because of cartographic generalisation

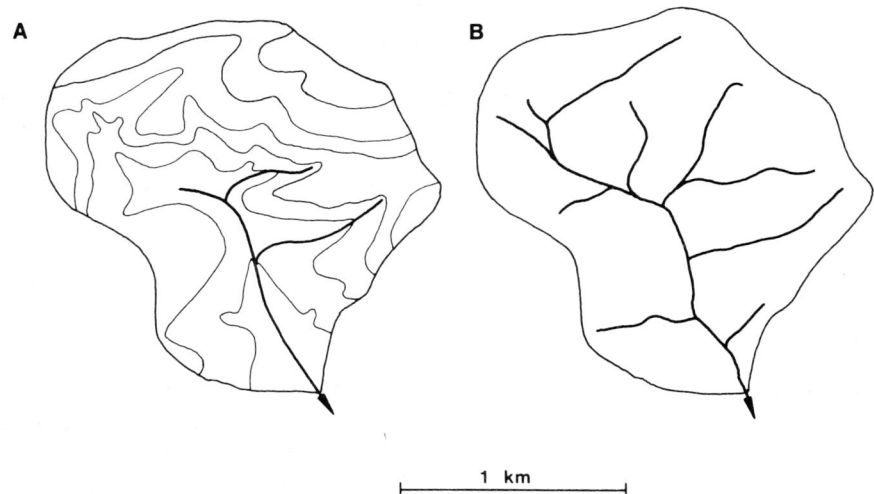

**Figure 6.1 Delineation of the valley network for a tributary of the River Fowey, Cornwall from a 1:25 000 ordnance survey map: contour crenulations and 'blue-line' network (A), and valley network (B)**

1 km

the importance of some dry valleys may be unrecognised.

Gregory (1976d) sampled valley densities for drainage basins ranging in size from 0.8 km$^2$ to 75 km$^2$ and including outcrops of chalk, Jurassic Limestone and Carboniferous Limestone. A consistent density of dry valleys was revealed for each of the six areas: the average valley density for all areas of 1.86 contrasts with the average stream density of 0.48, and in areas of Jurassic Limestone the valley network was found to be up to eight times longer than the network of the present-day stream. Valley networks have been identified also outside the limestone areas and in south-west England marked differences have been found between the total length of valley networks and the total length of the stream networks (Gregory 1966). For specific stream orders, the length of the valley network was consistently greater than the stream network lengths (*Table 6.1*) and the drainage density for the valley network of 3.44 contrasts with the value of 2.01 derived from the contemporary stream network.

**TABLE 6.1 STREAM AND VALLEY-NETWORK COMPOSITION, RIVER OTTER, DEVON. (BASED UPON GREGORY, 1966)**

| Stream order | Stream number | | Cumulative mean stream length (km) | |
| --- | --- | --- | --- | --- |
| | Stream-net | Valley-net | Stream-net | Valley-net |
| 1 | 226 | 681 | 0.64 | 0.97 |
| 2 | 60 | 178 | 1.61 | 2.90 |
| 3 | 17 | 45 | 3.70 | 7.08 |
| 4 | 4 | 7 | 10.30 | 35.40 |
| 5 | 1 | 1 | — | — |

As expected the number of network segments of each order are also greater for the valley system than for the contemporary stream system. Nevertheless, both sets of data conform to Horton's first two laws of drainage composition. For the Devon basins examined, Gregory concluded that the valley network appears to include valleys of different ages which developed and functioned at different times.

*B.*   *Misfit channel patterns.* In many areas it is possible to identify large winding (meandering) valleys which contain relatively straight rivers. The present day rivers may flow in a meandering pattern but this is commonly far less ample than the pattern of bends described by the valley. Such disparities between channel and valley forms can be easily recognised on maps and air photographs (*Figure 6.2*). Sometimes the trace of large meanders is clearly preserved by winding valley troughs but elsewhere a more careful examination of the valley-side contour pattern or valley form may be required. Nevertheless, such 'misfit' streams have been observed throughout much of Europe and North America.

In 1951, Dury first tested the hypothesis that if valley bends are authentic former meanders then former large channels should have been associated with them. The implications are that the meandering valleys represent the channel of former large streams, that a relationship exists between stream size and meander size, and that for some reason the

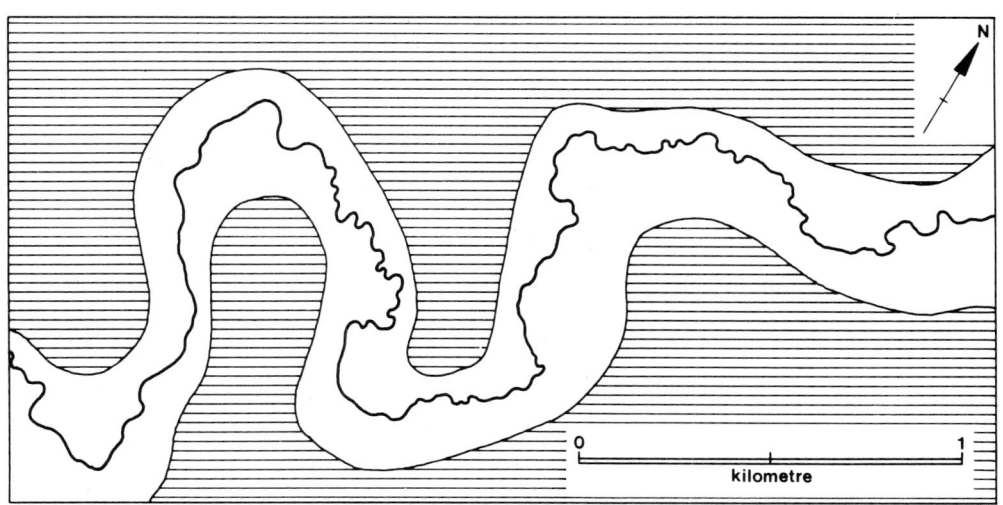

**Figure 6.2 The misfit channel of the River Leam, Warwickshire**

size of the streams has been subsequently reduced. Dury undertook subsurface exploration into the floodplain of the Warwickshire Itchen and established the presence of a large buried channel which meanders around the valley bends. Exploration also established that the buried channel was characterised by asymmetrical pools at the extremities of the bends and shallower, more regular cross-sections (riffles) between the bends. The ratio between valley meander wavelength and the bed-widths of the buried channels was found to average 13:1 and to be within the range of values obtained for the corresponding ratio on contemporary channels. Such streams which combine large former valley meanders with small present-day meandering channels, termed by Dury as *manifestly underfit*, have been identified in England, in France and in several areas of USA. An easily determined index of underfitness has been defined as the ratio of the wavelength of the valley meanders ($L$) to the wavelength of the contemporary stream channel meanders ($\ell$). Within lowland England values of $L/\ell$ were found to be in the range of 9:1 and 10:1, and in the USA the values ranged from 3:1 up to 10:1.

Some apparently underfit rivers were observed to have relatively straight channels flowing within wider, meandering valleys. Previously it had been observed that the pool-to-pool spacing is appropriate to the size of the channel and is commonly about five-times the channel bed width and one-half the meander wavelength. The apparently underfit streams were found to possess pools and riffles spaced appropriately to their bed-width but not to the wavelength of the valley meander. This type of underfitness (termed the **Osage type**) was first recognised for the Osage River in the Ozarks, USA. The river has a pool-to-pool spacing of 0.9 km and this is equivalent to about five bed-widths as expected within natural rivers. However, this pool-to-pool spacing should be associated with a meander wavelength of 1.8 km. The average wavelength of the meandering valley within which the Osage River flows is 6.1 km. Even though a meandering pattern may not be apparent (except where the channel is forcibly curved around the valley bends) the examination of contemporary pool-riffle sequences may demonstrate a misfit relationship with the meandering valley pattern. Thus streams with very high meander wavelength/bed-width ratios are probably Osage-type underfits.

*C.  River metamorphosis.* Long-term channel changes have provided an important theme for geographical study as a central component of landscape evolution. Until the 1950s the classical explanation for misfit streams was ***river capture***. In its simplest form river capture results from the relatively rapid development of subsequent drainage lines which cut the original, consequent streams and alter the drainage pattern. The captured headwater would provide a sudden enlargement in the source area of the subsequent stream. The consequent stream, however, deprived of its headwater drainage area, would receive reduced discharges, and its size would diminish; it would become a 'misfit' stream clearly too small to have produced the valley form which it occupies and the floodplain within which it flows.

Successful river capture requires that the pirate stream is incised to a lower level than the victim so that at the time of capture the victim will experience a sudden fall in base-level. Stream incision may result in a lowering of the water table and the contraction of affected tributary streams. A dry valley would also be formed at the head of the misfit stream. Evidence for river capture is provided then by sharp changes in a river's course ('elbow bends'), misfit streams, cols, dry valleys and knickpoints. Support for river capture may be found in the floodplain deposits of the misfit stream. Pebbles of a rock-type found only in the captured headwater area would support the inferred existence of a former consequent stream.

River capture is considered to be an important event in the erosional development of drainage systems but for several reasons the capture hypothesis is inapplicable to the majority of misfit streams. At the point of capture, the consequent stream (the "victim") will have a larger drainage area than the subsequent stream (the "pirate"). However, the pirate stream must be more deeply incised and have a higher capacity for erosion than its victim. This situation would require rigorous topographic and geological conditions. The breaching of basin divides and stream capture does occur during the early stages of drainage development and where the relative valley relief is low, for example as shown by the development of rills on man-made slopes. However, river capture becomes increasingly uncommon as the drainage network grows and is rare in large rivers. Thus, other factors are required to explain the widespread distribution of dry valleys and misfit streams.

The abandonment of dry valleys and river contraction to produce underfits may be explained alternatively by *climatic change*, that is, by recourse to climatic conditions substantially different from those of the present time. When considering the effect of climatic change upon the fluvial processes, the changing nature of the surface vegetation must be taken into account as the sediment loads in particular will be affected by the extent and effectiveness of the protective plant cover. Nevertheless, the regional effects of climatic change would be to alter river channel process and consequently to change channel form. Evidence of the long-term adjustment of entire river systems to the effects of climatic change has long been recognised by geologists in alluvial deposits. For example, within the alluvial plain of the sinuous Murrumbidgee River in south-eastern Australia three sinuous channels have been identified (Schumm, 1968). The character of the channels relates to the discharge and sediment load conditions existing when the channels were functioning (*Table 6.2*).

The present-day river drains a well vegetated basin, the source area is protected from erosion, and the river transports only small quantities of sediment. Although Palaeo-

**TABLE 6.2 CHANGES OF THE MURRUMBIDGEE RIVER, AUSTRALIA (AFTER SCHUMM, 1968).**

| | Channel capacity ($m^2$) | Width/depth ratio | Meander wavelength (m) | Sediment fill type | Suggested environmental conditions |
|---|---|---|---|---|---|
| Contemporary channel | 429 | 10 | 853 | Sand, silt and clay | Humid and well vegetated, moderate sediment loads and discharges. |
| Palaeochannel 1 | 1496 | 13 | 2134 | Silt and clay | Wetter climate, good vegetation cover, low sediment loads but high discharges. |
| Palaeochannel 2 | 502 | 67 | 5486 | Sand | Drier climate than present, poor vegetation cover, reduced discharges but much larger sediment loads. |

channel 1 differs little in shape it is filled with fine sediments, and is much larger, suggesting that it was formed under conditions of higher discharge but lower sediment loads. Such a situation could be found under a wetter climate than at present: higher precipitation could further improve the vegetation cover, and although runoff would increase the sediment yield would decrease. In contrast, a decrease in precipitation would decrease the amount of runoff but the vegetation cover could be reduced resulting in higher sediment loads. Wide and shallow channels may be expected to characterise such an environment and Palaeochannel 2 appears to have functioned under these conditions. The marked increase in meander wavelength and reduction of sinuosity associated with this phase of channel development describes an adjustment of channel slope. Wide, straight channels (Palaeochannel 2) with steep slopes are characteristic of high bed-load streams whereas relatively deep, sinuous, low-slope channels are characterised by the dominance of suspended sediment (Palaeochannel 1).

The adjustment of channel morphology to changes of the discharges and sediment loads has been termed 'River Metamorphosis' (Schumm, 1969), and the potential

**TABLE 6.3 MAJOR DIRECTIONS OF ADJUSTMENT OF CHANNEL FORM VARIABLES IN RESPONSE TO DISCHARGE OR SEDIMENT LOAD CHANGES. (AFTER SCHUMM, 1969)**

| Control variables | | Channel form variables | | | | | |
|---|---|---|---|---|---|---|---|
| Discharge | Bed-material load | Width | Depth | Width-depth ratio | Meander wavelength | Sinuosity | Slope |
| A  + | 0 | + | + |  | + |  | − |
| B  − | 0 | − | − |  | − |  | + |
| C  0 | + | + | − |  | + | − | + |
| D  0 | − | − | + |  | − | + | − |
| E  + | + | + | +/− | + | + | − | +/− |
| F  + | − | +/− | + | − | +/− | + | − |
| G  − | + | +/− | − | + | +/− | − | + |
| H  − | − | − | +/− | − | − | + | +/− |

+ = increase; − = decrease; 0 = no change

directions (larger or smaller) of channel change are described in *Table 6.3*. In situation A, for example, an increase in discharge without any change in sediment load would result in the enlargement of channel size in cross-section related to an increase in both the width and depth dimensions, an increase in meander wavelength and a decrease of channel slope. For the Murrumbidgee it was suggested that Palaeochannel 2 functioned under drier conditions than at the present time producing lower discharges but higher sediment loads. This is situation G, and a higher width/depth ratio (i.e. a relatively wider and shallower channel), with a lower sinuosity, should be expected: these channel changes were observed on the Murrumbidgee alluvial plain.

**6.1.2 Short-term channel changes**

In many areas with an extended cultural history, a range of historical data sources are often available for the examination of channel change. For the study of a single meander bend on the Missouri, Ruhe (1975) was able to use fifteen maps covering the period 1852−1970 and eleven air photographs from 1925−1966. Although such an availability of historical sources may be exceptional, several useful surveys covering the past one-hundred and forty years may be employed for channel change studies in Britain. Furthermore, these sources may often be supplemented by repeated field mapping using survey or photographic techniques to monitor the character of channel change, to assess the contribution of high magnitude discharges, and then to substantiate and complement the conclusions made from the comparison of historic data sources.

In Britain the 1:25 000 scale maps have proved the most useful for the measurement of channel planform. At this scale three classes of map are available for most parts of England — Ordnance Survey National Grid Series surveyed during the 1950s, Ordnance Survey County Series produced from a survey around 1900, and Tithe maps. The latter were produced for each tithe district, usually a parish, in compliance with the Tithe Commutation Act of 1838. However, it is obviously necessary to establish the accuracy and reliability of detail on the maps so that errors involved may be assessed. The Ordnance Survey undertake tests on the accuracy of the National Grid Series maps on which the river bank line is mapped as the 'normal winter level' of water. An accuracy of about 1 m is thought to generally apply to eroding river banks. The County Series are considered to be of the same order of accuracy.

Detailed tests on the accuracy of Tithe maps which vary considerably in standard of survey, cartography and presentation, have been carried out by Hooke and Perry (1976). A sample of twenty-three Tithe maps was employed and measurements of areas and distances were compared with corresponding measurements for the Ordnance Survey maps. The results demonstrated a mean absolute error in area of 3.94% and in linear measurements of 2.71%, and an estimated resolution of only 7.5 m on the ground. Despite the possible inaccuracies of the Tithe maps the two Ordnance Survey Series supplemented by recent field observations or aerial photographs can provide useful information, for example of planform change (e.g. *Plate 5.3*), for which there is no alternative.

River meanders consistently change their position and shape as a result of erosion around the outside of the bend and through deposition on the point bar. More dramatic changes may result from the formation of cutoffs. The pattern of broad channels will also change, new bars will be constructed and old bars destroyed and the whole channel

**Figure 6.3 Channel migration of the River Axe shown by the comparison of two maps. (From Hooke, 1977)**

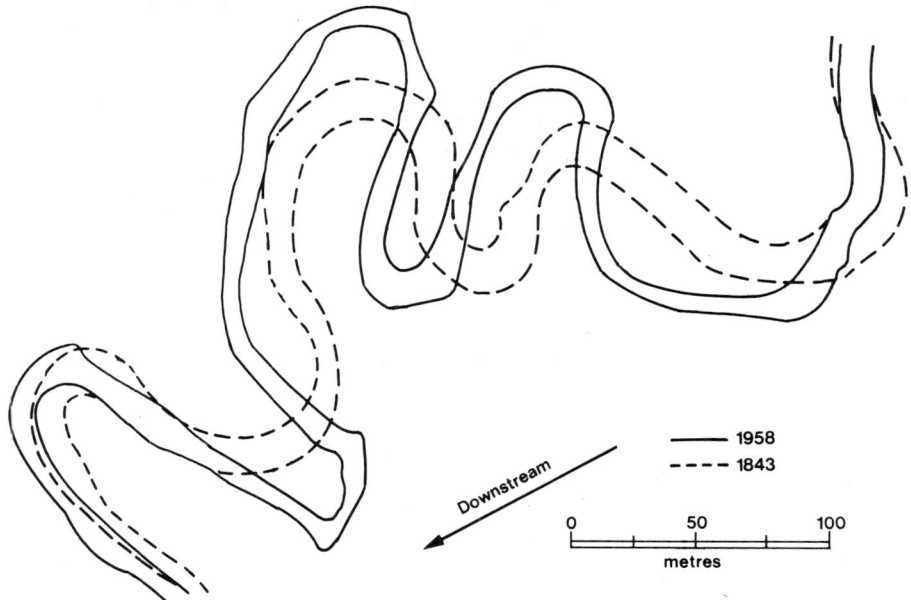

Downstream

——— 1958
‐ ‐ ‐ 1843

0          50          100
metres

system may shift across the floodplain. Such changes may of course be monitored by repeated field survey but a large amount of valuable information can be obtained from maps and aerial photographs. The accuracy and reliability of data derived from cartographic sources have been discussed earlier (*see* section 2.3). These sources of information may be supplemented by aerial photographs although the coverage is variable from area to area. Two examples of the information which can be obtained for pattern changes within mobile channels is given in *Figures 6.3* and *6.5*.

In the first example, Hooke (1977) has examined the changes of the meandering pattern of the River Axe in East Devon, England. Meanders were demonstrated to move in two ways (*Figure 6.4*). Firstly, by simple translation whereby the planform is main-

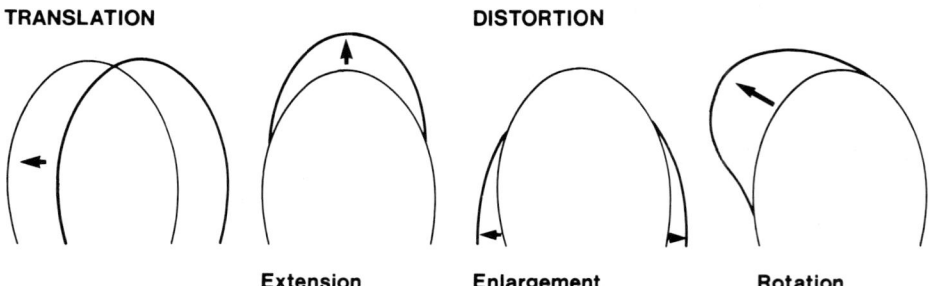

**TRANSLATION**          **DISTORTION**

Extension          Enlargement          Rotation

Figure 6.4 Primary forms of meander change. (After Daniel, 1971)

tained as the meander migrates laterally and downstream; secondly, by distortion when the movement is accompanied by a change in the form and characteristics of the pattern, for example where a channel has been straightened by a cutoff.

Distortion may involve extension, rotation or enlargement or indeed complex combinations of these primary movement types. It was estimated that 40% of the length of the River Axe has altered its course and 17% has also changed its form. Several prominent cutoffs were identified, as was a tendency for the amount of movement to increase with increasing discharge downstream though this was less noticeable than might be expected. Over a period of about sixty years the mean maximum movement was 36.4 m as determined by measuring the maximum distance the channel moved within each grid square along the length of the river. If completely stable reaches are excluded the mean maximum movement is 46.8 m and some individual locations moved by nearly 80 m.

Measurements of meander wavelength were also made from the different maps: the contemporary meander wavelength was found to increase downstream as expected. The channel was divided into sections of between 1.5 and 2.5 m in length. The data revealed that between 1843 and 1903 three-quarters of the sections decreased in mean wavelength, whereas between 1903 and 1958 fifty-eight percent experienced decreases. These were associated with increases of channel sinuosity of 55% and 69% respectively. Furthermore, of all the individual bends examined, over half experienced translation or extension or a combination of these movements. In the long term, however, the study demonstrated that movements of meanders tend to be gradual and consistent in time, taking place by progressive erosion and deposition rather than by sudden, catastrophic change causing cutoffs or complete alteration of the direction of movement.

**Figure 6.5 Short-term changes of Langden Brook detected by repeated field-survey and photography. (From Hitchcock, 1977)**

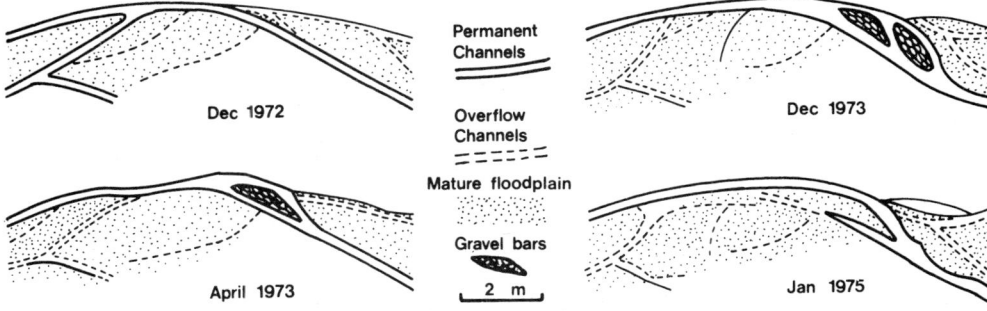

For the study of relatively short-term changes in braided reaches Hitchcock (1977) used evidence from air photographs and maps to identify those reaches which appear to experience extensive and repeated changes of channel pattern. An 800 m reach of the Langden Brook, Forest of Bowland, England, was then chosen for detailed study. Measurements of channel movements during 1972–1975 were made using simple field survey techniques supported by a photographic record. Between December 1972 and April 1975 changes of channel pattern were observed on seventeen occasions. These changes were classified into four categories representing a hierarchy of morphological changes:

A.  Local bank collapse, bed-material up to a mean diameter of 80 mm moved;
B.  Bank scour widespread, bars modified, larger stones moved;
C.  Extensive bank scour, bars completely changed, new channels appear, material of 200 mm diameter moved;
D.  Complete new channel system formed.

195

Measurements of peak flows undertaken at the site enabled the class of pattern changes to be related to discharge magnitude and frequencies. Class A changes were induced by flows exceeding 2.5 m$^3$ s$^{-1}$ having an expected frequency of 10 times per year on average. Extreme Class D changes were associated with larger floods exceeding 25 m$^3$ s$^{-1}$ having an average frequency of once every two years.

Although when viewed over the long-term (i.e. > 100 years) channel movements within systems of mobile meanders or braids appear to be steady and progressive, they are, of course, discontinuous in the short-term. Channel movements are related to high discharges and major channel movement episodes are associated with flows which may occur only two or three times a year.

## 6.2 DATING TECHNIQUES

The hydrological regime of a river acts as an important control of the channel-ward limit of some vegetation types. Within bed-rock channels the size-distribution of lichens is indicative of the degree of flow variability, and on floodplains the age distribution of trees may be used to detect the pattern and rate of channel migration.

### 6.2.1 Lichenometry

The technique of lichenometry was developed by Beschel (1950; translated 1973). It permits the dating of rock surfaces by measuring the diameter of approximately circular lichens. Comparison of field measurements with an established growth curve for the lichen species allows the age of an undated surface to be determined. Beschel observed that lichens may establish themselves immediately after the exposure of a rock surface so that they may provide an accurate age. However, to provide an estimate of age a suitable sequence of dated surfaces is required from which the curves for growth rate can be calibrated. The rate of growth of a particular lichen species depends primarily on the micro-climate (aspect and moisture availability) and the nature of the substrate is very important in governing the species found at any location. Rock-type can also influence growth rate.

Churchyard tombstones are generally not comparable enough with riverside habitats to give more than the vaguest notion of age. This is because the optimal water supply within the spray zone will result in lichens growing much faster than those without this abundant water supply. For some river locations bridges, weirs and riverside buildings may provide datable surfaces. In any case the diameter of the largest lichens can be used in a comparative way within a habitat to say a certain surface is older or younger than another without being quantitative. Useful information can also be derived by mapping lichen communities and dividing them into pioneer and more advanced successional stages.

A variety of species has been employed for dating rock surfaces but the yellow-green *Rhizocarpon* species has been very widely used for surfaces up to 5000 years old. For younger surfaces the more rapidly growing species of the *Parmelia*, *Lecidea*, *Huilia* and *Lecanora* groups have also been used. It is simply necessary to measure the maximum diameter of sub-circular individuals. The single largest lichen within an area of consistent size (studies often use between 25 m$^2$ and 250 m$^2$ depending on lichen abundance) is usually assumed to reflect the optimal growth rate and to represent most closely the minimum age of the substrate.

Measurements of lichen size on substrates of different age enable the derivation of age-size relationships. Artificial surfaces such as tombstones, old walls or buildings have been used to provide a range of datable surfaces for lichen measurement. In low altitude temperate environments the datable time period is limited by competition both by other lichens and higher plants as plant succession takes place so that the pioneer species may be replaced by more advanced forms. The technique contains many potential problems most of which relate to the need for acceptance of certain primary assumptions, not least that the largest lichen within a predetermined area is the oldest and of the same age as the surface on which it grows. Nevertheless, lichenometry has been applied to the analysis of river channel cross-sections in two ways — to provide dates for rock surfaces along the sides of river channels, and to indicate the frequency of inundation of the cross-section to particular levels.

Measurements of lichen diameter, using the *Parmelia conspersa* group, along streams within the basin of Commissioner's Water, New South Wales, Australia, distinguished several limits of lichen size. A lower limit clearly defined the contact of lichen cover with a lichen-free bedrock surface and this was attributed to sediment abrasion which cleans the rock surface up to the lichen limit. At one site the lichen limit could be related to stage board heights and it was found that this limit was associated with the 1.14 year recurrence interval discharge using the annual series. Moreover, the limits were generally consistent along each river so that lichens may be used to trace discharge levels between cross-sections.

An indication of the effect of Avon reservoir, Dartmoor, upon a bed-rock channel has been gained by the examination of lichen limits. Bedrock lines the channel along a reach between 1.8 and 3.5 km below the dam and two lichen limits are discernible. The lower limit separates a bare rock surface from a lichen-covered surface, although the cover is far from complete, and the upper limit marks the change to a denser surface cover with larger individuals. Between the two limits the rock surfaces are dominated by two lichen species: *Huilia tuberculosa* and *Rhizocarpon obscuratum* but all the thalli have diameters of less than 40 mm. Above the higher limit fifteen different species were identified including *Trapelia involuta*, *Parmelia* spp., *Huilia* spp., *Fuscidea cyathoides* and *Lecanora polytropa* — all lichens commonly found on acid rocks such as the Dartmoor granite.

Several lines of evidence point to the conclusion that the higher lichen limit represents the pre-reservoir lichen-bare rock contact which has been subsequently lowered as a result of a reduction of flood magnitudes by the dam exposing a new surface for colonisation (the area between the two limits). Firstly, *Huilia tuberculosa* and *Rhizocarpon obscuratum* are often pioneer species and suggest that the surface on which they were found had been exposed within the last thirty years. Secondly, measurements of *H. tuberculosa* and *R. obscuratum* on weirs, bridges and riverside structures of known age suggest that the maximum lichen diameter of 38 mm represents an age of fifteen years for the exposure of the lower surface. The dam was completed 16 years prior to this survey.

Lichenometry was also applied to the dating of storm discharges producing major bed-load movement. Gregory examined a granite channel containing rapids produced by very large granite blocks. One such block with a maximum dimension of 5 m had well-developed pot-holes up to 0.14 m deep on its under-side indicating that the block had been overturned. Lichens on the present surface were found to have a maximum diameter of 48 mm. A growth curve was established from 300 measurements on dated tombstones, and the diameter of 48 mm suggested a date of 1959 for the beginning of lichen growth. The second highest discharge on record at the upstream gauging station occurred in 1959 and this discharge was two and a half times greater than any subsequent flow.

## 6.2.2 Tree ring dating (dendrochronology)

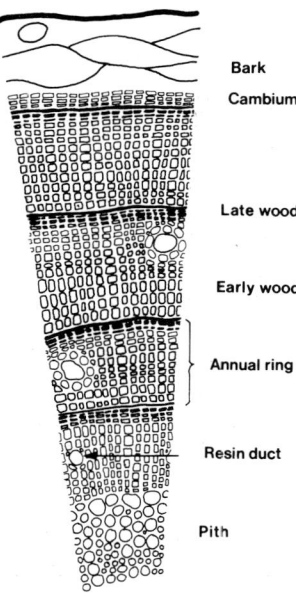

**Figure 6.6 Cross-section through a tree**

Dendrochronology uses annually produced rings, displayed in cross-section through trees, to date past events and to evaluate climatic history. The technique has been used for the dating of post-glacial landform changes to 7500 B. P. but is particularly useful for dating channel changes over the past 250 years. It is based upon the recognition, counting and correlation of annual growth rings exposed in transverse sections or in cores taken with a Swedish increment borer*. Stems of woody plants in cross-section are composed of an outer bark and an inner pith separated by layers of annual growth (*Figure 6.6*). Growth occurs by the division of the cambium cells and wood produced early in the growing season is characterised by large, thin walled cells whilst cells of later wood are small and thick walled. This different seasonal growth rate enables the recognition of distinct annual layers which appear as rings in cross-section and as layers in a core.

Variations in growth rate may cause problems of resolution. During periods of extremely slow growth rings of only a few cells thick may be added and resolution of individual rings will be poor. Also, extreme changes of the weather during a single year may interrupt the growth pattern to produce double or multiple rings. Growth rings may not be continuous nor concentric about the axis, nor uniform in width around the layer. Furthermore, the decay of the central old wood may require estimation of the "missing" time span as inferred from an average growth rate. In many floodplain areas the response of tree growth to short-term climatic fluctuations is relatively insensitive because of the availability of adequate moisture supplies. This is advantageous, however, for the dating of depositional landforms because the problem of false and missing rings is reduced.

* A Swedish increment borer is a standard item of forestry equipment for abstracting a core of about 4 mm diameter from a standard height above ground level (usually between 1.2 and 1.5 m). Note that the bore-hole should be plugged to prevent disease. Borers are supplied by Stobart & Son Ltd., 67-73 Worship Street, London EC2A 2EL.

Labels in Figure 6.6: Bark, Cambium, Late wood, Early wood, Annual ring, Resin duct, Pith

The establishment and maturation of trees on a new land surface (e.g. floodplain, point-bar or channel-side bench) is the result of an interrelated sequence in the timing of seed dissemination and germination, suitable soil and climatic conditions, and the flow regime of the river. The age of the oldest tree within a specified area or on a particular landform provides a minimum date for the establishment of the surface upon which it grows. Tree-ring counting provides a useful method of age determination for dating fluvial landforms and deposits and two examples will demonstrate the range of applications.

First, Everitt (1968) used cottonwood growth rings to map stages of channel change along the Little Missouri River, North Dakota. The height and diameter of the cotton-woods varied by as much as a factor of five but ages varied by no more than 10 percent in any one grove. The dates derived were portrayed as a contour map which described

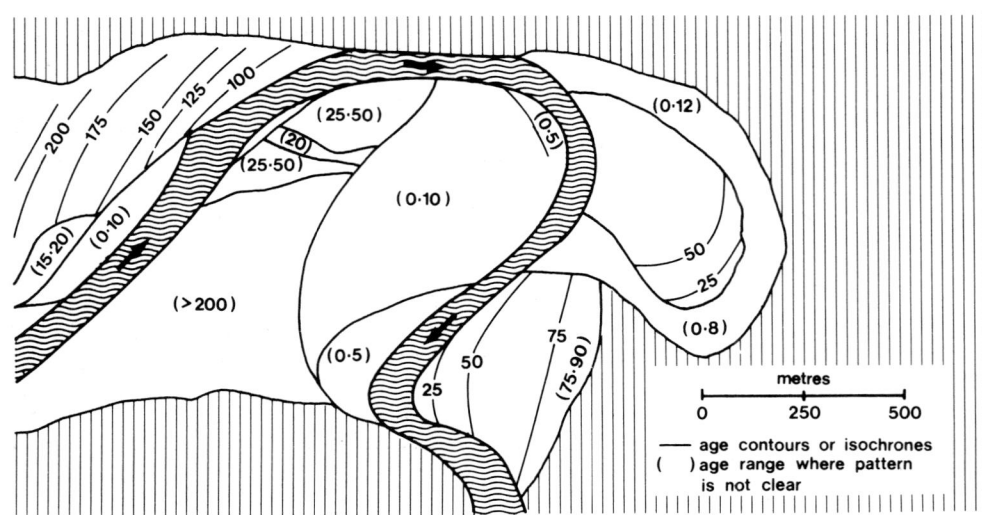

**Figure 6.7 Floodplain evolution along the Little Missouri River described by tree-ring dating. (From Everitt, 1968)**

the age of the floodplain forest (part is displayed in *Figure 6.7*) and this describes the recent history of channel migration and floodplain construction. The forest was found to be composed of a series of curved bands of trees. Cottonwood trees were found to be a pioneer coloniser of point bar and other deposits. They established on deposits 1.5 m above low water level but at intermediate elevations the saplings were severely damaged, uprooted or buried by floods. Each band began as a thicket of seedlings on a new deposit at the channel's edge and was then left stranded as part of the floodplain as the channel migrated.

Second, Graf (1979) used tree-ring dates from Ponderosa pines to date the development of a gully system in Colorado. An older gully system has been entrenched by a second gully system. No perceptible lithologic variation was found and the bench-like morphology of the gully is clearly of erosional origin with the shoulders cut into relatively uniform alluvium which forms the area's bedrock. The erosional history is described by the trees growing on the preserved gully forms. An increment borer was used to take a core from seventy-eight trees within the gully system and the oldest tree within each 15 m length of each gully was used to describe the age of surface exposure. As the first gully developed, newly exposed surfaces were colonised by Ponderosa pine, so that today younger trees are found in the headward parts of the gullies and in the gully bottom — the most recently exposed surfaces — and older trees are found on the upper slopes of the gullies towards the mouth of the system.

The tree-ring evidence indicated that the first gully system was initiated in 1826 and that by 1880 the headcut had eroded to 85% of its ultimate length. A Ponderosa pine over 40 years old growing 2 m downvalley from the headcut suggested that the first gully system has been stable since about 1927. Trees growing in the gully bottoms suggested that erosion began in about 1906. Both starting dates for erosion, 1826 and 1906, were found to coincide with the beginning of extended periods of more intense summer rainfall. Thus, short-term climatic fluctuations were concluded to have triggered gully erosion.

## 6.3 MAN'S IMPACT ON RIVERS

*"He (man) is not a figure in the landscape — he is a shaper of the landscape"*

*Bronowski, 1973, 19*

Throughout history man has directly altered the character of rivers and their drainage basins. River channels have been straightened and deepened to aid navigation and for flood control, and land-use changes involving agriculture, forestry, urbanisation and water supply development have markedly altered the pattern of water and sediment movement (*Figure 6.8*). The form of the river channel is adjusted to the fluvial processes so that the numerous changes that have taken place during settlement and allied land-use change, and industrialisation should be expected to have resulted in changes of land-form and these can be estimated from *Table 6.4*. Indeed, today a truly natural river is a rare phenomenon.

### 6.3.1 Process changes

Man's use of his environment may be considered under four headings — rural land-use change, urbanisation, water diversion and river impoundment. However, for many large rivers agriculture, forestry, housing and industrial development, water diversion and reservoirs, for example, may all alter the fluvial processes to produce complex changes of channel form.

The removal of a protective vegetation cover (deforestation, or turf destruction by ploughing, etc) is a particularly widespread impact which, in a variety of areas, has resulted in accelerated rates of soil erosion. Indeed, extensive soil erosion and gully development have been associated with forest clearance and cultivation during the period of land settlement and with subsequent overgrazing and heath burning. For example, the rise of the Yorkshire and Lancashire woollen industries during the late 18th Century was accompanied by increased sheep farming in the south Pennines, and extensive gully development has been attributed to overgrazing (Tallis, 1965). Forestry practices too, and especially logging and road construction, have increased sediment loads and peak streamflows. Restoration of the native vegetation cover, however, may be effective in the control and prevention of gully erosion and can reduce runoff rates.

In two American examples the reforestation of 58% of a drainage basin on the east coast was found to reduce winter and spring floods by up to 66% (Schneider, 1969),

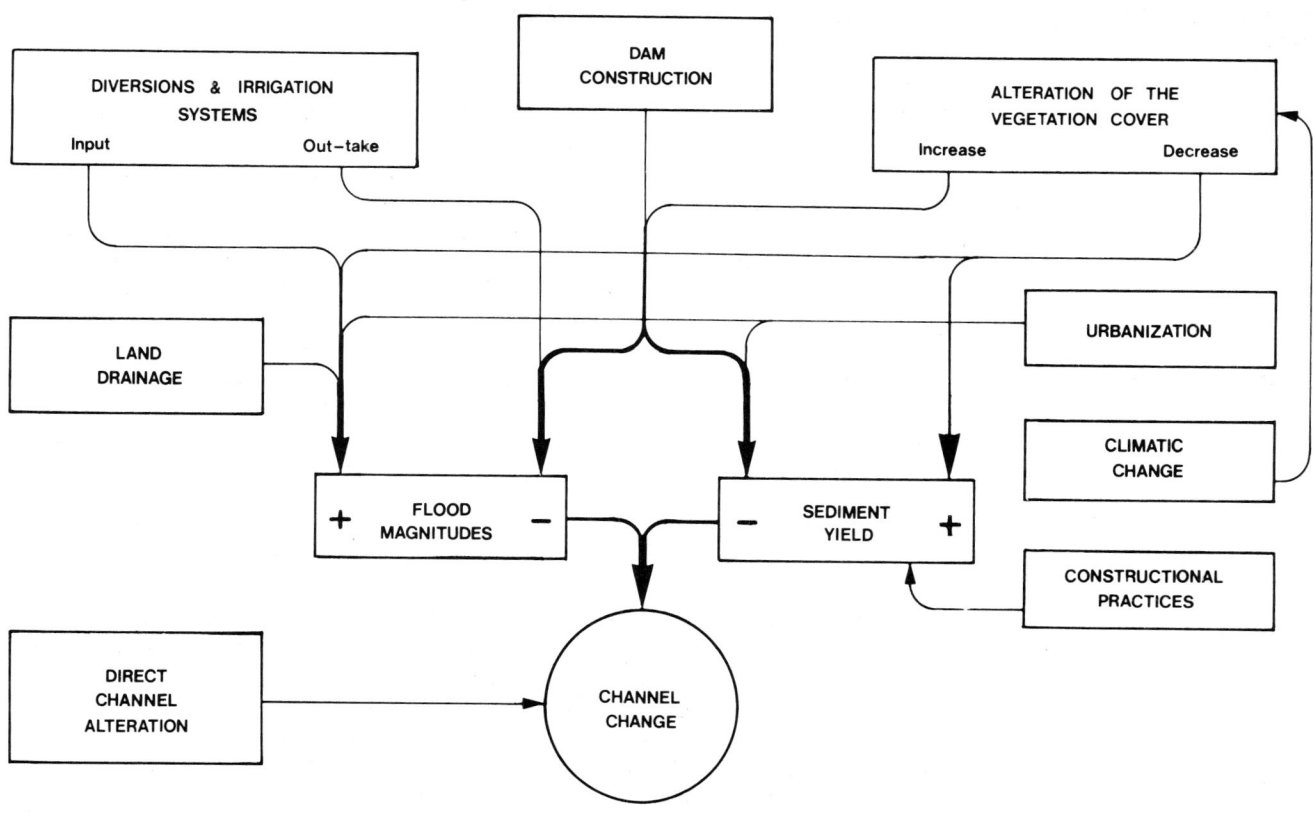

Figure 6.8 Man's impact upon fluvial
processes and channel form

while the planting of grasses, legumes and trees has significantly reduced rates of soil erosion from critical sediment-source areas (Gottschalk, 1962). Many land-use changes also involve land-drainage schemes which can reverse the beneficial effects of reforestation, for example. In Britain, one quarter of the agricultural land requires improved drainage for maximum output and upland areas often require drainage before afforestation can be undertaken. Land drainage effectively increases the length of the channel network and drainage densities are typically at least three times higher than natural channel densities. Such dramatic increases of the drainage network have resulted in a marked increase in the rate of runoff, and worsening flood problems have been attributed to the effects of land drainage.

Vegetation removal, soil disturbance and land drainage are also important during the construction phase of urban or industrial development. Such changes within the drainage basin can produce both high sediment loads and increased rates of runoff. However, once construction is complete the sediment supply to the river may be reduced by the cover of the soil surface and the channel boundaries with resistant materials. In contrast, runoff rates may be further increased. Since the turn of the century the most dramatic impact of man upon the environment has been the development of large urban areas. Indeed, major changes in runoff and sediment load have resulted from the conversion of rural land to an urban area. The construction of an impervious surface, for example of concrete, will reduce infiltration rates and the development of an extensive storm drainage network will increase storm runoff intensity. Lag times between rainfall and streamflow response will decrease and total flood volumes and flood peaks will increase. Commonly, flood peaks are between two and five times greater than under natural conditions. The precise effects, however, will depend upon the proportion of the area composed of impervious surfaces (roads, roofs, carparks, etc.) in relation to permeable surfaces (gardens, parks, etc.) and to the density of the storm sewer network.

Water is often abstracted directly from a river for domestic, industrial or agricultural supply and this results in the reduction of stream discharge without affecting the sediment load. Such changes may be expected to induce the deposition of sediment immediately downstream of the offtake. Indeed, the diversion of water for irrigation and supply has resulted in the reduction of channel width. In Britain, for example, Dury

(1973) reported the reduction of channel width on the River Ouse below mill-leat offtakes — an adjustment to the reduced discharges. The import of water into a river may be anticipated to initiate contrasting adjustments. The diversion of water into the River Tame has contributed to increased flood peaks such that a flow of 0.5 year return period is here increased by about 15% (Richards and Wood, 1976).

The construction of a reservoir within a river system is often undertaken in order to control streamflow and to manage the stream discharge for downstream abstraction. However, reservoirs are also built for flood control, water storage to supply urban areas by pipeline, and for hydro-electric power production. In any case, the dam will markedly alter the flow and sediment load characteristics of the river downstream. Virtually all the sediment transported by the headwater stream into the reservoir will be deposited and stored within the lake so that flows passing the dam will contain a negligible particulate sediment load.

Water retention behind a dam and its slow release downstream result in the reduction of both peak discharges and flow variability: the discharges are said to be regulated. Reservoirs are essentially designed for two purposes — water storage and flood control. The former requires that the reservoir is maintained at, or as near as possible to, maximum water storage capacity. Water supply reservoirs should be kept full to provide the greatest possible supply; they regulate the annual variation of streamflow so as to meet demand during dry periods. Temporary lake storage when the reservoir is full will reduce flood magnitudes downstream and this effect (known as reservoir attenuation) will be appreciable where the surface area of the lake is large — 2% or more of the drainage area. In contrast the basic concept of reservoir management for flood control is to maintain the reservoir empty so as to provide the maximum storage capacity for the absorption of flood discharges.

The impact of human activities upon the fluvial processes will not be constant: the variability relates to three characteristics.

1. **The effects of man's activities upon streamflows often have a seasonal character.**
This seasonality is related to the two distinct ways in which floods can be produced: during winter by long duration rainfalls, sometimes supplemented by snow melt, which produce saturated overland flow within the drainage basin; and short duration, high

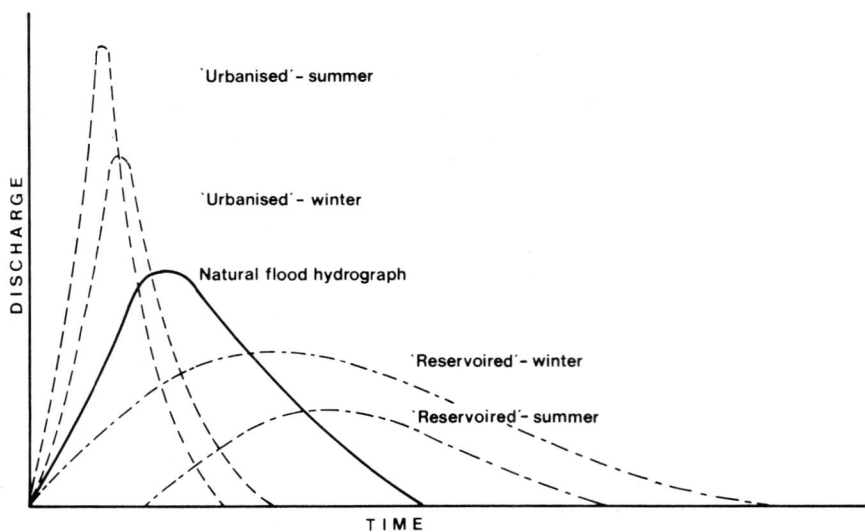

DISCHARGE

'Urbanised' – summer

'Urbanised' – winter

Natural flood hydrograph

'Reservoired' – winter

'Reservoired' – summer

TIME

Figure 6.9 Seasonal changes to flood
hydrographs within urbanized and
regulated rivers

intensity rainfalls in summer associated with thunderstorms. An impervious surface
for example may insignificantly alter rates of runoff during winter when the soil may be
at or near saturation but in summer the soil would be dry under natural conditions so
that urbanisation may markedly increase summer floods (*Figure 6.9*). Reservoirs too
will have a greater influence upon summer storm discharges because a greater storage
volume will normally be available during the 'dry season' for the absorption of streamflows.

2. **The effects are most marked for moderately frequent events and become less
apparent as the discharge decreases in frequency and increases in magnitude.** For
Charlotte, North Carolina, Martens (1968) predicted that urban development would
increase the mean annual flood by 58% whilst the twenty-year flood would increase by
only 17%. Similarly, below Stocks Reservoir in north-west England the mean annual

flood has been reduced by nearly 20% but the magnitude of the twenty-year flood is only about 5% less than experienced under natural conditions. Simply, the occurrence of extreme floods is controlled by factors which are unaffected by human impacts: extreme floods are commonly produced by both high intensity and long duration rains which negate the effects of urbanisation as rapid runoff would occur even under natural conditions, and river impoundment because reservoir storage may be insignificantly small in relation to the size of a large flood discharge.

3. **The effects of point impacts, such as dams or urban areas and land-use change confined to a particular area of the drainage basin, decrease downstream.** That is, the changes of discharge and sediment load become progressively less noticeable downstream as the contribution of water and sediment from unaffected parts of the basin increase in importance and eventually grow to mask any effects that the dam, for example, may have. In 1960 Ladybower Reservoir on the River Derwent, Derbyshire, reduced two floods by a total of 94.1 $m^3$ $s^{-1}$ immediately below the dam, a drainage area of 127 $km^2$, but at Matlock, 30 km downstream and with a drainage area of 700 $km^2$, the flow reduction was only 57.5 $m^3$ $s^{-1}$ (Nixon, 1963).

## 6.3.2 Evaluation of process changes

The effects of human activity upon channel processes can be examined by constructing hardware models to simulate the imposed conditions (*Plate 6.1*) but the application of such studies is limited because of the problems of scaling down the different morphological and process characteristics. The most likely changes that may result from a particular activity can be estimated, however, on the basis of past experience, that is, from observations made at locations changed or changing in response to a similar human interference. Three approaches are commonly used — continuous monitoring, paired basin studies and empirical modelling, and an historical approach. The ideal approach is to undertake a 'before, during and after' survey using the field measurement techniques described previously; that is, to establish the characteristics of streamflow and sediment loads under natural conditions and then to monitor the changes that occur during human disturbance. For example, Walling (1974) has documented the effects of building construction within a small, 0.26 $km^2$ drainage basin on the margins of Exeter, Devon. Between 1971 and 1973 constructional activity affected 25% of its area; the sod cover

Plate 6.1 A model of the Sacramento River. The model was constructed by the Department of Water Resources, University of California at Davis, to simulate channel processes at the proposed location for a flow diversion structure. The vertical and horizontal scales of the model are 1:50 and the length of river modelled is 3.4 km

was removed; and soil disturbance was associated with a network of roughly surfaced service roads, site preparation for houses, and the installation of sewer systems and road pavement drainage. A monitoring programme had been established five years prior to the constructional activity. The programme involved the collection of suspended sediment samples at ten minute intervals by using an automatic vacuum pump-sampler and continuous streamflow and rainfall recording. This enabled the comparison of suspended sediment loads produced by particular rainfall events before and during construction, and changes could be evaluated with respect to a control variable — rainfall — which had not changed. The data collected revealed that for individual storms suspended sediment loads generally increased between five and ten times and occasionally up to thirty times, when compared to the pre-construction period.

Before-and-after surveys are often prohibited by the lack of data describing the process characteristics under natural conditions. A commonly used alternative involves the comparison of field measurements of a river which is intuitively expected to have experienced streamflow or sediment load change with a 'natural' river assumed to represent the natural character of the river under investigation. For example, a 500 m long gully was observed within a small, 0.55 km² drainage basin, tributary to the River Burn, itself a tributary of the River Dart in Devon. Gullies are uncommon in Devon and its presence demanded explanation (Gregory and Park, 1976a). Cross-sections were surveyed at eight locations above the gully and across the gully itself to describe the changing character of the landform. The volume of the gully was then estimated by dividing it into eight sub-sections and the length of each sub-section was multiplied by the appropriate cross-sectional area. The volume derived, 1035 m³, contrasts with the estimate of channel volume of 195 m³ for an equivalent length and assuming a cross-sectional area equivalent to that of the channel above the gully head. This volumetric difference of 841 m³ represents a mass of 2 287.52 tonnes of soil.

Some indication of the processes taking place along the gully was obtained from measurements of bedload movement and by comparing the observed transport rates with three neighbouring tributaries. Slots were dug into the bed of the channels to a depth of 0.3 m and these were lined with concrete slabs. A box of marine ply was installed in each of the slots. Any bedload moved was trapped in the boxes; these were removed and weighed each week for twelve months. In the gully the bedload trap was inserted one-third of the distance along its length. During the measurement period the gullied tributary transported 0.631 tonnes in comparison to an average of 0.255 tonnes for the other tributaries. However, the drainage areas differ so that the data were expressed as a weight per unit area to facilitate comparison. This showed that bedload movement through the gully amounted to between two and fourteen times that moved through each of the three other channels. A transport rate of 0.631 $t$ yr$^{-1}$ would give the gully an age of over 500 years. However, it was estimated that only 5% of the sediment eroded from the gully

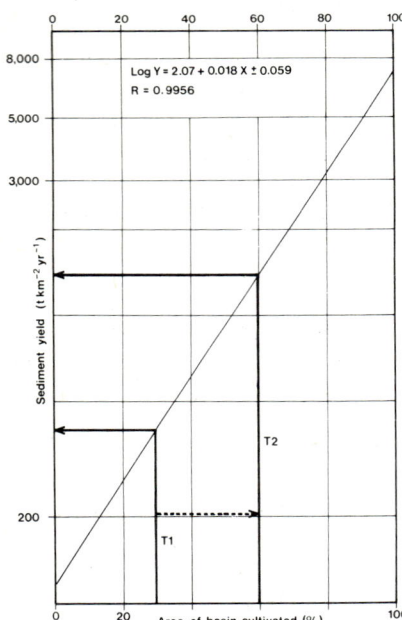

**Figure 6.10 Using empirical models to forecast process change. A regression relationship is established, here, between the area of basin cultivated and the annual sediment yield for a large number of 5 km² basins in the upper Mississippi area.**

would be transported as bedload, the remainder being moved in suspension; this would increase the total annual load to 12.620 $t$ $yr^{-1}$ so that the time taken to erode the gully would be about 29 years. A road drained by two ditches which feed into the stream was metalled 28 years previously and local residents recalled that the gully appeared only during the last 20—25 years. It was noted that the gully begins just above the point at which the uppermost drainage ditch reaches the stream. The road drainage system increases the drainage density by 1.66 $km^{-1}$ $km^2$ and the ditches collect runoff from the impervious road surface. Prior to road metalling most rain would have infiltrated into the soil but subsequently every storm would produce immediate runoff which is rapidly supplied through the ditch system to the main stream.

Comparative studies can be based also on the generation of empirical models. In section 4.1.3, solute loads were compared for streams draining basins of different land-use but otherwise similar character. A variation of this approach utilises a relationship between discharge or sediment load characteristics and a measure of basin character such as the proportion composed of a particular land-use, the area urbanised or the area draining into a reservoir. Thus, Meade (1969) derived an empirical model for the relationship between the percentage of cleared land within a basin and the annual sediment yield for a sample of rivers within the mid-Atlantic states, USA. By introducing into the model the proportion of cleared land for a basin in the same area whose sediment yield is unknown the annual yield of sediment can be estimated or predicted in cases of proposed land clearance. Meade demonstrated that the conversion of forests to croplands could increase sediment yields in the area studied by at least a factor of ten. The approach is illustrated in ***Figure 6.10*** and receives further discussion in section 6.3.3. From the models, at time one (T1) thirty per cent of another 5 km² basin is cultivated and the annual sediment yield of the river is 400 $t$ $km^{-2}$ $yr^{-1}$. If the cultivated area was doubled (T2) the model predicts that sediment yield would increase by more than three times to 1400 $t$ $km^{-2}$ $yr^{-1}$.

A second alternative, the historical approach, can provide valuable information about the pattern of land-use change within the drainage basin and the associated process changes during historic time. Lakes, natural and man-made, act as sediment traps for the material transported by the inflowing streams. The rate of sediment accumulation provides a

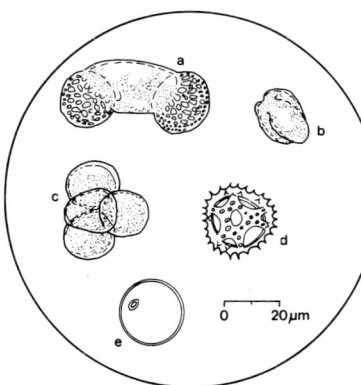

Some Characteristic Pollen Grains

a Pine (Pinus)
b Oak (Quercus)
c Heather (Calluna)
d Dandelion (Liguliflorae)
e Grass (Gramineae)

**Figure 6.11 Example of some pollen grains**

record of the erosion rates within the drainage basin, so that the examination of sediment sequences supported by dating techniques may be used to identify phases of land-use change. The deposits include not only inorganic sediments but also organic materials, such as the remains of aquatic insects and pollen, which provide a record of environmental characteristics at the time of deposition. Pollen grains in particular are relatively easy to classify according to the parent species (*Figure 6.11*). Palaeoecological techniques may therefore be usefully employed to reconstruct the environments of the time-periods identified. The study of lake sediments has grown into a broad area of study in its own right and discussion here will be confined to one example which demonstrates the potential use of such studies. Davis (1976) has used an historical approach to evaluate the effects of land-use change from forest in primaeval time to farmland during the past 146 years. Rates of sediment accumulation were examined in the small Frains Lake, Michigan, USA, having a drainage area of 0.18 km$^2$ and a relief of only 13 m. Short sediment cores were were collected by carefully pushing a simple corer into the sediment. The corer was a plastic tube with a check valve at the top end.

More sophisticated corers were used for deeper penetration. The cores were frozen while still in the upright position in order to prevent sediment mixing, and the core was pushed from the tube and chopped into 20 mm segments for subsequent analysis. Cores were collected along east-west and north-south transects across the basin as the pattern of sediment distribution is often uneven. One core in the centre of the lake contained 8 m of organic sediment overlying boulder-clay. Dates were obtained for two cores using the radiocarbon technique and these showed the cores to be composed of three parts. Erosion rates were calculated by dividing the total volume of sediment accumulated during a time period by the interval, and adjusted to a drainage basin of one square kilometre. The deeper part was related to an erosion rate of 9 $t$ km$^2$ yr$^{-1}$, the intermediate layer was associated with basin erosion rates some 30 to 80 times higher, and the surface layer was produced by erosion rates ten times higher than found in the deeper part.

The sudden change in erosion rates within the basin appeared to be coincident with the period of land settlement in the early nineteenth century. Within Frains Lake distinctive pollen-assemblages could be identified and pollen analyses, using the core segments, revealed a major change of the basin vegetation about 150 years ago (*Figure 6.12*). Tree

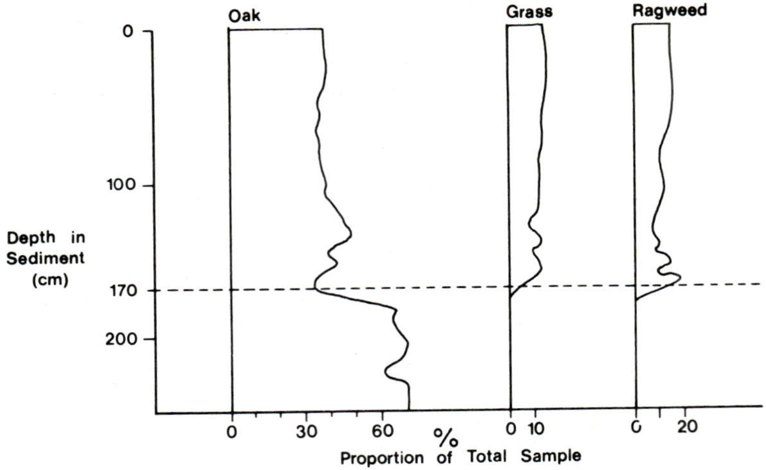

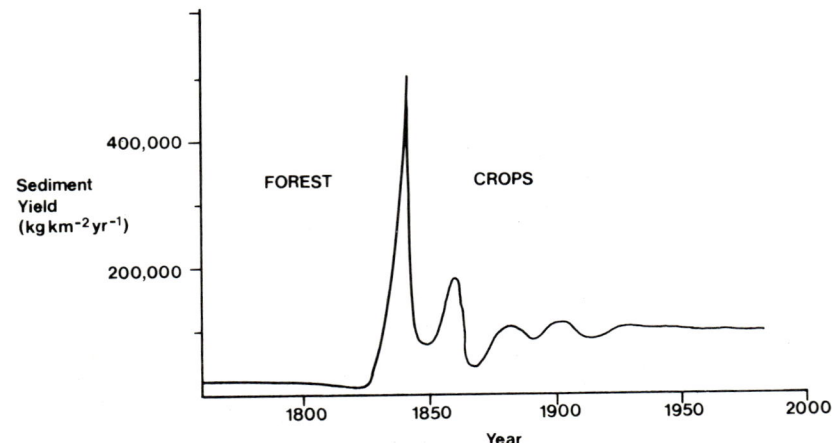

Figure 6.12 Typical pollen profiles: deposits from Frains Lake. (From Davis, 1976)

Figure 6.13 Land-use and sediment yield changes within Frains Lake catchment as interpreted from pollen and sediment-size data. (From Davis, 1976)

pollen, predominantly oak, accounted for 95% of the assemblage and the basin was clearly forested until about 1800. Tree pollen then declined sharply while pollen from agricultural weeds increased rapidly to dominate the assemblage. This evidence strongly supported the conclusion that accelerated erosion rates within the basin and the resulting accelerated rates of sedimentation were caused by deforestation, settlement and cropping during the early 1800s (*Figure 6.13*).

### 6.3.3 Evaluation of channel change

Under natural conditions it has been seen that channel form exhibits a longitudinal pattern in which the channel form parameters vary progressively downstream. Using regression analysis with logarithmically transformed data, simple linear relationships have been shown to exist between the channel cross-sectional dimensions and discharge or, in the absence of suitable flow data, a surrogate variable such as drainage area or total stream length. River channels are adjusted to the characteristics of water discharge and sediment loads provided by the drainage basin. Locally, channel forms may be modified by channel slope, bed-material composition, bank-material cohesion and vegetation character. Nevertheless, a regression 'model' (*see* section 2.5.4) can be used to describe the downstream variation of channel form parameters (width, mean depth, etc).

The development of such simple models for rivers draining basins of comparable climate, geology, relief and land-use reveals the existence of similar relationships between channel form parameters and the control variables of discharge, drainage area or total stream length. Therefore, the models may be used to contrast rivers draining basins of comparable climate, geology and relief but different land-use, that is, to identify the effect of human activity upon the longitudinal pattern of channel forms. The application of this *paired basin* approach is dependent upon establishing general similarity between basins in terms of their discharge, sediment load and channel form characteristics under natural conditions so that the observed differences can be genuinely ascribed to the effects of human activity.

In detail, the establishment of similarity is impossible for practical purposes so that a paired basin approach must be used with caution. Nevertheless, meaningful differences can be identified if the rivers and their basins are examined carefully for geomorphological and hydrological similarity, because the man-induced changes are often of a higher magnitude than the differences produced by local environmental conditions.

For small or geomorphologically homogeneous basins within which a significant length of the mainstream (at least 5 km) is available above an area of human activity (e.g. an urban area or reservoir) a *single basin approach* may be employed. A regression relationship is established between channel form parameters and discharge or a surrogate variable using field measurements of the channel upstream of man's influence. This linear relationship is then extended to provide an estimate of the 'natural' channel dimensions expected at downstream locations for comparison with field measurements of channel form.

The use of a simple regression model to provide estimates of channel form dimensions for downstream locations assumes, of course, that a linear relationship with discharge or drainage area would exist under natural conditions throughout the entire length of river under consideration. Within basins underlain by contrasting rock types, for example, the assumed linear relationship may be invalid. Statistically, it is unsound to extend a regression relationship beyond the range of the data from which it has been derived but geomorphologically the use of a regression model may be justified if the basin is examined carefully to ensure homogeneity downstream. For large basins of complex geology, or for surveys where a relatively long distance separates the upstream 'control' relationship from the channel section being examined for evidence of change, a paired basin approach should be used if a neighbouring basin of suitable character and size is available.

Regression analysis based upon quantitative data and field observations provides a useful technique for identifying channels which have experienced change in response to human activity. Differences between the estimated channel dimensions and field measurements — that is the identification of anomalies or discontinuities in the expected downstream variation of channel form — provide an indication of the nature, magnitude and direction of channel change.

The significance of the deviation of actual channel form measurements from the estimated values may be detected by reference to the confidence limits of the regression line. These define the probability of any measured channel dimension deviating from the estimated value within the 'natural river'.

More commonly, the actual channel dimension ($A$) is related to the expected dimension derived from the regression equation ($E$) as the channel-change ratio ($CR$) where

$$CR = A \div E$$

For most control relationships the majority of $CR$ values lie within the range 0.80 to 1.20 so that greater deviations by the sample data may reflect channel change. The interpretation of a variable pattern of channel form downstream may be aided by the division of the channel into a series of reaches each having a greater internal uniformity of character than that between neighbouring reaches. That is, **channel compartments** may be defined within which the variation of channel form is small in relation to the variation between compartments.

Major changes of discharge occur at tributary confluences so that the variation of channel form within the compartment above the confluence will be less than the difference between the upstream and downstream compartments. Channel compartments can be isolated on the basis of known control factors: tributary confluences, channel slope, bank sediment type, differences of bank vegetation, etc. For example, the planform of one compartment may be stabilised by trees lining the channel whereas downstream the channel may be able to migrate freely across the floodplain so that here a second compartment could be identified. Each compartment would receive the same discharges and sediment loads but different planforms are associated with different channel bank materials. This approach may be used to develop an appreciation of process-form associations by recognising that particular channel shapes or patterns, or locations of relatively rapid channel change, occur in compartments of particular character.

The establishment of a significantly different channel form does not, however, prove that the human activity being investigated caused the channel change. Unexpected channel forms immediately below a dam, for example, may have been produced before the dam was built. Therefore, an attempt should be made to determine the age of the channel forms. Archaeological materials, such as pottery and even car number plates and beer cans, found in river sediments, have been used to date deposits. Grossly erroneous dates may be derived, however, because the deposits may have been produced from the eroded sediments of an older deposit (i.e. the archaeological material may be inherited and considerably older than the deposit in which it has been found). Historical records such as documents, photographs, plans and maps (**see** section 2.3) are becoming increasingly important as records improve and become more complete, and other dating techniques (section 6.2) may have general application.

### 6.3.4 Channel change resulting from urbanisation (After Gregory and Park, 1976 b)

Urban development includes a wide range of activities including road construction, drainage, building construction and the creation of large impervious surfaces for carparks. Urbanisation commonly modifies the streamflow characteristics by increasing the frequency of high flows and one expected consequence of such changes in discharge (*Table 6.4 A or F*) is the enlargement of channel dimensions.

In order to ascertain whether urbanisation has a detectable influence upon channel capacity, four basins were selected to embrace locations above, within and below the urban area of Catterick Garrison in north-west Yorkshire. Measurements of channel form were made at thirty sites on rural channels unaffected by Catterick Garrison, six sites were located on channels below the urban area and a further twelve sites were derived from streams within the urban area itself. The rural sites were selected to provide a representative sample of channel locations with drainage areas ranging from 0.04 to 4.5 km². For the purpose of analysis the measurements of channel form must be related to some measure of spatial location and as suitable discharge records were not available drainage area was again adopted. The regression relationship of drainage area and channel capacity for the rural streams allowed a comparison to be made between the rural channels and those which receive runoff from the urban area.

The channels within and below the urban area are usually larger and up to twice the size of the rural channels (*Figure 6.14*). In two cases the urban channels are smaller than the estimate derived from the regression equation and these sites are associated with local channel modification and the presence of flood-control structures. For all sites affected by urban runoff the ratio of actual to predicted channel capacity averages 1.95; major differences were observed between the within-urban and below-urban sites. Within the urban area the ratio averages 1.66. This contrasts with the five sites immediately below Catterick Garrison which have an average ratio of 2.62 and the measured channel capacities were found to be between twice and four times the expected values. At these downstream sites the channel form has adjusted to the total effects of the urban runoff from the paved and sewered area of Catterick Garrison.

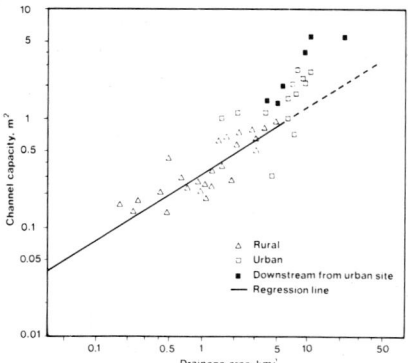

**Figure 6.14 Channel-capacity variation above, within and below Catterick Garrison. (From Gregory, 1976c)**

## 6.3.5 Channel changes below a reservoir

Reservoirs have two effects upon channel processes: the sediment loads of inflowing streams will be trapped behind the dam so that headwater sediment sources will be isolated from the river downstream; and flood magnitudes will be reduced by storage within the reservoir. Clear-water discharges from a dam may produce channel-bed erosion (*Table 6.4D and H*) but some impounded rivers are lined by gravels which, in the absence of high floods, provide a non-transportable 'armour' layer preventing erosion.

Also, if the natural bed-load is low the effect of reservoirs on bed-load supply will be negligible. Under such conditions, it is to be expected (*Table 6.4B*) that the channel dimensions will become smaller as the channel form adjusts to discharges of lower magnitude.

The South Teign River was impounded in 1942 with the completion of Fernworthy Reservoir. Thirty sites were surveyed within the 3.5 km long channel between Fernworthy Reservoir and the confluence with the North Teign River. Upstream of the reservoir the streams are small, having drainage areas of less than 2.5 km$^2$, whereas the first site below the dam has a drainage area of 9.95 km$^2$. Data were also collected, therefore, from adjacent streams. Seventeen sites were measured on the neighbouring North Teign and Bovey rivers to extend the data over the range of drainage areas for the measurements on the South Teign below the dam. The data are shown in *Figure 6.15* and the solid line represents the regression line relating channel capacity to drainage area for natural channels. The capacity of the channel below Fernworthy Reservoir is generally much smaller than that expected from the natural channel data although at locations the channel capacity is closely comparable to the expected values, that is, not all channel locations have as yet responded to the effects of flow regulation and sediment load abstraction by the reservoir. Nevertheless, channel capacities at 70% of the locations surveyed deviated from the estimated values by more than 30%.

The 3.5 km length of channel between Fernworthy Reservoir and the confluence with the North Teign River is not uniform in character but is affected by an important tributary joining 0.4 km below the dam and two significant changes of channel slope; three compartments were therefore delimited (*Table 6.5*). Within the first compartment,

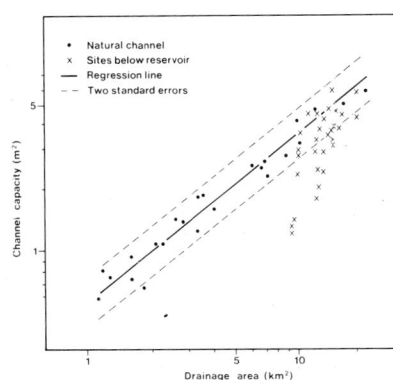

**Figure 6.15 Channel-capacity variation within the upper Teign river, Dartmoor**

## TABLE 6.5 CHANNEL COMPARTMENTS AND TREE-RING COUNTS, SOUTH TEIGN RIVER

| Compartment | | Distance below dam (km) | Channel slope ( m km$^{-1}$ ) | Channel type | Channel-change ratio | Age of trees (years) | | Latest formation date | |
|---|---|---|---|---|---|---|---|---|---|
| | | | | | | Lower surface | Upper surface | Lower surface | Upper surface |
| 1 | 1A | 0.0—0.2 | 33.83 | Stable | 0.35 | 16—22 | 24—49 | 1955 | 1928 |
| | 1B | 0.2—0.4 | | | 0.83 | | | | |
| | | TRIBUTARY | | | | | | | |
| 2 | 2A | 0.4—0.8 | 16.92 | Meandering | 0.48 | 15—28+ | 33—80+ | 1949 | 1897 |
| | 2B | | | Stable | 0.82 | | | | |
| 3 | | 0.8—4.1 | 30.08 | Stable | 0.84 | — | — | — | — |

immediately below the dam, a marked bench borders the river channel which has a capacity of only one-third of the expected value. The bed-material is composed of coarse cobbles and occasional small boulders forming an armoured layer which protects the channel bed from erosion by the sediment-free discharges. Downstream the channel capacity rapidly approaches the estimated value and the channel change ratio reaches 0.99. Throughout the middle compartment individual locations contain evidence of active channel migration, albeit on a small scale. Surveyed cross-sections differed markedly in their dimensions and two groups of cross-section were identified. The first group were all associated with sites of channel migration (i.e. active erosion and deposition) and channel capacities were consistently reduced to less than 70% of the estimated values. However, at stable sites, usually having well wooded banks, the channel dimensions were generally comparable to the values expected from the data obtained from neighbouring streams.

Channel changes within the third compartment are less apparent although the majority of the sample sections had channel capacities smaller than the best estimate provided by the regression equation. The channel here is commonly lined by trees which stabilise the bank materials and the bed is often composed of coarse gravel and boulders. Such stable channel forms which lack an input of sediment for the creation of channel side benches will respond only slowly to changes of process.

The channel of the South Teign River below Fernworthy Reservoir has a compound cross-section with a discontinuous bench inside the larger channel form which is defined by a sharp contact with the adjacent valley floor. Datable material along the river is sparse but tree-ring counting using cores taken with a Swedish increment borer provides a minimum age for the different surfaces identified. Twenty-eight cores were examined, and trees growing on the inner bench were consistently younger than neighbouring trees on the valley floor. The ages obtained suggest that the lower surface (the channel side bench) defines the limit of the contemporary channel so that the higher surface, possible a former floodplain, is now a terrace above the level of regular inundation. For both compartments the inner bench, and the contemporary channel to which it relates, are younger than the reservoir: the dam was completed in 1942.

# REFERENCES

Beschel, R.E. (1973) 'Lichens as a measure of the age of recent moraines', *Arctic and Alpine Research* 5,4,303–309.

Bleasdale, A. and Douglas, C.K.M. (1952) 'Storm over Exmoor on August 15, 1952', *Meteorological Magazine* 18,353–67.

Briggs, D. (1977) *Sediments*, London, Butterworths.

Bronowski, J. (1973) *The ascent of man*, B.B.C.

Browne, T.J. and Foster I.D.L. (1978) 'The measurement of low streamflow by dilution gauging', *Revue de Geomorphologie Dynamique* 17,21–28.

Chorley, R.J. (1962) 'Geomorphology and general systems theory', *United States Geological Survey, Professional Paper* 500–3.

Costa, J.E. (1974) 'Stratigraphic, morphologic and pedologic evidence of large floods in humid environments', *Geology* 2,6.

Daniel, J.F. (1971) 'Channel movement of meandering Indiana streams', *United States Geological Survey, Professional Paper* 732–A.

Davis, M.B. (1976) 'Erosion rates and land-use history in southern Michigan', *Environmental Conservation*, 3,2, 139–147.

Department of the Environment (1972) *Analysis of raw, potable and wastewaters*, H.M.S.O.

Dunne, T. and Leopold, L.B. (1978) *Water in Environmental Planning*, San Francisco, Freeman.

Dury, G.H. (1973) 'Magnitude and frequency analysis and channel morphometry' in *Fluvial Geomorphology* (Morisawa, H.E. (ed.)) State University of New York 91–121.

Everitt, B.L. (1968) 'Use of the cottonwood in an investigation of the recent history of a floodplain', *American Journal of Science* 266,417–439.

Finlayson, B. and Statham, I. (1980) *Hillslope Analysis*, London, Butterworths.

Folk, R.L. and Ward, W.C. (1957) 'Brazos River Bar: a study in the significance of grain-size parameters', *Journal of Sedimentary Petrology* 27,1,3–26.

Foster, I.D.L. (1979) 'Intra-catchment variability in solute response: an east Devon example', *Earth Surface Processes* 4,381–394.

Gibbs, R. (1970) 'Mechanisms controlling world water chemistry', *Science* 170,1088–90.

Gottschalk, L.C. (1962) 'Effects of watershed protection measures on reduction of erosion and sediment damage in the United States', *International Association of Scientific Hydrology Publication* 59, 426–47.

Graf, W.L. (1979) 'The development of Montaine Arroys and Gullies', *Earth Surface Processes*, 4,1–14.

Gregory, K.J. (1966) 'Dry valleys and the composition of the drainage net', *Journal of Hydrology* 4,327–40.

Gregory, K.J. (1976a) 'Changing drainage basins', *Geographical Journal* 142,237–247.

Gregory, K.J. (1976b) 'Drainage networks and climate, in *Geomorphology and Climate* (Derbyshire, E. (ed.)) Wiley 287–315.

Gregory, K.J. (1976c) 'Lichens and the determination of river channel capacity', *Earth Surface Processes*, 1,273–285.

Gregory, K.J. (1977) *Channel Changes*, Chichester, Wiley.

Gregory, K.J. (1978) 'A physical geography equation', *National Geographer* 12,13–141.

Gregory, K.J. and Gardiner, V. (1975) 'Drainage density and climate', *Zeitschrift fur geomorphologie* 19,3,287–298.

Gregory, K.J. and Park, C.C. (1976) 'The development of a Devon gully and man', *Geography* 16,2,77–82.

Gregory, K.J. and Park C.C. (1976) 'Stream channel morphology in northwest Yorkshire', *Revue de Geomorphologie Dynamique* 15,2,63–72.

Gregory, K.J. and Walling, D.E. (1971) Field measurements in the drainage basin, *Geography* 56,277–92.

Harvey, A.M. (1974) 'Gully erosion and sediment yield in the Howgill Fells, Westmorland', in *Institute of British Geographers Special Publication* 6 (Gregory, K.J. and Walling, D.E. (eds.)) 45–58.

Hellawell, J.M. (1978) *A biological surveillance of rivers: a biological monitoring handbook*, Natural Environment Research Council.

Hewlett, J.D. and Hibbert, A.R. (1967) 'Factors affecting the response of small watersheds to precipitation in humid areas', in *International Symposium on Forest Hydrology* (Sopper, W.E. and Lull, H.W. (eds.)) 275–90.

Hitchcock, D. (1977) 'Channel pattern changes in divided reaches: an example in the coarse bed-material of the Forest of Bowland', in *River Channel Changes* (K.J. Gregory (ed.)) Wiley 207–220.

Holeman, J.N. (1968) 'The sediment yield of major rivers of the world', *Water Resources Research*, 4,737–747.

Hooke, J.M. (1977) 'The distribution and nature of changes in river channel patterns: the example of Devon', in *River Channel Changes* (K.J. Gregory (ed.)) Wiley 265–280.

Hooke, J.M. (1980) 'Magnitude and distribution of rates of river bank erosion', *Earth Surface Processes* 5,143–157.

Hooke, J.M. and Perry, R.A. (1976) 'The planimetric accuracy of tithe maps', *Cartographic Journal*, Dec. 177–183.

Horten, R.E. (1945) Erosional development of streams and their drainage basins: hydrophysical approach to quantitative morphology', *Geological Society of America Bulletin* 56,275–370.

Kidson, C. (1953) 'The Exmoor storm and the Lynmouth floods', *Geography* 38,1–9.

Kirkby, M.J. and Chorley, R.J. (1967) 'Throughflow, overland flow, and erosion', *Bulletin of the International Association of Scientific Hydrology* 12,3,5–21.

Langbein, W.B. and Schumm, S.A. (1958) 'Yield of sediment in relation to mean annual precipitation', *Transactions of the American Geophysical Union*, 39,1076–1084.

Leopold, L.B. and Maddock, T. (1953) 'The hydraulic geometry of stream channels and some physiographic implications', *United States Geological Survey, Professional Paper* 252.

Leopold, L.B. and Wolman, M.G. (1957) 'River Channel Patterns', *United States Geological Survey, Professional Paper* 282—B.

MacCurdy, E. (1938) *The Notebooks of Leonardo da Vinci*, 2 vols. London, Reprint Society.

Makkaveyev, N.I. (1970) 'The impact of large water engineering projects on geomorphic processes in stream valleys', *Geomorfologiya* 2,28—34.

Martens, L.A. (1968) 'Flood inundation and effects of urbanisation in Metropolitan Charlotte, N. Carolina', *United States Geological Survey, Water Supply Paper* 159C, (60pp).

Meade, R.H. (1969) 'Errors in using modern stream—load data to estimate natural rates of denudation', *Geological Society of America Bulletin* 80,1265—74.

Murdoch, J. and Barnes, J.A. (1974) *Statistical Tables for Science, Engineering, Management and Business Studies*, 2nd revised edition, London, Macmillan.

Newson, M.D. (1971) 'A model of subterranean limestone erosion in the British Isles based on hydrology', *Transactions of the Institute of British Geographers* 54,55—70.

Nixon, M. (1963) 'Flood regulation and river training in England and Wales', in *Conservation of Water Resources*, Institute of Civil Engineering, London 137—50.

Park, C.C. (1977) World-wide variations of hydraulic-geometry, *Journal of Hydrology*, 23,133—146.

Penning-Rowsell, E.C. and Townshend, J.R.G. (1978) 'The influence of scale on the factors affecting stream channel slope', *Transaction of the Institute of British Geographers* 3,4,395—415.

Powers, M. (1953) 'A new random scale for sedimentary particles', *Journal of Sedimentary Petrology* 25,117—119.

Pugh, J.C. (1975) *Surveying for field scientists*, Metheun, London.

Richards, K.S. and Wood, R. (1976) 'Urbanization, water redistribution, and their effect on channel processes', in *River Channel Changes* (K.J. Gregory (ed.)) Wiley 369—388.

Ruhe, R.V. (1975) *Geomorphology*, Houghton Mifflin Co.

Schneider, W.J. (1969) 'Reforestation effects on winter and spring flood peaks in central New York State', pp. 780—787 in *Floods and their computation*, 2. Publication No; 85 AIHS, IASH, Gentbrugge, Belgium.

Schumm, S.A. (1968) 'River adjustment to altered hydrologic regimen — Murrumbidgee River and palaeochannels, Australia', *United States Geological Survey, Professional Paper 598* (65pp).

Schumm, S.A. (1969) 'River Metamorphosis', Proceedings of the American *Society of Civil Engineers, Journal of the Hydraulic Division* HY1,6352,255—73.

Sherman, L.K. (1932) 'Stream flow from rainfall by the unit-graph method', *Engineering News Record* 108,501—5.

Strahler, A.N. (1952) 'Dynamic basis of geomorphology', *Geological Society of America Bulletin* 63,923—38.

Sundberg, A. (1967) 'Some aspects on fluvial sediments and fluvial morphology', *Geografiska Annaler* 49A,333—43.

Tallis, J.H. (1965) 'Studies on Southern Pennine Peats of IV: evidence of recent erosion', *Journal of Ecology* 53,509—520.

Tanner, W.F. (1968) 'Rivers — meandering and braiding', in *Encyclopaedia of Geomorphology*, New York, Reinhold Book Corporation.

Trudgill, S.T. (1983) *Weathering and Erosion*, London, Butterworths.

Twain, M. (1904) *Life on the Mississippi*, London, Chatto and Windus.

Walling, D.E. (1971) 'Sediment dynamics of small instrumented catchments in south-east Devon', *Transactions of the Devonshire Association* 103,147—65.

Walling, D.E. (1974) 'Suspended sediment and solute yields from a small catchment prior to urbanisation', in *Fluvial processes in instrumented watersheds*, Institute of British Geographers Special Publication 6,169—192.

Walling, D.E. and Webb, B.N. (1975) 'Spatial variation of river water quality: a survey of the River Exe', *Transactions of the Institute of British Geographers* 65,155—169.

Water Resources Board (1974) *Surface Water Year Book of Great Britain 1966—1970*, H.M.S.O.

Wentworth, C.K. (1922) 'A scale of grade and class terms for clastic sediments', *Journal of Geology* 30,377—392.

## ADDITIONAL REFERENCES

Chorley, R.J. (ed.) (1969) *Water, earth and man*, London, Methuen.

Davidson, D.A. (1978) *Science for physical geographers*, London, Edward Arnold.

Golterman, H.L., Clymo, R.S. and Ohnstad, M.A.M. (1978) *Methods for physical and chemical analyses of fresh waters* (2nd edition), Oxford, Blackwell Scientific.

Goudie, A. (ed.) (1981) *Geomorphological techniques*, London, Allen and Unwin.

Goudie, A. (1981) *The human impact*, Oxford, Basil Blackwell.

Gregory, K.J. and Walling, D.E. (1973) *Drainage basin form and process*, London, Edward Arnold.

Hooke, J.M. and Kain, R. (1982) *Historical change in the physical environment*, London, Butterworths.

King, A.M. (1966) *Techniques in geomorphology*, London, Edward Arnold.

Lewin, J. (ed.) (1981) *British rivers*, London, Allen and Unwin.

Till, R. (1974) *Statistical methods for the earth scientist*, London, Macmillan.

Townsend, C.R. (1980) *The ecology of streams and rivers*, London, Edward Arnold.

# GLOSSARY

**Aggradation**   The progressive accumulation of sediment.

**Alluvium**   Fine sediment deposited by rivers.

**Aquifer**   A body of rock capable of storing and transmitting water.

**Bar**   An accumulation of sand or gravel in a stream.

**Baseflow**   Streamflow sustained during periods of no rainfall by the slow release of water from storage within the soils and rocks of the drainage basin.

**Base level**   The limiting level of effective stream erosion.

**Bedding**   Layers of sediment composed of particles having a range of sizes and/or an arrangement which is distinguishable from layers above and below.

**Bedload**   Sediment carried along the river bed.

**Benthic**   Living in and on the sediments of the channel bed.

**Berm**   An accumulation of sand or gravel which forms a linear deposit along a river bank and having a level surface.

**Biological indicators**   Species of animal or plant which have well-defined living conditions.

**Braided river**   A river which is divided into several interlinked channels.

**Capacity**   The maximum amount of sediment of a given size that a river can carry.

**Channel compartment**   A length of channel within which the morphological characteristics show less variation than between it and adjacent compartments.

**Competence**   The ability of a stream to transport sediment.

**Correlation**   The average relationship or interdependence between two variables.

**Degradation**   The progressive erosion of a river channel.

**Dendrochronology**   The study of tree growth-rings applied to dating past events and evaluating climatic history.

**Denudation**   The lowering of the land surface by all processes involved in the weathering and transport of rock materials.

**Discharge**   The volume of water flowing past a fixed point in a river during a specific period of time.

**Drainage basin**   The geographical region drained by a river.

| | | | |
|---|---|---|---|
| **Drainage density** | The length of stream channel per unit area. | **Laminae** | Thin layers of fine sediment. |
| **Equilibrium** | A balance between form and process. | **Lichenometry** | The study of lichen growth applied to the dating of rock surfaces. |
| **Eutrophication** | The process of nutrient enrichment of water bodies. | **Lotic** | Of, or belonging to, running water. |
| **Floodplain** | An accumulation of river-transported sediment produced by the lateral migration of channels and forming a level surface adjacent to the river which is flooded periodically. | **Meandering river** | A river channel with a winding or sinuous course. |
| | | **Morphology** | The form of surface features. |
| | | **Phylum** | A biological term describing a division of fauna or flora which consists of species having the same general form. |
| **Fluvial** | Of, or belonging to, rivers. | | |
| **Gauging** | The measurement of streamflow. | **Phi** | A logarithmic transformation of particle-size. |
| **Hydrograph** | A graph of discharge against time. | | |
| **Hydrological cycle** | The movement and exchange of water between the atmosphere, oceans and the land. | **Point-bar** | An accumulation of sediment on the inside of a meander bend. |
| | | **Pool-and-riffle** | Sequence of deeps and shallows occuring at regular intervals along the channel bed. |
| **Hysteresis** | A relationship between two variables which has the form of a loop rather than a straight line. | **Porosity** | The volume of open space in a soil or rock. |
| **Imbrication** | The stacking of plate-like particles, one leaning against the other, in a deposit. | **Permeability** | The capacity of soil or rock to transmit water. |
| **Infiltration** | The vertical movement of water into the soil. | **Probability** | The chance of an event occuring described as a precise value. |
| **Ion** | An electrically charged atom or molecule. | **Quasi-equilibrium** | A state of near equilibrium applied to the relationship between channel morphology and stream channel processes. |
| **Lag deposit** | Coarse sediment left after erosion of finer particles. | | |

| | |
|---|---|
| **Recurrence interval (return period)** | The average period of time separating events of similar magnitude. |
| **Resurgence** | Reappearance of a stream from an underground cave system common in limestone basins. |
| **Sample** | The small selected part of a statistical population which represents the character of the whole. |
| **Storm runoff** | Streamflow generated by the rapid movement of water over and through hillslopes during or soon after rainfall. |
| **Substrate** | The material forming the bed of the river. |
| **Suspended load** | Fine sediment transported by suspension in water. |
| **Variable** | Any quantity or value which can change. |